Misconceptions in Primary Science

Second Edition

Michael Allen

Open University Press

Open University Press
McGraw-Hill Education
McGraw-Hill House
Shoppenhangers Road
Maidenhead
Berkshire
England
SL6 2QL

email: enquiries@openup.co.uk
world wide web: www.openup.co.uk

and Two Penn Plaza, New York, NY 10121-2289, USA

First published 2010
First published in this second edition 2014
Copyright © Michael Allen, 2014

A catalogue record of this book is available from the British Library

ISBN-13: 978-0-33-526266-3 (pb)
ISBN-10: 0-33-526266-X (pb)
eISBN: 978-0-33-526267-0

Library of Congress Cataloging-in-Publication Data
CIP data applied for

Typesetting and e-book compilations by
RefineCatch Limited, Bungay, Suffolk

Misconceptions in Primary Science

Praise for this book

"This essential, clear and readable text is a must! As well as identifying the main misconceptions it succinctly explains the science content for teachers to refresh their own understanding and offers really useful guidance and ideas to help reconstruct learners' misconceptions. It is a most welcome resource for anyone involved in primary science teaching and should be in every classroom."

Sue Dale Tunnicliffe, Institute of Education, University of London, UK

"Michael Allen's book is excellent. He writes specifically for primary teachers to catalogue a strong list of children's common ideas and misconceptions in early science, and suggest constructive ways in which these can be addressed in the course of classroom discussion and activities. This is an enormously valuable resource, each section outlines the form of common misconceptions and suggests lucid and effective tactics that might easily be used. The text is authoritative and well sourced, the figures and drawings are clear and constructive. The admirable key to the book is that, of course, not all the learning to take place will be that of the pupils."

Mike Watts, Professor of Education, Brunel University, UK

Contents

Figures

Boxes

Preface

A key aspiration for this publication was to produce a science book that was accessible to readers who have not experienced a scientific education beyond the years of their compulsory schooling. Yet, the end product is not by any means a comprehensive 'one-stop shop' for primary teachers who wish to supplement their science knowledge and understanding. There are other, very good publications on the market that would better fulfil that role. What *Misconceptions in Primary Science* does is give a very detailed treatment of selected science concepts that other generalized primary science books lack, precisely because they are devoted to an all-inclusive approach with respect to the science curriculum. For this reason, this book should be used in conjunction with one of the more comprehensive texts.

The purpose of this book is twofold. Its chief aim is to help teachers raise standards in primary schools by recognizing their pupils' science misconceptions, and helping them to restructure these, as and when they arise in the classroom. It attempts to achieve this by creating an awareness of the multitude of misconceptions that have been uncovered by research, the rationale being that if one has prior knowledge of what pupils might be thinking then one is more likely to notice their misconceptions. As with any problem, a misconception has to be first identified and characterized before it can be dealt with.

It is hoped that as a result of using the book, readers become more cognizant of the ideas that learners bring to a lesson that differ from the concepts embodied in National Curriculum primary science. They should appreciate that, after being exposed to teaching, pupils may construct ideas that do not agree with a teacher's intended learning outcomes. As stated, the science misconceptions included in the book do not take into account every science concept in the entire curriculum, only the parts that have been studied by misconception researchers. The book does, however, include concepts from all of the topics contained within the new science **Programme of Study** for **KS1** and **KS2** that comes into force in September 2014. Coverage reflects the proportion of attention that researchers have given to each science area, with physics concepts occupying the lion's share of the book, and chemistry somewhat less. Misconceptions relating to experimental work, predicting, collecting and interpreting evidence, drawing conclusions, and so on are not included in the book as the aim was to concentrate on substantive content only. A future publication devoted solely to these aspects might do justice to the myriad of misconceptions relating to this important area of school science.

This second edition of *Misconceptions in Primary Science* also offers tried and tested examples of a variety of practical and other **pedagogies** that would help bring learners' ideas into line with accepted science. Teachers are encouraged to use the principles of constructivist teaching in order to achieve this aim.

The second broad purpose of the book is to enhance readers' own science subject knowledge, which is a convenient side effect of studying the nature of pupils' misconceptions. The concepts that are discussed go beyond KS2 level in order to elucidate their meanings, and generally speaking the deeper the understanding a teacher has about a topic area, the more likely they are to offer clear explanations to their pupils. In any case, the level of science taught to pupils in many primary schools in England frequently goes well beyond the requirements of the KS2 National Curriculum, embracing abstract concepts such as those centred on **particles** and **energy**.

For this second, expanded edition brand new misconceptions are included most of which mirror the 2014 changes to the new KS1 and KS2 Programmes of Study. As well, additional information is added to the pre-existing misconception entries. This new material reflects the most recent research from the science education literature bringing the book up to date with latest findings. Part One is longer, with a new section discussing the relevance of scientific evidence to primary teaching, and to everyday life. Specific references now denote the research studies for each misconception in order to help students who are writing course assignments correctly cite the source. Children's own drawings and quotations help breathe life into the discussions about scientific conceptions. There is also a renewed focus on activities that are suitable for KS1 children, including simple experiments and recommendations for story books that help engage younger pupils with scientific ideas.

Although each misconception entry has a part entitled 'reconstruction', a disclaimer must be made at this point to assert that reconstruction is not always guaranteed! Some misconceptions are very tenacious, and pupils will need lots of time in order to construct and assimilate the scientific idea. The ideas tendered in the book are suggestions that will facilitate these long-term processes. If we are to ultimately generate a scientifically literate population, KS1 and KS2 teachers have a vital part to play by helping their pupils to successfully construct acceptable scientific concepts, so laying firm foundations for the more complex ideas that they will encounter in secondary school and beyond. This can only be achieved if teachers are able to elicit and recognize pupils' science misconceptions, then help them to reconstruct them.

Acknowledgements

Continued thanks go to the friendly people at Avanquest Software Publishing Ltd. for their kind permission in allowing the use of images from the software package *80,000 Pictures* in this second edition

A special thank you goes to the talented artist Marianne Johns, who drew the anatomical outlines used in Part Two.

How to use this book

It is intended that readers will be able to use *Misconceptions in Primary Science* in a number of different ways. Most commonly you will read the relevant entries before delivering a science topic, so becoming aware of the possible misconceptions that pupils may either bring to the lesson, or construct as a consequence of teaching. This awareness may prompt you to carry out an elicitation exercise at the beginning of the topic in order to have a clear idea of where pupils are starting from. This can be followed by the modification of assessment tools such as end-of-topic tests or more formative instruments, taking into account the possibility of misconception construction before or during teaching.

You may wish to incorporate misconceptions into your personal lesson notes, and create teaching strategies that will seek out and rectify them when they arise in the classroom. More formally, a science coordinator may choose to build misconception material into school schemes of work, helping to moderate the quality of science teaching school-wide.

Particularly with KS1 classes some of the concepts and pedagogies that are described in the main text may not be applicable because they are too advanced for the children, for instance some **forces** misconceptions in Year 1. Nevertheless, younger pupils may demonstrate to you that they have constructed misconceptions that need addressing, and the level to which you take your science teaching is up to you. Along with other factors, this is dependent on the general ability of your class and the science curriculum that is specific to your school. In the main text whenever a topic is mentioned in association with a specific year group, it refers to the National Curriculum Programme of Study for Science (the 'POS').

Part One of the book gives a theoretical background, covering misconception research, constructivist pedagogies and the nature of scientific evidence. The main body of the book is divided into three sections that reflect the traditional organization of school science and will be familiar to most teachers: biology, chemistry and physics. Within each of the three sections are the misconception entries, laid out using the following structure:

Misconception. This comprises a scientifically incorrect statement expressed in words that a pupil might be likely to use, accompanied by a pictorial representation when necessary.

Scientific conception. This offers a scientifically accurate explanation, illustrated by diagrams if required. The science concepts discussed here are usually above KS2 level and so are not necessarily to be shared with pupils, but instead are there to enhance the reader's subject knowledge. This section may include a short discussion of the origins and thought processes involved in specific misconception construction.

Reconstruction. Pedagogical approaches are suggested that are likely to enable learners to successfully construct accepted scientific concepts. Where possible, corrective measures are of a practical nature, with pupils using scientific enquiry in order to take control of the learning process and refute the misconception themselves.

Sources. Research from the science education literature is cited here. A good deal of the groundwork for misconception research took place during the 1980s and 1990s and so most of the references are taken from this intense period of research activity. Many other citations refer to more recent work, however.

The writing is intended to be as accessible as possible – although, unavoidably, scientific terms are frequently used throughout. To assist readers who may have little formal science background there is a glossary to be found at the back of the book. When a glossary word is first used in the text it has been highlighted in bold face. Figures are used to support and elucidate statements in the main text, and represent illustrations of correct scientific ideas unless labelled 'misconception'.

The reader will find that within each misconception entry there is often cross-referencing to other parts of the book. A misconception rarely exists in isolation within a learner's mind, and instead is constructed or 'bolted onto' related misconceptions that all share the same faulty underpinnings. Together, they form part of a complex lattice of understanding called a **meaningful erroneous conceptual network**. Sometimes a teacher cannot successfully address a misconception without first dealing with other, more fundamental, misunderstandings. One tip is to leave a permanent stick-on bookmark at the contents page so that, during reading, other misconceptions in the book can be quickly cross-referenced when they are cited in the text. As an aside to the main narrative thrust, three varieties of boxes give supplementary information that might appeal to pupils: *Did you know? Famous scientists* and *Be safe!*.

Finally, the bibliography provides source material that interested readers might want to refer to for further information about the misconceptions included in this book. The publications are mainly research reports that will probably prove quite difficult to access unless the reader is a member of a university library. In fact a driving force behind the book was to open up these 'hidden gems' to a wider audience, instead of allowing them to continue to sit in academic library collections gathering dust. That said, the Association for Science Education (ASE) journals *Primary Science* and *School Science Review* often contain articles on misconceptions and are posted out to ASE members on a regular basis (membership is open to all).

PART ONE

Introduction

A

How do people learn science?

What is constructivism?

Over the course of several million years, evolution has provided humans with the capacity to develop explanatory mental models that help them make sense of the world around them. For instance, the Aztecs 'knew' that the sun was a god who moved across the sky bestowing his power onto growing crops. The sun god needed to be kept continually appeased through worship and tribute, otherwise one day he might fail to rise and cause famine. In an everyday sense people similarly create mental models that help them meet the challenges posed by daily events, e.g. associating a summer's day with warm temperatures and deciding that an overcoat is unnecessary. Individuals sometimes develop their models of natural phenomena to a high level of complexity, and go on to reason that the weather is warmer in summer because the Earth is nearer to the sun at this time of the year.

People reflect upon their past life experiences when devising their mental models, or *constructions*. In order for a new fact or concept to make sense it needs to fit in somewhere with an already established model that has been previously constructed, and if it fails to do so it is less probable that the learner will be able to recall the new information at a later date. These cognitive processes take place continually in the classroom, where pupils do not simply absorb facts like a sponge but instead will subconsciously and automatically search for existing constructions on which to hang new material that is presented to them in lessons. This idea is *constructivism*.

Learners' constructions are quite idiosyncratic in the sense that after a teacher has explained a brand new concept to a class of 30 pupils, each child will have constructed their own personal version of that concept that is different to some degree from everyone else's. This is because each learner comes to the classroom with different life experiences, so at the end of the lesson the teacher will be faced with up to 30 different ideas, some of which will be more aligned with the teacher's original concept than others. In practice, however, there is usually a small number of specific conceptions that are common, appearing in the same form within different samples of learners who are geographically widespread. An aim of this book is to give the reader a greater awareness of these different conceptions.

Historically, and also in many contemporary contexts, teaching and learning have been seen as the transfer of facts from teacher to learner, with the pupil either 'getting it' or 'not getting it'; this has been called a *transmission* view of learning, with knowledge being passed (transmitted) unchanged from mentor to pupil. The popularity of the positivist theory of behaviourism in the twentieth century has provided a theoretical justification for these ideas, with successful learning being associated with the replication of desired behaviours, accompanied by appropriate stimuli, reinforcements and punishments. These influences persist today with older students (and curriculum designers) commonly following positivist beliefs, and successful students tend to be rote learners oriented to achieving high grades. Such learning strategies are used because science particularly is perceived as being merely a collection of facts that need to be memorized and reinforced or practised. In many cases learners do not find things out on their own but rely on teachers and peers to 'spoonfeed' them, delivering knowledge that must be assimilated unchanged, and view science as static, with only one correct answer existing that will be valid for ever.

There have been revolts against behaviourist pedagogies. At the turn of the twentieth century John Dewey advocated that students learn best from discovery situations, where free interaction with the environment promotes active learning, as opposed to the passive receipt of unchanged knowledge. About 50 years ago the Swiss psychologist Jean Piaget, the 'father of constructivism', proposed developmental cognitive stages where learners reached the next level by building personal theories based on the previous stage. Later thinkers such as David Ausubel extended constructivist theory, emphasizing the importance of linking new material with ideas that learners have already in place. It is thought that students using constructivist pedagogies (see later) use more meaningful learning strategies, engage in more active learning and carry out practical work without supervision to arrive at answers; science is dynamic to them, and they seek general principles to connect their bits of scientific knowledge.

As discussed, learners construct common ideas that researchers have found to reappear again and again in different samples, so showing a worldwide commonality in human thought; however, some ideas are specific to certain cultures. Today in southern Africa scientific ideas are sometimes rejected by pupils in favour of traditional beliefs based on folk medicine and witchcraft. Cases such as this suggest that learners do not construct their mental models in isolation but instead are influenced by the ideas of people around them, who can play a big part in moulding their thoughts. In the 1930s the Russian psychologist Lev Vygotsky asserted that all knowledge is socially constructed in this way, and contemporary scholarly writing on constructivism within the education literature tends to concur with this view. An example is how during group work in science lessons pupils will socially construct knowledge by discussing and debating how each of them has individually interpreted the results of an experiment, eventually arriving at one agreed shared meaning; this is conceptual convergence.

What is a science misconception?

From the preceding discussion it will be apparent that children will 'know' some areas of science before ever having been taught them at school, and an individual's constructions are not drawn on a blank slate, but instead build on previously created structures. Since the prior ideas of students gained from both previous educational experiences and informal events are of vital consideration, in order to facilitate meaningful learning it is preferable that at the start of a topic or lesson teachers try to discover their pupils' current ideas that are relevant to the science concepts that are about to be introduced. Existing constructions that are at odds with accepted science can provide a shaky foundation for new concepts, and there are vast quantities of constructivist research within the science education literature, much of which deals with such incorrectly constructed scientific concepts, or misconceptions.[1] Two different science misconceptions pertaining to the nature of Earth's association with the sun were given at the very beginning of this section: that the sun is a sentient god, and that during summer the Earth is nearest to the sun.

In many cases, once learners construct models that make perfect sense to them and have successfully explained a variety of phenomena, they are difficult to change or shed, particularly if constructed in early childhood, which is clearly a problem if these models reflect misconceptions. Many mental models are the result of everyday trial and error experimentation; for instance, deep-seated knowledge of how forces behave in the real world is thought to be constructed during informal play in the early years, and can be a source of misconceptions that become revealed later on when the child studies physics at school. Alternatively, pupils may not have met certain concepts in their everyday lives before exposure to them during a science lesson, for instance the rules governing the depiction of food chains, and so may construct misconceptions during the lesson itself. Constructions can be quite sophisticated where several misconceptions link together in the mind of a pupil in a sensible way, which has the tendency to strengthen them because each supports the other, becoming a meaningful erroneous conceptual network. An example would be the interrelated ideas that the lungs' job is to pump air to the heart, and during exercise the heart beats faster to supply the muscles with more pumped air (see 3.2 and 4.2 in Part Two of the book).

It is well established that science misconceptions represent a barrier to learning at all levels of education. The misconceptions contained within this book have been reported in published research articles since the mid-1970s; some are commonly seen 'classic' misconceptions; others are less well known. A main aim of this book is to provide teachers with the awareness that their pupils are capable of creating their own ideas that are different from those that were intended, exactly what form those ideas might take, and suggested ways to change these ideas into acceptable scientific variants.

Can a misconception be corrected?

Identification of a pupil's misconception is often the easy part for teachers, with correction being more complex and less attainable. The literature carries a multitude of constructivist-inspired attempts to transform misconceptions into scientifically acceptable ideas (conceptual change), which can be traced to Piaget's idea of accommodation, where new ideas conflict with existing models resulting in a change in the latter, or equilibration. More recent explanations have focused less on Piagetian stage theory and more on the nature of learners' ideas with respect to scientific phenomena. Since the early 1980s research has centred largely on how students construct ideas from observations of natural phenomena, with many studies focusing on Vygotskyian ideas of social constructivism and constructing knowledge in a social setting.

The origins of the modern conceptual change model stem from the frequently cited 1982 paper of Cornell University's Posner, Strike, Hewson and Gertzog, who claim that learners tend only to accept new concepts if *dissatisfaction* with the current constructs exists (it does not solve a current problem). The new, replacement theory needs to be *intelligible* (it can be understood), *plausible* (it actually works, and is able to solve present discrepancies) and *fruitful* (it can solve future problems presented in a different context that are not resolvable using current conceptions). An important quality of conceptual change interventions is the building of new concepts giving due regard to students' prior ideas, and learning should be embedded in classroom conditions that support this process. However, many studies have found misconceptions to be resistant to modification, which may be due in part to them serving a useful function for the learner in explaining everyday life phenomena.

A conceptual change approach signifies that if dissatisfaction is encountered with respect to an idea that is already held, learners will restructure the idea until it fits the latest evidence. Constructivist pedagogies have provided such opportunities for *cognitive conflict* in pupils' thinking by introducing a problem situation such as experimental evidence that disagrees with pupils' conceptions to create cognitive disequilibrium. Exposure to alternative concepts helps students think more deeply about their own ideas, and they either reject, modify or hold on to those views. Also, awareness of one's own existing concept is necessary for any conceptual change.

Research shows that even if pupils successfully construct scientific ideas during exposure to a classroom event, they may revert back to their initial misconceptions either at a later time, or when a problem is presented to them differently from the way they learned it, with the misconception frequently persisting into adulthood. It appears that a pupil's misconception might never be truly extinguished, instead existing side-by-side with the correct scientific concept, with either of the two being recalled depending on the circumstances. In this situation, ideas compete with each other for dominance within a learner's mind, and this has been termed *conceptual competition*. The fact that many misconceptions are difficult to treat is due to the fact that there are accepted scientific ideas, some of which are fundamental to science, which are counterintuitive and go against basic common sense. For instance, the previously described misconception that the Earth is closer to the sun during summertime makes more sense than the actual situation – during the month of July the Earth is actually the furthest away from the sun than at any other time of year (see 18.9).

What is scientific evidence?

Something that can come as a surprise to beginning primary teachers is that during science lessons we expect children to think slightly differently from how they would do in any other lesson. In fact, in many ways thinking scientifically is different to thinking 'normally' in everyday life. As will hopefully become apparent from the following discussion, when we think scientifically *the standard of evidence is usually higher* than is required in day-to-day settings.

When asked to define science, primary children usually encounter some difficulty. They may cite the paraphernalia of science lessons, for example 'science is when we get the test tubes out'. A simple definition of science would be 'a way of making sense of natural phenomena'. In children's language we could say 'science is finding out how things work', although not just mechanical things like a car engine, but nature in general. These things would include the universe, living organisms and systems, energy and the human mind, and the way a scientist goes about finding out how things work follows a system called the scientific method. Vital aspects of the method include the premise that any knowledge claim the scientist makes must be supported by empirical evidence (i.e. evidence verifiable by observation), and that evidence must have been collected as objectively as possible. It is not enough for a scientist to merely form an opinion, no matter how well founded, unless there is convincing experimental or observational evidence to warrant it.

Of course, in everyday situations people form opinions all the time based on flimsy or absent evidence; one example would be UFOs having an extraterrestrial source. It would be socially acceptable in the polite setting of a dinner party for two people to hold opposing views regarding the origin of UFOs. However, such a claim would not be published in scientific journals because of the current lack of convincing evidence. Opinions are based on personal judgement and not necessarily objective evidence. They are acceptable in everyday life as statements of free expression, and are sometimes necessary for normal social functioning. For example, a manager might have an opinion about a particular employee that they want to promote to a higher grade, with decisions being made partly on subjective 'gut-feelings' about the person, such as they will respond well to taking on extra responsibility. A different manager might hold a different opinion about that same person, that the employee would be unable to handle extra responsibility. Religious belief is a form of personal opinion as it does not require evidence to test ideas; faith in the ideas alone will suffice. Unlike with science, criticism of fundamental religious ideas is not possible so ideas remain unchanged over time, and many religious people see this as a strength, to maintain stable core values that were first passed down many thousands of years ago. In contrast, the scientific method advocates the interaction of an existing body of knowledge with new evidence, which may lead to a reinterpretation of phenomena and processes. Core scientific ideas have changed over time as more convincing models have emerged and will continue to do so in future – it is a common myth that once a scientific theory has been 'proved' then it is set in stone for eternity.

Opinions may be erroneous because they have not been supported by reliable, objective evidence. On the other hand they may also be accurate, and anyone has a perfect right to hold any opinion, but it is unscientific to make an unsupported claim. Opinion can become a scientific theory only once there is enough convincing evidence available to support it. The success of science over the past few hundred years has been due to the efforts of scientists actively attempting to falsify any existing theory, so accepted scientific ideas have been continually scrutinized and challenged by sceptical researchers. Under this withering pressure only the most convincing and valid ideas survive, with fruitless **pseudosciences** that were once completely accepted being refuted; these include astrology, alchemy, witchcraft, Creationism and forms of paranormal activity. However, note that, unlike religion, science does not deal in absolutes. It may be the case in the future that with some of these pseusdosciences convincing empirical evidence does emerge, in which case they may be promoted to the level of accepted science. With science, no idea is completely dismissed out-of-hand as invalid forever.

One can imagine scientific theory and evidence as being two separated entities (Figure A.1). René Descartes (1596–1650), the French mathematician and philosopher, noticed when travelling by boat that the oars appeared bent when they were dipped in the water due to an optical illusion.[2] He realized that his senses were deluding him, and that in the case of the bent oar the outside world was different from how he perceived it. Taking this line of thinking further he questioned whether any of his senses could ever give him a correct impression of the world, and even doubted the existence of the outside world because he could not directly access that world, other than by his unreliable senses. He pondered whether he was perhaps merely dreaming the outside world. He finally began to doubt that he actually existed himself, but baulked at that step, famously asserting *cogito ergo sum* (I think, therefore I am). Modern ideas within the philosophy of science still carry the essence of Descartes' dualism, that there is an inside world (the mind) that is separate to an outside world (reality) and the two are not directly connected to each other than by senses that are sometimes unreliable.

In the classroom teachers can explain evidence to children as something in the outside world that they can use to see if their ideas are correct. It is important to disconnect evidence as something they observe or measure during an experiment,

Figure A.1 The basic relationship between theory and evidence

from theory (or a prediction, hypothesis or conclusion), which is something they can imagine in their minds. Children need to appreciate that in science it is not enough to believe something in your mind in order to show it is 'true' or 'accurate', you have also to collect evidence, which needs to be credible.

Summary

Humans routinely construct mental models in order to make sense of the world around them (constructivism). If these constructions conflict with accepted scientific ideas they are misconceptions, and act as a barrier, preventing successful learning in science. A good deal of educational research has been geared towards the identification and correction of science misconceptions by means of conceptual change, aligned with the learning theories of Piaget, Vygotsky and others. Attempts to replace learners' misconceptions with scientific ideas have met with mixed success. There are differences between scientific and everyday thinking, and science lessons reflect this by requiring any theory, hypothesis, prediction or conclusion be backed up by plausible empirical evidence.

Notes

1. The literature also refers to misconceptions as children's science, naive conceptions, private concepts, alternative conceptions, alternative frameworks, intuitive theories, preconceptions, and limited or inappropriate propositional hierarchies.
2. This illusion is well known today and commonly reproduced using a pencil in a glass of water.

B

How can we elicit, recognize and reconstruct science misconceptions?

The driving forces behind the initial idea for this book were an acknowledgement that science misconceptions have been and remain a significant problem at all levels of education, along with a recognition of the importance of 'catching them young' by starting to address misconceptions at the primary stage. The book aims to make teachers aware of the myriad of alternative ideas that their pupils may construct either before the formal introduction of science concepts in the classroom, or as a consequence of teaching. Once teachers have an awareness of the misconceptions that they might encounter during the delivery of a particular topic, they will be more equipped to recognize them when pupils say or write something that suggests they may hold a misconception. That said, instead of passively waiting for misconceptions to arise during the course of normal teaching it is preferable that teachers actively search by introducing specialized activities that are designed to highlight them; this is *elicitation*.

Elicitation

This section gives ways in which teachers can elicit the ideas of their pupils, so exposing misconceivers and correct conceivers alike. As well as informing teachers, elicitation will make each learner explicitly aware of what they really believe about scientific phenomena, which is fundamental to any future reconstruction.

Ask pupils directly about their ideas

The most straightforward way in which to find out what someone is thinking is to ask them in a direct manner face-to-face. This can sometimes reap benefits; often, however, asking pupils directly tends to end up in them giving you the answer they think you want to hear, and not what they really believe. More indirect methods, detailed below, may be necessary in order to provide a more valid form of assessment. Direct questions can be asked to the whole class and used in conjunction with pupils' dry pen mini-whiteboards in order to survey understanding, e.g. by means of a true/false plenary session. Some misconception entries in this book offer specific teacher questions that have been found to be useful when eliciting learners' ideas.

Self-completion exercises

These can take the form of worksheets that ask probing questions related to a science concept, written tests, computer-based quizzes such as found on the BBC *Bitesize* website, etc. There is also an element with these exercises of not revealing children's true beliefs, although perhaps less so than with face-to-face encounters. If you want to elicit the ideas of all pupils it is best that the class complete these activities as individuals instead of as a group effort, which usually ends up eliciting just the concepts held by the dominant member(s) of each group.

Card sorts

With younger classes where children have difficulty expressing their ideas in writing, more kinaesthetic tasks are preferred, for instance asking them to categorize a number of cards. An example of a common card sort activity in primary science is to have a collection of cards with pictures of materials, with the aim being to place them into sets of solids, liquids and gases. These non-verbal approaches also have the advantage of being more accessible to learners with lower literacy skills or who normally use English as a second language. A traditional method is to have pupils first sort their cards into the groups that they think are correct, then swap seats with other pupils so that different arrangements can be examined. The teacher can walk around the room and readily see any misconceptions held by individuals or the class as a whole.

Pupils' drawings

Asking children to draw a picture, for instance, of 'different animals' can give the teacher an indication of any restrictive sets or incorrect categorization. In this particular case if a child has drawn only furry four-legged animals you could ask them why they have not drawn animals such as a fish or an earthworm. Reading a story can be used as an orientation towards a science concept that the teacher would like to elicit, with learners being asked to draw pictures afterwards that offer personal visualizations of certain events in the story, a familiar example being Eric Carle's *The Very Hungry Caterpillar* (1969) being used to elicit misconceptions related to life cycles. Researchers have used pupils' own diagrams as a basis for asking questions in order to explore their ideas in intricate detail.

Concept maps

These are usually a helpful way in which to elicit misconceptions as well as acting as a revision exercise to assess understanding after the delivery of a topic. There are several concept-mapping techniques, with perhaps the most basic being the variant where the teacher provides all the words that will be used on a printed sheet. Working in pairs, pupils are given a list of key words that relate to a topic to cut out. Pupils then arrange the words onto a sheet of sugar paper and associated words are glued down and linked with a drawn pencil line. Each line must be accompanied by a written comment explaining why the words are connected, e.g.

Sand_____Both solids_____Wood

Concept cartoons

Concept Cartoons in Science Education, a well-known book and CD-ROM by Naylor, Keogh and Mitchell (2000), was written for KS3 pupils but many of the ideas are very relevant to the primary stage. Scientific ideas are presented in pictorial scenes where cartoon characters express different views about an illustrated situation. Pupils then decide which character is correct, or offer their own explanation, so eliciting any misconceptions.

Using toys

It is often the case that a more valid indicator of what a person is thinking/feeling is reflected in how they behave and not what they tell you, this premise forming the basis of the study of body language. When children play with toys they become relaxed and absorbed in the moment, entering into a different world and dropping their guard, allowing an informed observer the chance to glean valuable information about their scientific beliefs. For instance, pupils are asked to build a car from Lego that will travel as far as possible down an inclined ramp. If given free rein and lots of time, some will go for big wheels, others will add weights, some will combine different variables, and so on.

Using scientific apparatus

Observing the behaviour of pupils can be extended from playing with toys to more formal exercises involving scientific apparatus that require them to perform a systematic experiment. An example would be a boy who believes all metals are magnetic trying to attract an aluminium drinks can (which is non-magnetic). When the can fails to stick to his magnet, he frantically searches for other magnets to try because he believes his must be broken. Watching how pupils manipulate apparatus during PE lessons may be helpful in eliciting some misconceptions about forces.

Role play

It is sometimes easier for children to express their true thoughts and feelings when they are pretending to be someone/something else. Research into self-expression by pupils through hand puppets has suggested that this could be a useful way forward, with the teacher asking the puppet (and not the pupil) direct questions relating to scientific concepts, within an appropriate imaginary setting.

Word association games

Researchers have revealed learners' misconceptions by describing a context and then asking the child to say out loud the first situation that immediately comes to mind. An example would be 'the Earth in space at summertime', followed by a child's response 'the Earth is very near to the sun'. Spontaneous responses are thought to be linked with what a person strongly believes, as with Freudian slips of the tongue, being governed by unconscious processes the person is unaware of and so has no control over.

Listening to pupils talking

Eavesdropping on what children say to one another during group work or when engaged with their talking partners on the carpet can be used as a valuable gauge of their ideas.

Recognition

It is intended that the misconception entries in this book act as prompts for teachers during elicitation exercises so that they are able to recognize any misconceptions displayed by pupils if they arise. The rationale is that reading about them beforehand primes the teacher to be ready for them should they appear in class. If teachers are unaware of the variety of misconceptions that are associated with a particular topic or concept, they might overlook them, especially if the misconception is closely aligned with the scientific concept, i.e. is nearly right, but not quite.

Reconstruction

Once misconceptions have been elicited and recognized, the next step is reconstruction. Explicit ideas for reconstructing misconceptions are given in the main body of the book; that said, there are general principles of constructivist pedagogy which when applied are useful for reconstructing misconceptions, and are given in this section. Box I, at the end of this section, offers some general qualities of a constructivist teaching approach.

A vital starting point for misconception reconstruction is the linking of any intervention with the prior knowledge of the learners. This can be done by using data from a classroom elicitation exercise to guide the subsequent intervention; e.g. using a reconstruction method that applies to the most common misconception that is prevalent with your particular class. It can be done at a more simple level by merely linking an activity with the prior, familiar experiences of children, perhaps popular TV programmes that (incorrectly) show loud explosions occurring in space, or how the volume control on an MP3 player limits the **current** in a circuit. As stated, an important principle of constructivist psychology is the assumption that we remember more effectively when we can integrate new knowledge into constructions that we have already in place.

Another fundamental assumption is that people often learn best when they are performing a hands-on task; in the case of science learning this would be taking part in an experiment. To this end, pupils in primary (and secondary) schools are taught to act like 'little scientists', planning experiments, observing phenomena, recording and interpreting results, drawing conclusions and finally evaluating the whole process by reflecting on what they did. A constructivist approach usually advocates a particular way of experimenting where, instead of being given a strict 'recipe' of instructions to follow, pupils are allowed a certain amount of freedom to plan and perform practical activities. They begin by making a prediction, then test out that prediction using scientific apparatus in order to see if their prediction was correct. A pupil may predict that a heavy object will fall faster than a light object, though when two different-sized glass marbles are dropped they are both seen to land at the same time. Thus, their prediction has been shown to be false, which triggers cognitive conflict and ideally ends up with the pupil rejecting their original view and assimilating the scientific concept (**mass** has no effect on the speed of freefall) in its place; we say that the misconception has been *refuted*. A more involved approach is to give pupils a number of different outcomes or hypotheses and ask them to carry out tests in order to ascertain which one is correct.

The principle behind constructivist practical work is to allow learners to construct a scientific concept from what they have found out by themselves, and not be told the answer didactically by the teacher. That said, constructivist pedagogies tend not to resemble pure discovery learning where children are left mainly to their own devices with little or no supervision. Instead, there is usually some degree of teacher direction involved so that learners are able to focus on relevant phenomena. Also, practical outcomes need to be reliable in the sense that the scientific concept is reflected by the results that pupils collect, otherwise misconceptions will be reinforced, and not refuted. Note that it may be the case that reconstruction is not necessary because pupils already hold the scientific view, so exercises need to reinforce this view as well as refuting misconceptions.

The familiar view of the professional scientist as a solitary soul who is happy working alone in a laboratory discovering theories is really the antithesis of constructivist learning, which assumes people learn science better when they interact in groups and are permitted to freely discuss the phenomena they observe. In a constructivist classroom, predictions and results are openly expressed and interpretations debated; this is closer to how scientists actually work, since theories are suppositions that have been collectively agreed upon by a community of experts as being a 'best guess'. School science in general should be viewed as a shared activity where the assistance and input of peers are of vital importance.

Over the course of a topic it is sometimes useful to track the ideas of pupils in order to see how they have changed. Floor books are a good way to achieve this, with children sticking down pieces of relevant work, teachers writing down interesting things that pupils have said, photographs of experiments along with predictions and results, etc. Alternatively, the same result can be achieved using class posters or wall displays.

Did you know?

Typical constructivist pedagogies

- Facilitating students' personal construction of knowledge, and integration of this knowledge with prior ideas (assimilation).

- Learning that involves not only acquisition and extension of new concepts but also reorganization or rejection of old ones (accommodation).
- Providing laboratory practical work to help construction of knowledge through personal experience of the physical world.
- Providing experiences such as discrepant events that challenge existing hypotheses using empirical data (cognitive conflict).
- Using a social setting for learning.
- Allowing student autonomy, engagement, motivation and initiative.
- Presenting open-ended questions.
- Promoting higher-level thinking.
- Encouraging peer dialogue.
- Leaving the final responsibility for learning with the pupil.

Summary

Science misconceptions are addressed using a constructivist approach by means of elicitation, teacher recognition and then reconstruction. Whenever possible, learners should construct science concepts using hands-on activities that allow some freedom in planning, execution and interpretation. The input of peers is of vital importance during these processes. Activities need to clearly refute misconceptions so triggering cognitive conflict in order that the pupil successfully assimilates acceptable science.

PART TWO

Biology

1

Concept of living

1.1 When is something 'alive'?

> **Misconception**
>
> *Fire is a living thing because it moves, breathes, reproduces, grows, excretes and consumes.*

Scientific conception

Before we can classify something as being alive it needs to be capable of all of the seven **processes of life** (as given by the acronym MRS GREN):

Movement
Respiration
Sensitivity
Growth
Reproduction
Excretion
Nutrition

Fire appears to fulfil six of these characteristics, but since a fire cannot sense its surroundings it cannot be categorized as a living thing. As is the case with the misconception statement, learners sometimes incorrectly classify entities as living things by applying only some of the seven characteristics, two of the most popular being movement and **breathing**.[1] For instance, the sun, cars, robots, air (wind) and clouds can be considered to be alive. These are cases of faulty reasoning of the necessary/sufficient type – in order to be called living, although it is *necessary* for an entity to be capable of moving, this condition alone is not *sufficient*.

Reconstruction

At the start of the topic/lesson, first ask pupils what they deem the important characteristics of life to be. This will reveal any learners who have a more restricted view of life when compared to the more comprehensive MRS GREN list.

Pupils may debate with you about the 'living' status of non-living things; e.g. they may insist that fire is able to sense its surroundings because it knows what to burn next. One criterion not covered by the MRS GREN acronym is the requirement to be made from **cells**, which would discount fire and the other examples given above.

Did you know?

Viruses. Viruses are extremely tiny infectious units that appear to fulfil all of the MRS GREN requirements. However, they are not cellular, which has created debate within the scientific community as to whether they are actually living creatures or not.

Sources: Arnold and Simpson (1979); Piaget (1929); Sere (1983).

1.2 Seeds

Misconception

Seeds are not alive.

Scientific conception

Learners may believe a seed only becomes alive once it has been planted and begins to grow. It may be the case that learners have applied the MRS GREN characteristics (1.1) to a seed and come to the (apparently) appropriate conclusion of 'non-living' – in this case the normally useful MRS GREN method in effect breaks down. A seed that has yet to germinate does not respire, grow, etc.; however, because it is capable of these things given the right conditions it is regarded as being alive but **dormant**. Dormancy is a very effective way for a plant (in the form of a seed) to survive unfavourable conditions for long periods, for instance a 2000-year-old date palm seed recovered from Herod's palace in Masada, Israel, has been successfully germinated and grown.

Learners who think seeds are not alive are having problems understanding that during an organism's life cycle there can be no breaks that include a temporary non-living state. A related misconception is the belief that although a caterpillar is alive, when it becomes a pupa (chrysalis) it dies, then when it appears as a butterfly it becomes alive again.

Reconstruction

Application of the MRS GREN characteristics would do little to convince learners that seeds are alive. As in 1.1, show learners that since a seed is composed of viable cells it can be considered to be a living thing. Also emphasize that any breaks in a life cycle would mean an organism dies permanently, analogous to the journey of the Olympic torch. Pupils' understandings would be facilitated if these discussions took place in the context of the familiar primary school activity of growing broad bean seeds or incubating butterfly pupae.

Sources: Stavy and Wax (1989); Tamir *et al.* (1981).

Note

1. Some plants are not regarded as being alive by pupils because they are not thought to move or respire – see 1.2.

2
Classification

2.1 What is an animal?

> **Misconception**
> *Animals are furry and have four legs.*

Scientific conception

Learners sometimes confuse the everyday meanings of words with scientific definitions. Colloquially, the 'animals' that young children tend to talk about the most are
mammals commonly encountered on land, especially in the home or on farms, or
played with as soft toys. They have fur/hair, walk on four legs and make their own
peculiar noise. Anything else may not be considered as being an animal – this is especially the case with **invertebrates** such as jellyfish, snails, earthworms, crabs and
insects. **Vertebrates** that fail to meet this furry/terrestrial/quadruped standard also
may not be thought of as animals, e.g. fish, snakes and birds.

Taxonomically speaking, living organisms are categorized into five kingdoms.
Figure 2.1 shows the hierarchy. Note that protoctists are usually simple, single-celled
life forms, e.g. an amoeba; prokaryotes are bacteria.

For an organism to be categorized as an animal it must be able to consume **food**
(instead of making its own food by **photosynthesis**) and be capable of movement,
and it is usually **multicellular**. Using deduction, if an organism that a learner thinks is
not an animal (such as a shark) cannot be placed in any of the other kingdoms then it
has to be an animal. All of the organisms named in the first paragraph are part of the
animal kingdom.

Reconstruction

Misconceptions can be elicited by asking pupils to write down what they think something has to be like before it can be called an animal. Alternatively, pupils can draw
'some animals'.

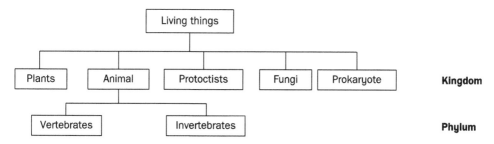

Figure 2.1 The hierarchy of living things

At the primary level the hierarchy can be simplified if teachers only revealed four 'kingdoms' to pupils: plant, animal, fungus and 'single cell' (so merging protoctists and prokaryotes). Have these four kingdoms diagrammatically on display in the classroom to remind learners of the choices they have to make when categorizing a living thing. Ask learners *could a shark be called a plant, a fungus or a 'single cell'?* Sharks clearly cannot be placed in any of these kingdoms, so by default the only remaining group left is 'animal'. This could be extended to a whole-class exercise with Venn-type representations that use hoops and photographs (2.2). The Venn-diagram approach could be used with any classification concept in order to make the taxonomic system as visually clear as possible for pupils. Alternatively, a cut–and-paste paper worksheet or a drag-and-drop activity with the interactive whiteboard could be used.

Sources: Bell (1981); Patrick and Tunnicliffe (2011); Trowbridge and Mintzes, (1985, 1988).

Famous scientists

Carl von Linné. Known better by his Latinized name *Linnaeus*, this eighteenth-century Swedish botanist devised his own system of classifying living things that biologists still use today (in an adapted form) nearly 240 years after his death. He also created a binomial taxonomic nomenclature that can be applied to every species; for example, humans are **Homo sapiens**. Unlike the five kingdoms we accept today, Linnaeus initially recognized only three – the animal, vegetable and mineral kingdoms.

2.2 Is an insect an animal?

Misconception

A bee is not an animal . . . because it is an insect.

Scientific conception

A bee is indeed an insect, although the pupil making this misconception statement has not recognized that the set 'insect' is subsumed within the overarching set 'animal'. It needs to be made clear that a bee can be both an insect and an animal at the same time.

Reconstruction

The use of Venn-type diagrams may help pupils appreciate the hierarchy – these are simplifications, but easier for younger children to understand if compared with the more usual 'tree of life' depictions of animal classification. Pupils could be asked to sort animal picture cards into sets using different-sized plastic hoops (Figure 2.2).

Source: Leach *et al.* (1992).

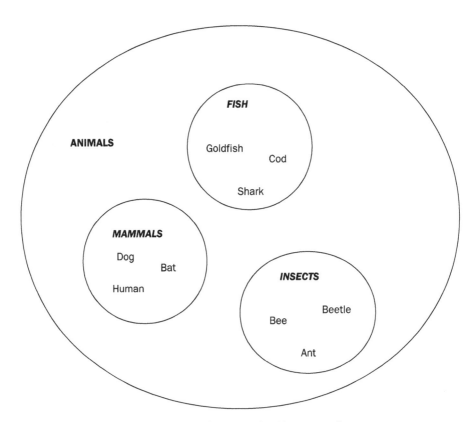

Figure 2.2 Showing hierarchy of classification using Venn-type diagrams

2.3 The similarity between amphibians and reptiles

Misconception

Lizards and snakes are amphibians.

Scientific conception

From an early age children in schools in England and Wales traditionally learn about familiar creatures that live in nearby ponds. Teachers discuss the life cycle of frogs, sometimes keeping frogspawn, tadpoles or immature frogs in a small fish tank in the classroom. Because of this coverage many pupils are aware that frogs, and to a lesser extent newts, are amphibians.

In the UK and other temperate countries sightings of wild reptiles are rare; lizards are only common in certain rural areas and snakes are very shy. When pupils are presented with pictures of reptiles they may note similarities between the pond animals they are already familiar with such as frogs and newts, including green/brown skin, the laying of eggs, and the fact that all of these animals are cold blooded, and then assume reptiles are amphibians too. There is a striking visual correspondence between newts and lizards that compounds the error (Figures 2.3a and 2.3b).

Reconstruction

Remind pupils of the taxonomic differences between reptiles and amphibians: reptiles have scaly skin, lay leathery eggs and cannot breathe under water, while amphibians have smooth skin, lay soft eggs and are able to breathe both in air and under water. Particularly emphasize the semi-aquatic lifestyle of amphibians. Bringing a pet reptile into school such as a gecko or a snake to compare with the class's frogs and newts would help to reinforce these differences.

Before pupils first start placing animals into sets for classification, as a prelude ask them to place familiar objects into sets based on physical appearance. These objects could be the contents of a pencil case or commonly used scientific apparatus. Tell them that when assigning an object to a particular set it must have at least one thing in common with every other member of the set. This exercise is followed by the more usual tasks where pupils place pictures of living things into sets such as

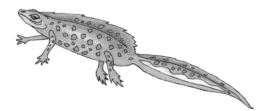

Figure 2.3a A newt

Figure 2.3b A lizard

plant/animal. The prelude exercise would encourage pupils to categorize using the observable features of living things.

Play the game *Who am I?*, where a volunteer secretly takes on the identity of a living thing and answers questions from the class relating to physical characteristics by responding either yes or no, with the class having to guess what the pupil is pretending to be from the responses. Introduce amphibians and their complex life cycles to KS1 by reading the story book *Oscar and the Frog* by Geoff Waring.

Sources: Allen and Choudhary (2012); Trowbridge and Mintzes (1988); Waring (2009).

2.4 Sea-dwelling mammals

Misconception

A whale is a fish because it lives in the sea.

Scientific conception

Learners sometimes use an organism's habitat in order to determine classification instead of observable, physical features. Other common errors include thinking that seals, penguins and turtles are amphibians because they live both on land and in the sea, and that a bat is a type of bird because it flies. These ideas may be reinforced by the fact that the physical features of some of these animals do not make correct classification easy, e.g. whales and bats are not typical mammals, and penguins not typical birds, nor turtles typical reptiles.

With a related type of misconception pupils are distracted by an organism's name and conclude, for instance, that starfish and jellyfish are types of fish.

Reconstruction

Remind pupils that classification is based largely on how an organism's body is put together, not where it lives. Recapping the characteristics of vertebrate and other taxonomic groups can help refute the above examples, e.g. a whale is not a fish because it does not have gills or a scaly skin; a bat is not a bird because it has fur instead of feathers; a penguin is not an amphibian because it has feathers, and although it spends its time on land and in the sea, like proper amphibians it cannot breathe both in air and under water. A simple rule of thumb when deciding whether a sea animal is a whale or a fish is to look at the tail – whales and other cetaceans such as dolphins have their tails fins oriented in the horizontal plane, and fish have theirs in the vertical plane (Figure 2.4a).

For an exercise in observation, pupils can be asked to compare pictures of a variety of animals that look different but are classified within the same taxonomic group, e.g. different fish. Using a tick list, they can look at the pictures and try to spot as many of these characteristics as possible (Figure 2.4b). Conclude by saying that, to be called a fish, an organism needs to tick *all* of these boxes. Note that a problem of using such simplified taxonomy means that exceptions sometimes crop up, such as the fact a seahorse has no scales but is still technically a fish. Nicola Davies' *Big Blue Whale* is a good story book with which to introduce the concept to KS1 children.

Sources: Davies (1997); Trowbridge and Mintzes (1988).

Figure 2.4a Comparing the tails of a killer whale (left) and a swordfish (right)

Animal	Scales?	Gills?	Fins?
Shark			
Goldfish			
Puffer fish			

Figure 2.4b Observable features of different animals of the same taxonomic group (fish)

2.5 What is the difference between a vertebrate and an invertebrate?

Misconception

A crab is a vertebrate because it has a hard shell on its back

Scientific conception

Adults and older children generally know that animals with backbones are called vertebrates and those without a backbone are invertebrates. Crabs do not possess a backbone despite appearances that may suggest the contrary. When children are deciding whether or not a particular animal has a backbone they tend to look at its anatomical features, particularly its overall body shape, texture, flexibility and the curvature of its back. Some children think that organisms with soft bodies are entirely boneless so do not possess a backbone. They commonly consider the turtle to be an invertebrate because learners imagine a soft, boneless body underneath its shell, and for that reason it needs its shell to provide support. In a similar way children describe animals that are very flexible when moving, such as fish, as invertebrates because they are deemed to be 'too bendy' to have a backbone. For the same reason, they know that snakes can coil up tightly because they are flexible and so must be invertebrates, or are too long and thin to house something as substantial as a backbone (also see 2.6). However, turtles, fish and snakes are all vertebrates. In contrast, learners (correctly) believe animals with pronouncedly curved backs such as the elephant and gerbil are vertebrates. They may also mistakenly think that **arthropods** such as the crab and centipede are vertebrates because the backs of their bodies are covered by a hard **exoskeleton**.

As was seen from the previous figure, 2.1, the animal kingdom can be divided into two broad sections, vertebrates (Figure 2.5a) and 'invertebrates' (Figure 2.5b); that said, Figure 2.1 is a simplification as there are eight invertebrate phyla. The word invertebrate is used in biology to refer to any animal without a backbone, although there is no taxonomic level called *invertebrate* – it is merely a convenience word used to group together non-vertebrates.

Reconstruction

Research has shown that children who have seen skeletons of fish and snakes in museums and elsewhere quickly realize that they are vertebrates. Children who have eaten bony fish such as trout where parents have dissected the backbone and ribs prior to eating can be reminded that fish are indeed vertebrates.

Sources: Braund (1998); Prokop *et al.* (2008); Trowbridge and Mintzes (1985, 1988).

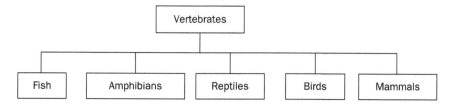

Figure 2.5a Vertebrate classification

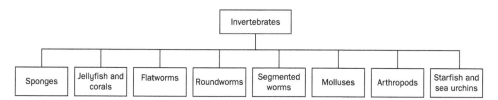

Figure 2.5b Invertebrate classification

Figure 2.5c Some examples of invertebrates

2.6 Snakes and earthworms

Misconception

Like earthworms, snakes are invertebrates.

Scientific conception

In many cases this misconception would be a result of the visual similarity of snakes and earthworms – both have tubular bodies with no limbs and move with a crawling motion. Some pupils who have correctly learned that earthworms have no backbones and so are invertebrates go on to automatically include snakes within the same category. Snakes do have backbones, being part of the reptiles class, which is subsumed under the overarching vertebrates **phylum** (see Figure 2.5a).

As seen previously in 2.5, related misconceptions include the belief that eels (fish) and turtles (reptiles) are invertebrates. Pupils can make these errors if the outward appearance of an animal does not obviously suggest that a backbone or even any bony structure exists.

Reconstruction

Show the class a picture of a snake skeleton, or if possible a real snake skeleton, and it should be clear that the animal is a vertebrate because the skeleton seems to be all backbone and ribs. Compare with a photo/diagram of the inside of an earthworm, which has no bones. An earthworm's insides are mainly soft and liquidy, and the outward (hydrostatic) pressure of this liquid helps the worm maintain its shape, keeping it 'inflated', and also plays a role in movement. In contrast, as is the case with humans, a bony skeleton supports a snake's body, which also is important in movement.

Remind pupils of the rules of taxonomy that assert snakes belong in the reptiles set because they have scaly skins and lay leathery eggs, and that reptiles are included within the larger vertebrates set (Figure 2.5a). As well as having no backbone, earthworms have moist, smooth skins, and so are neither reptiles nor vertebrates.

A model backbone can be made by children in the classroom by cutting a drinks straw into short lengths and then threading them through with string. This can help demonstrate that although the backbone has only limited flexibility in humans, vertebrates such as snakes are able to coil their bodies tightly because their backbones are very bendy.

Source: Trowbridge and Mintzes (1988).

2.7 What exactly is an insect?

Misconception

All 'creepy crawlies' are insects.

Scientific conception

The statement reflects a common over-generalization of the category 'insect', and can emerge when animal classification is first introduced in Year 1. As well as *bone fide* insects, a learner may include other arthropods within the category such as arachnids (e.g. spiders, mites and scorpions), myriapods (e.g. centipedes and millipedes) or crustaceans (e.g. woodlice).

In taxonomy, insects are characterized from other arthropods by having three body sections (head, **thorax**, abdomen), one pair of antennae and three pairs of legs (Figure 2.7). Spiders have only two body parts and four pairs of legs; myriapods such as centipedes and millipedes have numerous body segments (a 'myriad') with one or two pairs of legs on each. Crustaceans have a variable number of body parts and legs. When presented with unfamiliar arthropods children may automatically call them 'insects' and not refer to the taxonomic rubric; for instance, a frequent error is to call the household wingless daddy long legs an insect, although it is actually a type of arachnid called a harvestman. Another common misnomer is to think that a woodlouse is an insect when it is in fact a crustacean.

Figure 2.7 Comparing insects, arachnids and crustaceans (respectively)

Reconstruction

In common with other classification misconceptions covered in this book, it is advised that pupils get into the habit of referring to the rubric that is unique to individual sets, e.g. for an animal to be called an insect it first has to have six legs, etc. Keeping arthropods such as locusts, giant cockroaches or giant millipedes as class pets would aid this process.

The use of **keys** will help pupils differentiate between different arthropod groups by means of examining physical characteristics. These can be done as paper exercises or by using real animals captured from soil samples. Such activities can be extended by research-style lessons where pupils have to find out about a particular arthropod using library books or the internet with a view to producing an information poster.

KS1 children can capture insects and other small soil-dwelling animals by using pitfall traps. Dig a hole in the soil so that a small tub or cup can be placed inside, making it deep enough so that the lip of the tub is flush with the surface of the soil. Cover the trap with a small roof made from plastic or wood to keep the rain out, remembering to leave a gap at the lip of the cup to allow animals to enter. Use a little sugar or fruit as bait then wait overnight. Any captured animals can be taken to the classroom and studied using magnifying glasses. Ask children to treat the animals with respect, and at the end of the lesson return them to where they were captured, removing your pitfall traps.

For KS1 classes, books such as *The Very Hungry Caterpillar* by Eric Carle are good for helping to explain the complex life cycle that many insects undergo.

Sources: Carle (1969); Shepardson (2002).

2.8 More about insects

Misconception

Insects have a pair of legs attached to each body segment.

Scientific conception

The pupil has depicted the ant as having one pair of legs per body section plus a pair of antennae on the head (Figure 2.8a). Typical characteristics that pupils learn when classifying insects are the three body parts (head, thorax, abdomen), one pair of antennae and three pairs of legs; teachers often compare insect morphology to that of arachnids (e.g. spiders) which tend to have only two body sections but four pairs of legs. All six legs on an adult insect are joined to the middle body section – the thorax (Figure 2.8b). In contrast, the creature at the larval stage (e.g. grubs, caterpillars and maggots) often has many body segments with one pair of legs per segment, which may be one reason for the confusion. In addition, with some insects such as bumble bees the three body sections are difficult to distinguish and it is not clear from where the legs originate.

A related misconception involves counting the antennae as legs, and so mistaking insects for eight-legged arachnids.

Reconstruction

Showing pictures of a variety of adult insects to the class will demonstrate that although there is a wide diversity of insect body shapes, in all instances the legs are

Figure 2.8a Incorrect drawing of an ant (misconception)

Figure 2.8b All six of an ant's legs attach to the thorax

joined to the thorax. The exercise can also be used to reinforce other characteristics common to all insects such as a hard exoskeleton and antennae.

Source: Brass and Jobling (1994).

2.9 Are humans animals?

> **Misconception**
> *We are not animals because we are people.*

[The little girl is not an animal because] she lives at home, she picks flowers in the garden . . . and she is human too. (Pupil, 7 years old; Chen and Ku, 1998, p60)

Scientific conception

It is a fairly widespread belief amongst children and adults alike that humans are not considered as animals. Some of the reasons learners give are related to the fact that humans do not match the terrestrial/quadruped/furry archetype expected of animals (see 2.1). Other reasons centre around a child's ethical/religious experience; for instance an animal is thought of as something less than human and bestial. In contrast human beings are a unique kind of living thing that occupy a special place in the world, and exist outside the rules of classification. When we call another person 'an animal' it can be meant as an insult, referring to something debased and degenerate.

All living things have their place within a biological taxonomic system, including the species *Homo sapiens*, which is classified alongside similar species such as chimpanzees and gorillas in the family Hominidae (apes). This family is subsumed within the primate order, mammal class, vertebrate phylum and the animal kingdom; therefore, taxonomically humans are classified as a type of animal.

A related misconception is that death may not be related to living things other than human beings.

Reconstruction

As with other taxonomic misconceptions, making children aware of the place that human beings occupy within the animal kingdom can be achieved by offering them a view of exactly where our species fits into the 'big picture'. Teaching the five kingdoms, perhaps as a tree-of-life depiction, will make it clear that humans are indeed a type of animal. Discussing similarities between humans and other apes can lead into a discussion about human **evolution**, and how all apes (including humans) have evolved from a common ancestor that is now extinct (see 8.7 for more).

Sensitivity may need to be observed, as some young children will be surprised or even taken aback to hear that they are actually a type of animal, with all the negative connotations allied with the everyday, bestial meaning. In addition, bear in mind that with any discussion about human evolution the scientific view may conflict with the beliefs of children having strong religious ideals.

Sources: Chen and Ku (1998); Inagaki and Hatano (1987); Sequeria and Freitas (1986); Tema (1989); Yen *et al.* (2007).

2.10 What is a plant?

Misconception

All plants have flowers with coloured petals, green leaves and a stem. They can be grown in a plant pot.

Scientific conception

Indeed, many plants fulfil the criteria as laid out in this statement. Others that fail the criteria may not be judged by pupils as being plants, e.g. trees, grass, vegetables, and non-flowering plants such as mosses and ferns. These ideas may be underpinned by the related misconception that 'a flower' is the whole plant, including petals, stem and leaves, as in 'a bunch of flowers'. The origins of these misconceptions probably lie partly in the fact that domestic plants in pots and gardens are the most familiar to children and tend to have large, attractive coloured petals because they serve a decorative function around the home. An associated misconception is that in a garden there are two types of things that grow – plants and weeds – the defining criterion in this case being human cultivation.

Taxonomically there is a wide variety of organisms in the plant kingdom (Figure 2.10). An important criterion that must be met before something is called a plant is that it uses sunlight to make its own food, or photosynthesizes. So as a rule of thumb anything that looks plant-like and is green is likely to be a plant because plants have the green photosynthetic pigment **chlorophyll**. That said, there are a small minority of plants that do not photosynthesize (the myco-heterotrophs), and instead are parasites, gaining nutrients from other living things.

Some learners classify fungi as plants because on first inspection they appear to be plant-like and many are rooted in the soil. Fungi used to be classified as plants, but

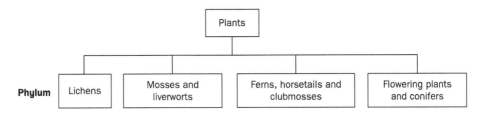

Figure 2.10 The plant kingdom

modern taxonomy has allocated them their own kingdom because they are all exclusively non-photosynthetic, which is why mushrooms, toadstools and yeasts are rarely green. Some single-celled creatures such as chlamydomonas can photosynthesize, but are not classified as plants, instead falling within the kingdom Protoctista (single-celled, not bacteria), which serves to further complicate the situation.

Did you know?

The algae. These include the seaweeds and phytoplankton and are perhaps surprisingly not classified as plants regardless of the fact that they photosynthesize. Because they lack the true differentiation of roots, stems and leaves that is normally found in plants, algae instead belong to the Protoctista kingdom (2.1).

Reconstruction

As with 2.1, the four kingdoms of animal, plant, fungi and 'single cell' could be shown to pupils who are then asked *which category would a fern best fall into?* In addition, although the material is beyond KS2, if the hierarchy in Figure 2.10 can be successfully explained to pupils then this would help them appreciate the variety of life found in the plant kingdom. This could be extended by asking learners to classify pictures or living examples of a variety of plants belonging to different phyla.

Source: Bell (1981).

3

Circulation

3.1 Location of the heart

> **Misconception**
> *The heart lies at the left side of the chest.*

Scientific conception

Pupils frequently draw the heart as a valentine cartoon heart shape on the left portion of the chest (Figure 3.1a).[1] Culturally derived practices such as holding the left side of the chest at around the nipple level when doing a 'broken heart' action signify the widespread nature of the myth, as do popular comic strips and films.

The heart lies at the centre of the chest, behind the breastbone, and is about the size of its owner's clenched fist (Figure 3.1b). The shape of the human heart *approximately* resembles a valentine cartoon heart shape, having a pointy bottom and a minor indentation at the top (separating the two atria), though it should be made clear to children that drawing a cartoon heart is scientifically inaccurate; an asymmetric pointed oval is a better simplified representation at primary level (Figure 3.1c). Note that the bottom of the heart points over towards the left and so slightly more of the heart's mass is actually in the left half of the chest (Figure 3.1b).

The 'heartbeat' (pulse) can be felt if the palm of the hand is pressed firmly just below the left nipple; if you place the hand over the breastbone over where the heart actually is there is no discernible pulse. This is a likely source for the misconception, although what you can feel on the left side of the chest is not the heartbeat directly, but instead the pulse **wave** transmitted through the aorta and the great arteries that exit the heart on the left side.

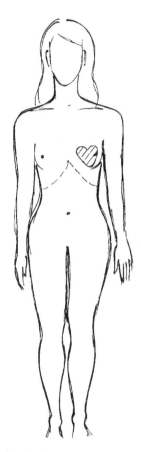

Figure 3.1a My heart is situated at the left side of my chest (misconception)

Reconstruction

As with 5.1, posters or organ vests will prove useful for the elicitation of ideas, end-of-topic assessment or to reinforce previous learning, as will demonstrating the heart's position using commercial plastic anatomical models.

Ask pupils to feel with their left hands where the bottom of their breastbone ends, just where the squashy abdomen begins, and keep the left hand at that position. Make a clenched fist with the right hand and sit it on top of the left – this will locate the position and give the approximate size of the heart. Mention that during **CPR** the heart is massaged indirectly by pressing onto the breastbone and not on the left surface of the chest.

Sources: Bartoszeck *et al.* (2011); Osborne *et al.* (1992).

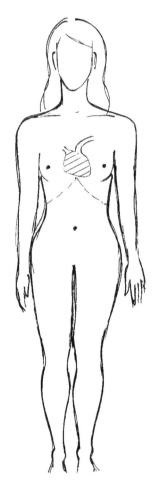

Figure 3.1b Anatomical position of the heart

Figure 3.1c A simple way to draw the heart

3.2 Are the heart and muscles joined together?

Misconception

Our heart beats faster during exercise in order to work our muscles.

Scientific conception

Some learners believe that the heart and muscles are connected by a kind of **pneumatic**-style machine system, and when the heart 'pumps' then this directly causes muscles to move because air (instead of blood) is sent down hollow tubes that connect the two. The idea may derive from experience with bicycle pumps, where if you put work into the system at the hand pump end, air is forced through tubes and something is inflated at the other end.

The heart pumps liquid blood and not gaseous air around the body. As blood moves away from the heart and towards muscles it contains oxygen and food that the muscle cells need in order to sustain themselves (for use in **cellular respiration**). During exercise, muscles work harder and so need a greater supply of oxygen and food. In response the heart beats faster and with more force in order to speed up blood flow and deliver these much needed materials to muscles at an increased rate. Blood also removes wastes such as carbon dioxide from muscle cells. During exercise more waste materials are produced and since blood is moving faster they are removed more quickly.

A related misconception that may form part of a meaningful erroneous conceptual network is that breathing rate increases during exercise in order to supply the muscles with 'more air' (also see 3.3).

Reconstruction

The muscular system is a new addition to the Primary National Curriculum (Year 3), and although beyond the simple ideas laid out in the Programme of Study, a basic understanding of the exchange of materials between cells and the blood would help learners to construct an appropriate mental model: the blood system delivers oxygen and food to muscles, and takes away carbon dioxide and other wastes (Figure 3.2). Integrating these ideas into the wider context of circulation, including the role of the lungs, would provide for a more holistic explanation. This model of the exchange of materials can be practised by means of a role-play exercise where pupils circulate around the classroom acting as 'the blood', dropping off and picking up substances at appropriate points in the room that represent different parts of the body. This role play of the exchanges at body cells can be linked in simultaneously with role plays involving other bodily processes such as **gaseous exchange** at the lungs, and the addition of food to the general circulation at the liver.

There are commercially available anatomical models available that show how the biceps and triceps muscles contract and relax in opposition to move the arm.

Because these model muscles are driven by an air pump system this can reinforce the misconception, so if a model is used, pupils must be reminded that muscles are not in reality driven by air.

Source: Westbrook and Marek (1992).

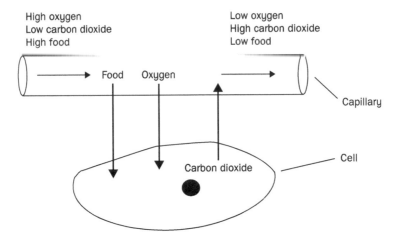

High oxygen
Low carbon dioxide
High food

Low oxygen
High carbon dioxide
Low food

Figure 3.2 Exchange of materials between blood and cell

3.3 What makes your heart rate increase?

Misconception

Exercising is the only time when my heart beats more quickly.

Scientific conception

Children who believe misconceptions such as 'the heart pumps just to make the muscles work' (see 3.2) can further assume that if the muscles are not working vigorously then there is no need for the heart to beat any faster, no matter what the circumstances. However, during periods when the body is at rest a person's heart rate may still be elevated. Drugs such as caffeine, nicotine, cocaine, ecstasy and asthma medicines all increase heart rate in the absence of exercise. Being ill can also elevate heart rate, for instance having a thyroid abnormality, anxiety disorder, high blood pressure, or simply having raised body temperature due to infection.

Humans (and vertebrates generally) have evolved bodily responses to any perceived threat that help them deal with dangerous situations – these are called *fight-or-flight* adaptations. The body is prepared for immediate physical action by increasing the supply of blood to the muscles so they can work more effectively, in order to fight the threat or run away. Blood pressure becomes raised, breathing is deeper and more rapid to enhance oxygen levels in the blood, more sugar is released into the blood to provide food for muscles, and the digestive system is shut down to allow more blood to be diverted to muscles. The fight-or-flight response can also be triggered by relatively non-threatening situations such as anxiety during a job interview, riding a roller-coaster or watching a scary film.

A related misconception is that during exercise, heart and breathing rates increase to keep the body at the same temperature.

Reconstruction

A traditional activity is to have children measure their resting heart rates using stop-watches, then take part in some vigorous physical activity such as doing steps on a bench. Immediately after the activity, measure the heart rate again to see how much it has been raised, and repeat every two minutes until the resting rate is regained. The speed at which the resting rate is reached after exercise has finished is a measure of fitness, and is called the recovery rate. Children often have difficulties finding their pulse and it is generally easier for them to locate their carotid pulse (neck) and not their radial pulse (wrist). The quickest way to find the carotid pulse is to make a cup shape with your hand, then place the fingers and thumb either side of the Adam's apple, or larynx, touching it on both sides. Press the hand gently inwards *around* the larynx, and the pulse should be felt. Do not press directly onto the larynx at any time. Note that contrary to popular belief girls also have an Adam's apple, but it is less pronounced. Alternately, use an electronic pulse meter that children can wear on the wrist – these can be purchased for about £10 each.

To dispel the misconception that only exercising can affect heart rate, it will be necessary to have a child experience a short period of minor stress. Obtain a paper dot-to-dot puzzle but Tippex out one of the numbers in the middle of the sequence, then photocopy the puzzle so that it is not apparent that the number has been erased. Have a child wear an electronic pulse meter, preferably one that can be connected to a computer so that pulse rate can be visually displayed for the rest of the class to see. Have the child start the puzzle but say that this will be a timed exercise where the object is to finish as quickly as possible. When the child cannot find the missing number, a transient period of anxiety will occur as they search frantically for something that is not there. Pulse rate should notably increase during this time as the body senses a threat and reacts with a fight-or-flight response. After pulse rate elevation has been demonstrated, stop the activity and let the child in on the secret, explaining that one does not always need to exercise in order to make one's heart beat more quickly.

Source: Westbrook and Marek (1992).

3.4 The colour of blood

Misconception

The blood in our veins is blue.

Scientific conception

It is commonly believed that **arterial** blood is red and **venous** blood is blue. The assumption is that blood rich in oxygen is bright red, and as this blood travels around the body, oxygen levels are depleted as cells take oxygen and dump carbon dioxide into it (Figure 3.2). The resultant low-oxygen (deoxygenated) blood then enters the venous system, being dark blue or purple in colour. Learners may also believe that when venous blood makes contact with the air, for instance as a result of injury, the blue blood turns immediately bright red as it absorbs atmospheric oxygen.

In fact, venous blood is deep red, as can be witnessed when a doctor draws a blood sample from a vein using a transparent syringe; arterial blood is a brighter red because of increased oxygen levels. The chemical haemoglobin gives blood its red colour, changing its shade in response to whether oxygen is present or absent. The blue colour of veins as seen through paler skins acts as a source for this misconception, which is further reinforced by diagrams in textbooks that (accurately) show the arterial system as red and the venous system as blue.

Despite venous blood being dark red, it appears to be blue due to a false impression of colour – the bluish tinge of venous blood is merely an optical illusion (partly caused by a phenomenon known as *Rayleigh scattering*). As light is reflected from red deoxygenated blood in veins and up through the skin towards an observer's eyes, the blue parts of the reflected light spread out and penetrate the most so that only blue light leaves the surface of the skin, making the blood appear blue. This effect can also be seen during *cyanosis*, a symptom of low blood oxygen that presents in asthma attacks, heart failure, asphyxiation and other conditions, giving rise to blue lips and skin.

Reconstruction

Even though the study of blood and blood vessels is new to the Year 6 Programme of Study, an explanation of the science behind the illusion of blue venous blood is probably beyond the abilities of most KS2 classes. However, showing a video clip of venous blood being drawn from a patient would help learners remember that the blood in veins is actually red. Such a video can be readily sourced using an internet search; be aware of sensitivity issues – some children may find this uncomfortable viewing.

Source: Schoon and Boone (1998).

Note

1. Note that the dotted inverted 'V' in the anatomical outlines represents the bottom of the ribs.

4

Breathing

4.1 Why do we breathe?

> **Misconception**
>
> *Air is just breathed in and out, serving no physiological function.*

Scientific conception

Young pupils who have received little instruction about the role of the human respiratory system will be aware that they need to breathe air in order to survive. Some will associate breathing with the lungs, being able to locate these organs somewhere in the chest cavity or neck area. They may have little understanding of the reasons for breathing other than 'to stay alive', and have no reason to think that after it has been breathed, air changes its composition.

As will be explained in 4.3, there are some differences between inhaled and exhaled air, although not as stark as is commonly expected. The differences reflect the processes of oxygen absorption along with carbon dioxide and water excretion, discussed elsewhere (4.2). A related misconception is the idea that after air is inhaled it remains inside the head merely circulating around briefly before being immediately exhaled, without change.

Reconstruction

This misconception needs to be addressed in the wider context of the role of the respiratory system as an absorber of oxygen and a remover of carbon dioxide and water. Demonstrating that there are differences between inhaled and exhaled air would help children understand that there are changes taking place deep within their lungs. Place a burning candle under two inverted tall glasses in turn, one containing exhaled air and the other atmospheric (normal) air, and time how long it takes each to extinguish (Figure 4.1). The reason the candle goes out is due to using up the oxygen and the

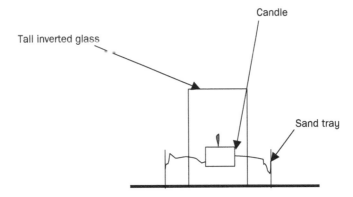

Figure 4.1 Comparing the compositions of exhaled and atmospheric air

production of carbon dioxide within the sealed containers – in exhaled air the candle flame gutters and goes out first because it has higher levels of carbon dioxide and lower levels of oxygen.

Be aware that showing that inhaled and exhaled air are different can act as a trigger for the misconception that exhaled air *is* carbon dioxide (4.3) which may need separate refutation.

Sources: Arnaudin and Mintzes (1985); Gellert (1962).

4.2 How are the heart and lungs connected?

> **Misconception**
>
> *Air tubes connect the lungs to the heart.*

[Your heart] helps you to breathe. (Pupil, aged 9 years; Osborne *et al.*, 1992, p33)

Scientific conception

At primary level pupils learn that during breathing air enters the body through the mouth and nose and travels down the 'air tubes'[1] to the lungs (Figure 4.2a). Pupils also learn that oxygen from the air enters the blood, which then transports the oxygen (along with other materials, such as food) around the body. For many learners the transfer of gaseous oxygen from the air into the liquid blood is a mysterious process, and they may rationalize it by assuming that the air that they breathe into their lungs travels directly to their heart via further air tubes and then enters the bloodstream at the heart (Figure 4.2a).

In reality the process is more complex. After a breath of air is inhaled it eventually ends up in air sacs (**alveoli**) deep within the interior of the lungs. At the alveoli, oxygen in that air sample dissolves into the blood across tiny thin-walled blood vessels

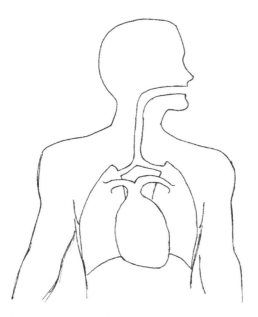

Figure 4.2a Air tubes lead from lungs to heart (misconception)

called **capillaries** (Figure 4.2b). At the same time carbon dioxide, a waste gas produced by all body cells, leaves the blood and enters the alveoli, ready to be exhaled and removed from the body in expired air. When the blood, which is being continuously pumped through the capillaries in the lungs, leaves the alveoli it is 'refreshed', being rich in oxygen and low in carbon dioxide. On the other hand the air that leaves the lungs is 'spent', and is higher in carbon dioxide and lower in oxygen.

The heart really does two separate jobs. The first is well known – to pump blood around the body, so delivering oxygen to cells and removing carbon dioxide from those same cells (Figure 4.2). Its second job is to replenish the blood's oxygen and get rid of its carbon dioxide, which it does by sending blood on a separate journey around the lungs (Figure 4.2c). As this diagram shows, the circulatory system can be thought of as two separate circuits that meet in the heart. 'Used' blood low in oxygen and high in carbon dioxide enters the heart after a trip around the body. This blood needs refreshing so is sent to the lungs; when the blood returns to the heart it is now high in oxygen and low in carbon dioxide, and so ready for another trip around the body. These ideas were first put forward by the English physician William Harvey in the seventeenth century (see box, p47).

Considering the complexity of the double circulation, it is not surprising that some learners rationalize how oxygen enters the blood by assuming open tubes exist so that air can pass from the lungs to the heart, allowing oxygen to directly enter the blood (Figure 4.2a).

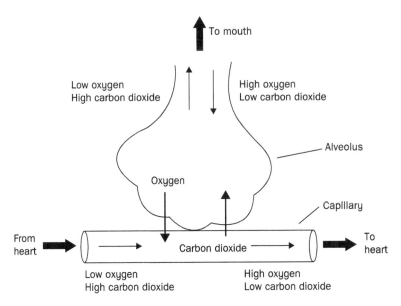

Figure 4.2b Gaseous exchange in the lungs

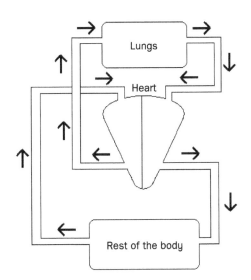

Figure 4.2c Simplified diagram of the double circulation

Reconstruction

Using an anatomical plastic model of a human torso will show that air tubes connect the mouth to the lungs, but not the lungs to the heart. This can be supplemented by reference to the internet: there are several useful animations available showing how the pulmonary circulation connects to the systemic circulation (try Googling 'animation pulmonary circulation'). Traditionally, a lamb's heart and lungs dissection has been used to show how the circulatory and respiratory systems are linked, although in some schools there may be ethical issues with using this pedagogy.

Sources: Arnaudin and Mintzes (1985); Garcia-Barros *et al.* (2011); Osborne *et al.* (1992); Symons *et al.* (1994); Tracana *et al.* (2012).

Famous scientists

William Harvey. Before Harvey proposed his double circulation model in 1628, physicians believed the teachings of Galen, a medical scientist who had lived in Ancient Roman times. Galen had judged that the human arterial and venous systems were completely separated and that the purpose of the lungs was merely to cool the blood, while the heart in turn heated the blood. These beliefs were blended with mystical views of the heart as the place where the human spirit resided. Many contemporary physicians did not accept Harvey's theory despite clear anatomical evidence, since at the time medical thinking was generally very conservative and did not accept new ideas readily.

4.3 What is in the air we breathe out?

Misconception

Exhaled air is mainly carbon dioxide and very low in oxygen.

Scientific conception

This is a common misunderstanding, often expressed as *we breathe in oxygen and breathe out carbon dioxide*. Pupils learn that the job of the lungs is to absorb oxygen and excrete unwanted carbon dioxide, so it makes sense to them that most/all of what humans breathe out will contain this waste gas. This idea may link in with the related misconception that atmospheric (inhaled) air is pure oxygen, to form a meaningful though erroneous conceptual network.

In fact, exhaled air only contains around 4 per cent carbon dioxide; this compares to levels of about 0.04 per cent in inhaled air. Furthermore, the air we breathe into our lungs (atmospheric air) has an oxygen content of 21 per cent, and contrary to popular opinion our lungs do not absorb all of this oxygen, only around a fifth of it. It could be argued therefore that the air we breathe out is not immensely different from that we breathe in, despite the fact that carbon dioxide is 100 times more concentrated (Figure 4.3a). The gas that makes up most of both inhaled and exhaled air is neither oxygen nor carbon dioxide, but nitrogen, which enters and leaves the lungs at the same concentration level (78 per cent). Note that the values given are for dry samples of air. Inhaled air will normally contain **water vapour**, the amount of which depends on environmental humidity (up to 5 per cent of the total). Because the respiratory tract is very moist, exhaled air is saturated with water which makes up around 5 per cent of the total composition, which is why on cold days we are able to see water droplets as a fine mist when we breathe out.

This misconception is not helped by a popular diagram that pupils are generally good at recalling, which implies that trees give out only oxygen and humans give out only carbon dioxide (Figure 4.3b).

Gas	Inhaled air (%)	Exhaled air (%)
Carbon dioxide	0.04	4
Oxygen	21	17
Nitrogen	78	78
Others	1	1

Figure 4.3a Comparative compositions of inhaled and exhaled air by volume of dry samples

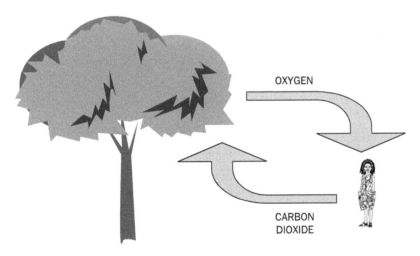

Figure 4.3b Animals give carbon dioxide to trees and trees give oxygen to animals

Reconstruction

Ask pupils to carefully waft a gentle breeze onto a **glowing splint** using a piece of stiff material such as a piece of A4 card – why does it glow more brightly? We are feeding the smouldering fire with a stream of atmospheric air that contains 21 per cent oxygen, which increases the rate of burning, so causing the glow. Next, ask them to gently blow at the splint using a straw – as before, the splint glows more brightly. When we blow on something we are passing exhaled air from our lungs over it, and the splint glows brightly because this air still contains significant levels of oxygen, which at 17 per cent is just 4 per cent less concentrated than atmospheric (inhaled) air. If we breathed out pure or highly concentrated carbon dioxide then the smouldering splint would be extinguished.

To reinforce this idea mention to pupils that mouth-to-mouth resuscitation would not work if exhaled air was high in carbon dioxide and low in oxygen.

Source: Yip (1998).

Note

1. The term 'air tubes' is a simplification; more anatomical terms are the trachea, bronchi and bronchioles.

5

Nutrition

5.1 Where exactly is the stomach located?

> **Misconception**
>
> *The stomach is located around the navel area.*

Scientific conception

In Figure 5.1a the stomach has been drawn as a large organ that lies around the level of the navel. This popular idea derives from the colloquial use of the word 'stomach' to describe the whole area at the front of the body that lies below the ribs and above the pelvis; for instance, stomach/tummy/belly ache is discomfort felt from anywhere around this region.

The stomach is actually sited at the level of the ribs on the left side of the body, and is much smaller than people generally realize (Figure 5.1b). The shaded area in Figure 5.1a, colloquially understood to be the stomach, is anatomically part of the *abdomen*, and contains several organs including the intestines, liver, spleen, bladder, pancreas and the stomach itself. Note that after a large meal the stomach temporarily expands (distends) more into the abdomen, acting as a food storage area and initiating a feeling of 'being full'.

Reconstruction

Ask learners to produce a life-sized poster of their bodies with stuck-on paper organs in the correct position. Alternatively, a fabric 'vest' can be made that requires different organ shapes to be cut out of spare pieces of material and glued/sewn onto an old T-shirt, with the finished article able to be worn by pupils as an item of clothing. These activities can be used at the beginning of a topic if the teacher wishes to elicit misconceptions; at the end of the topic the process may be repeated to make pupils aware of how their learning has progressed. A common problem is that pupils tend not to

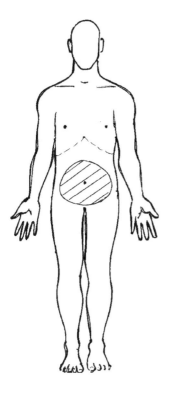

Figure 5.1a The stomach is a large organ situated around the navel area (misconception)

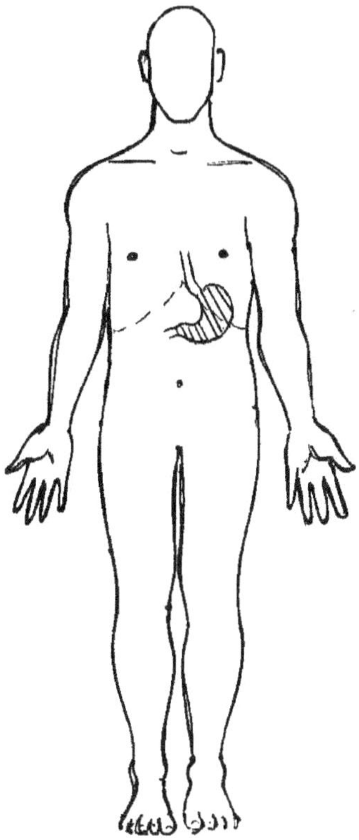

Figure 5.1b Anatomical position of the stomach

overlap organs when they create a two-dimensional poster or drawing, which results in errors in the size and position of organs. For instance, in reality the stomach overlaps or is overlapped by the large intestine and the left lung, the heart overlaps the lungs, and the kidneys are tucked away at the back of the body, being overlapped by several organs.

Ask pupils to physically locate their own stomachs by feeling for the bottom of their ribs just left of the breastbone. Demonstration using a commercially available plastic anatomical model of the human torso is very useful, helping to reinforce the real position and size of the stomach.

Source: Mintzes (1984).

5.2 How the digestive system deals with food and drink

Misconception

The digestive system consists of two separate tubes, one for faeces, the other for urine.

Scientific conception

Before exposure to the formal teaching of digestive processes some pupils may believe that any food they eat passes down a 'solids' tube inside their body, and anything they drink travels down a separate 'liquids' tube (Figure 5.2). The solids tube is directly connected to the anus, where faeces leaves the body as waste once the goodness has been taken out of food. Similarly, the liquids tube is connected to the urinary system, which disposes of what is left over once the body has extracted all it needs from what the person has drunk.

These misconceptions are a result of learners' attempts to construct a rational explanation to link the processes of eating with defecating, and drinking with urinating. They realize that there is a cause-and-effect relationship between what goes into and what leaves their bodies, particularly the knowledge that the desire to urinate follows drinking a significant **volume** of liquid. They have clear understandings of the start and end events, but intervening processes are a mystery to them, taking place inside the unfathomable 'black box' of their bodies.

Anything that is ingested, whether food or drink, follows the same pathway through the digestive system. As many children will appreciate, 'solid' food goes on a journey from the mouth to the anus; nutrients are absorbed from the food into the bloodstream at many waypoints during the course of this trip. Ingested 'liquids' (such

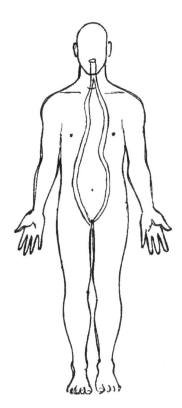

Figure 5.2 The digestive system is two separate tubes (misconception)

as drinks, soups, yoghurts) normally have a high water content yet travel precisely the same route, with water being absorbed into the blood at the stomach, large intestine and other sites. The brain then detects that there is now an excess of water in the blood and 'tells' the kidneys to expel more water, so redressing the balance (see box) and producing the familiar feeling of the need to urinate after drinking liquids. As is the case with more solid foods, any nutrients contained within the liquids are absorbed by the digestive system and enter the blood, e.g. sugar in soft drinks, protein in milk (although these proteins are first broken down into simpler units, or **digested**).

A fuller appreciation can be gained by referring to the function of the urinary system as a waste mechanism for the metabolism of the whole body, which clarifies the point that urine is not merely the direct product of spent liquids that have been previously ingested (see box). Related misconceptions include that digested food is melted, and the stomach acts as a filtering organ sorting out the goodness from the useless parts of food.

Did you know?

The urinary system. School children and adults alike tend not to fully understand the reasons why they urinate, although there is an obvious association between drinking liquids and urinating. Blood enters the kidneys which then act as filters, extracting waste substances the body does not need, especially urea (a by-product of protein metabolism), and drugs such as alcohol. It is acceptable to say in simple terms that the kidneys clean the blood. In order to get rid of these waste materials from the body they have to be dissolved in water, hence urine is a liquid. There is more sophistication to the process as the kidneys are able to adjust the amount of water they excrete according to the body's needs. For instance, on hot days we lose lots of water via sweating through the skin, and so urine is smaller in volume because the body needs to conserve water to avoid dehydration. If both kidneys fail then death is imminent due to the build-up of waste toxins in the blood.

Reconstruction

The original misconception of there being a food tube and a liquid tube is partly accurate, and so can be used as a foundation on which to build more correct scientific ideas. Say to pupils that if they reject their idea of a liquid tube then they are on the right lines, and that all ingested material whether liquid or solid follows the path of the 'food tube' and is treated in a similar way by the digestive system.

Mention that urine colour does not change in response to any drink that was previously ingested – it does not matter whether you drink water, coca cola or milk, urine is still yellow. Incidentally, if large amounts of milk are drunk habitually, stools often take on a whiter shade due to having a higher fat content, so supporting the scientific view of a single food tube for liquids and solids. Further discussion could cover some simple ideas underpinning water balance, e.g. the fact that urine can change its shade not because of the colour of drunk liquids, but in response to whether the body is conserving or shedding water – on hot days our bodies lose less water in urine because larger quantities have been lost during sweating, so urine has a more concentrated deep yellow tone because it contains less water.

Sources: Brinkman and Boschhuizen (1989); Equit *et al.* (2013).

5.3 The body's interior

> **Misconception**
>
> *The entire inside of the body is a hollow bag where blood, food and wastes are contained.*

Scientific conception

Even though they understand that the human body contains a variety of things, younger children particularly may not differentiate specific areas inside their bodies where life processes such as digestion or excretion are carried out. To them, the whole body is a large bag where food which has been eaten floats around, mixing freely with the other things that are recognized as being present internally. For instance, some children have drawn food entering this bag and then slowly making its way downwards to the legs, which are also hollow areas (Figure 5.3).

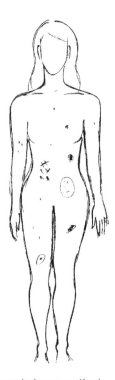

Figure 5.3 The body is a hollow bag (misconception)

Since the interior of their bodies cannot be directly observed it is not surprising that children use their imaginations in order to construct rational depictions of how the things inside of them might look (also see 3.1 and 5.1).

Reconstruction

When pupils are taught the general location of major body organs in association with the role each fulfils, it should become clear to them that the 'hollow bag' view is not sustainable. The pedagogies used in 5.1 can be used to clarify the correct locations of internal body organs, especially three-dimensional representations such as plastic models that refute the idea that an interior empty space exists. Note that using a skeleton during teaching may actually reinforce the 'hollow bag' misconception since knowledge of the presence of the ribs, spine and pelvis would be consistent with the erroneous view of an empty internal space.

Sources: Fraiberg (1959); Osborne *et al.* (1992).

5.4 Why do we have to eat food?

Misconception

The only reason we eat food is to give us energy.

Scientific conception

Analogous to a 'fuel', food provides the body with the energy needed to carry out life processes (1.1); the energy content of a specific food is given in kilojoules or kilocalories.

Pupils can forget, however, that many nutrients carry out additional functions within the body. After proteins and fats in the diet have been digested and absorbed into the blood they are often reassembled into new protein and fat **molecules** that then become a lasting part of our body structure. For example, amino acids from proteins in a beef burger can end up becoming part of our biceps muscle; animal fat components from the same burger eventually become integrated within the membranes of cells within the lining of our lungs. Thus, food is important during the growing years as a source of raw material for building our bodies, and even after we stop growing is still vital as the body is continually repairing itself due to loss of cells during everyday wear and tear, and illness.

Furthermore, carbohydrates (e.g. from fruits, bread, rice, sugar) are normally broken down into glucose by the body for use as the 'fuel' in respiration, providing energy, although if eaten in excessive amounts they become converted into body fat and stored under the skin, around the midriff, etc. The same outcome ensues when an excess of dietary fat is consumed. **Minerals** can similarly become integrated into bodily structures, such as calcium in bones and teeth; vitamins are important for certain chemical reactions inside the body. Dietary fibre is indigestible, though is needed for the effective movement of material through the intestines.

Reconstruction

Primary pupils are generally aware that their bodies will not grow if they do not eat enough of the 'right' food, a belief that is undoubtedly reinforced by parental reminders at mealtimes. Conversely, they are warned that eating an excessive amount of the 'wrong' food can make them overweight. These are good starting points from which to introduce the idea that nutrients not only supply energy but also can become a physical part of our bodies, or *we are what we eat*.

Babies increase in size rapidly during the first months of life, growth then continuing at a lesser pace up until the mid/late teens. Ask the class the question, *where has all this extra body mass come from?* It cannot have just appeared without a source, and if science was advanced enough we perhaps would be able to look inside our bodies and relate every piece of ourselves to a particular meal that we ate on a specific day in the past.

Sources: Smith and Anderson (1986).

5.5 Why is eating proteins important?

Misconception

It is important to eat protein because it is the body's main source of energy.

Scientific conception

This idea is related to the misconception that the only reason humans eat food is as a source of energy to drive life processes (5.4), with the notion that food can also act as raw material for growth and repair being sometimes forgotten. The importance of protein as a vital nutritional component is well known and reinforced by the media and health education. In the statement above the pupil has merged a (correct) under-standing of the essentiality of proteins in the diet with the (correct) concept that we eat partly to provide our bodies with energy. However, the nutritional role of protein is not as a provider of energy, and is discussed further in 5.4; instead it is carbohy-drates and fats in the diet that constitute the main sources of energy for the body. Note that in certain circumstances, for instance during starvation, fasting or intense exercise, the body *is* able to use proteins as an 'emergency' energy supply in the place of carbohydrates, but this process is far from the norm.

Related misconceptions include the ideas that water and vitamins are important sources of energy for the body.

Reconstruction

The pedagogies described in 5.4 are applicable here.

Sources: Boyes and Stanisstreet (1990); Dreyfus and Jungwirth (1988); Lucas (1987).

5.6 Can eating fat be good for you?

Misconception

All fat is bad for you.

Scientific conception

A major focus of public health education both inside and outside schools is the problem of increasing levels of obesity in the developed world. Resulting health issues such as heart disease (and other cardiovascular illness), type II diabetes, arthritis, and lowered self-esteem are a bane for the UK population and a drain on medical resources. The ingestion of animal fat from foods such as meat, butter and other dairy products has been particularly singled out as a significant factor in the onset and maintenance of obesity, which has led to the current popularity of preventative measures such as low-fat diets.

The conspicuousness of these ideas in the public domain has led to the mistaken belief that *any* intake of dietary fat is a bad thing. In fact, fats are vital for maintaining life processes (Figure 5.6a), and if we stopped eating fats we would become ill. Sources vary, but it is usually recommended that a balanced diet contains 45–65 per cent carbohydrates, 10–35 per cent proteins and 20–35 per cent fats (Figure 5.6b). Instead of a total avoidance of fats, nutritionists advise that in order to fend off obesity this recommended intake not be exceeded as part of a calorie-restricted diet. A main role of dietary fat is to provide the body with energy, as is the case with carbohydrates; in fact the same mass of fat provides double the amount of energy of carbohydrate, and it is this high calorific content that contributes to the obesity problem. Some kinds of dietary fats are less healthy than others, for instance saturated fats (e.g. dairy products, red meat) have been linked to serious cardiovascular conditions and cancer. Unsaturated fats (e.g. fish oils, olive oil, nuts) are associated with fewer health

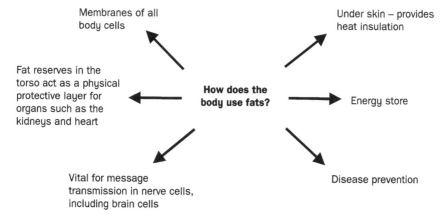

Figure 5.6a The importance of fats inside the body

problems, an exception being unsaturated trans-fats (e.g. butter, some cooking oils), which have been strongly linked to heart disease.

Reconstruction

As part of a topic on healthy eating in Year 5 it is usual to make pupils aware of which foods are abundant in particular nutrients (e.g. meat, fish, eggs, etc. contain proteins), and this is normally presented as a pie chart which comprises pictures of different foods occupying sectors within the circle whose size represents the proportion that should be eaten as part of a balanced diet (Figure 5.6b gives a simple depiction). The Food Standards Agency in the UK has published its own version, the *Eatwell Plate*. These

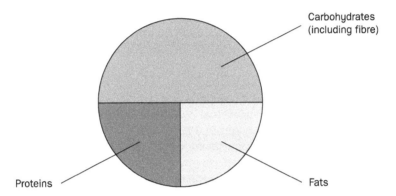

Figure 5.6b The proportion of nutrients recommended for a balanced diet

ideas can be extended by using the nutritional information labels found on packaged food to plan an 'expedition menu', where pupils have to decide which foods to take on a three-day expedition to the desert, bearing in mind the requirements for a balanced diet.

Using the library or the internet as a resource, ask pupils to produce a poster of the body that shows where fat reserves are found, and also where fats play an important role in metabolism.[1] Remind them that the well-known Atkins diet recommends a long-term intake of significantly higher-than-normal percentages of fat that appears to have no lasting deleterious effects on adherents, who tend to lose body mass due to restricted dietary carbohydrate.

Source: Turner (1997).

5.7 The nutritional value of dairy foods

Misconception

All dairy products are good for you.

Scientific conception

In the UK, from the 1950s until the early 1990s, cow's milk and its derivatives (e.g. butter, cheese, cream, yoghurt, ice cream, milk chocolate) had been heavily marketed as nutritionally beneficial foods. Advertising campaigns telling us to drink a pint of milk a day have helped embed the idea into the national consciousness that dairy foods are an essential part of a healthy lifestyle. Indeed, milk particularly has nutritious constituents. Whole milk 'straight from the cow' has approximately 4 per cent fat, 4 per cent sugar, 4 per cent protein, less than 1 per cent minerals (including calcium), the remainder being water. As milk is artificially processed, essential vitamins and minerals are added. Dairy products generally are high-energy foods due to their significant fat content, with the proportion being higher in derivatives such as cheese and cream (both up to 50 per cent fat), and butter (up to 80 per cent fat).

Considering these figures, milk products could be included as part of a balanced diet where the total fat intake is advised to be 20–35 per cent; the detrimental effects of excessive consumption of high-fat foods have been discussed elsewhere in this book, including the presence of saturated fats in dairy foods that have been associated with heart disease (5.6). Lower-fat, 'healthier' varieties of processed milk are available in the form of semi-skimmed and skimmed milk (1.5 per cent and 0.25 per cent fat, respectively). Inclusion of lower-fat milk into the diet has been linked to a fall in obesity levels and reduced cardiovascular disease. An added problem with dairy products is lactose intolerance, which affects 4 per cent of the population in the UK. Also, there have been widely reported controversies centred on the fact that cow's milk contains trace amounts of bovine drugs such as anabolic steroids, growth hormone and antibiotics; to date, no clear detrimental health effects have been uncovered regarding these particular constituents.

Reconstruction

Inform pupils that dairy products contain many beneficial nutrients including proteins, sugars, fats, vitamins and minerals (calcium included). A problem lies in the varying amounts of fats found in the different dairy foods – with skimmed milk, fat content is low and so is less of an issue. However, butter, cream and full-fat cheese, for instance, are high-fat foods and so should be taken in moderation as part of a healthy balanced diet.

Source: Turner (1997).

5.8 Which foods contain fats?

Misconception

Food only contains fat if the fat can be seen.

Scientific conception

Some meats have obvious fatty areas (e.g. bacon rind, lamb joint, pork chops, ham), with these parts often being removed by health-conscious diners and left uneaten. Pupils may believe that other foods rich in fats but without visible fatty regions are fat-free (e.g. crisps, nuts, cheese, cream, pastries).

Reconstruction

Having an *Eatwell Plate* type poster (Figure 5.6b) on display in the classroom will help pupils understand that a variety of foods are rich in fats, and not just meats that have visible fat. Examining food nutrition labels would help to reinforce these ideas. A rule of thumb is that if your fingers feel greasy after eating a particular food then it contains comparatively high levels of fats (e.g. crisps, chips, spare ribs).

The teacher can demonstrate the energy content of different foods by burning equal masses of samples and measuring the temperature rise of a small container of water held over the flame (Figure 5.8). Foods like crisps and cashew nuts heat the water more intensely than crispbreads or pasta due to their higher fat content, because fats contain twice as much energy as carbohydrates.[2]

Source: Turner (1997).

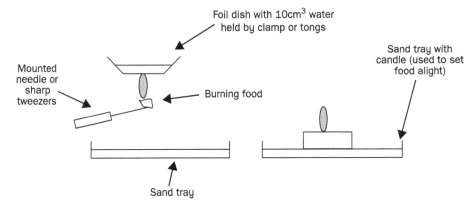

Figure 5.8 An experiment to show the energy values of different foods

Be safe!

Using naked flames in the classroom. Naked flames in the form of candles are both potentially a fire and injury hazard and so require a little thought before they are employed in the classroom. The shape of many traditional candles makes them inherently unstable and prone to being knocked over when alight. Before lighting candles place them in a small sand tray consisting of a disposable foil baking dish approximately 20cm in diameter. Make sure the base of the candle is adequately sunk into the sand so that it will not fall over easily. Tea light candles have a low centre of gravity and are the safest type so should be used whenever possible. Inform pupils of the dangers of working with naked flames including the risk of burnt fingers and clothing. Know where the fire extinguisher is in the room and how to use it correctly (read the label), and have it close to hand during these activities. The decision about whether to use candles with your class is a matter for risk assessment, but generally they are quite safe with well-behaved upper KS2 pupils. It is good practice *not* to let pupils light their own candles with matches or splints, instead the teacher should go around the class and light the candles her/himself.

5.9 Do plants need food?

Misconception

Plants get their food from the soil.

Scientific conception

This very common idea makes sense to learners because they have constructed a link between two pieces of knowledge – a plant's roots take in water/goodness from the soil, and the plant is constantly growing. It is correct to say that some substances vital for life processes are absorbed into a plant via the roots, e.g. water, nitrates for protein synthesis, and magnesium for chlorophyll production. However, even though the plant takes in these nutrients (in a similar way to an animal eating) these substances are not food in a strictly scientific sense. For a chemical to be classed as food it has to be able to supply energy to the organism during cellular respiration, therefore in plants only carbohydrates such as glucose and starch are technically food. Carbohydrates are made during the process of photosynthesis, where the plant converts carbon dioxide and water into glucose (food) and oxygen, in the presence of sunlight. Thus, a plant does not take in food directly from the environment as an animal would, but instead is a kind of food factory, manufacturing its own glucose from raw materials and storing it as starch (Figure 5.9).

In an everyday sense, to state that plants absorb food from the soil is true since 'food' is colloquially understood to be anything an organism takes in for nourishment, so any nutrients absorbed from the soil would fall into this category. This is an instance where everyday and scientific meanings clash and create confusion; the commercial availability of garden fertilizers labelled 'plant food' reinforces this scientifically erroneous, though everyday meaning.

The misconception can be elicited with questions such as *over many years this tree has grown from an acorn to become a mighty oak . . . where did all this extra mass come from?* It is important to remember that some of the plant's mass did in fact originate from the soil in the form of water absorbed by the roots that becomes converted into carbohydrate, and also remains as water in the plant's tissues. However, this water cannot be called *food* because in the form it is absorbed it cannot act as a source of energy for the plant.

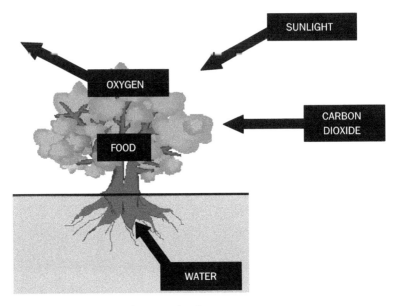

Figure 5.9 The components of photosynthesis

Reconstruction

A simple way to refute the misconception is to ask pupils to plant a seedling such as a broad bean in a pot containing soil. At the beginning, weigh the soil and pot together without the seedling, and then the seedling on its own. Allow it to grow for a few weeks, keeping well watered in a bright area of the classroom, then reweigh both soil/pot, and plant, again separately. The plant will have increased in mass, though the soil/pot's mass will remain fairly constant. Point out to pupils that obviously the soil could not have been responsible for the plant's significant increase in mass, even if the soil/pot ends up being slightly lighter than before. Use this idea as a starting point to explain that water in the soil and carbon dioxide in the air were responsible for the extra mass.

A traditional KS1 activity is making leaf prints. Use leaves as a template by painting one side and them pressing them down firmly onto sugar paper to make striking patterns. The story book *Fran's Flower* by Lisa Bruce can provide an appropriate entry into the subject of plant nutrition for young children.

Sources: Barker (1985); Bell and Brook (1984); Bruce (2000); Smith and Anderson (1984); Stavy *et al.* (1987); Wandersee (1983).

5.10 Are all drugs harmful?

Misconception

Drugs are harmful, illegal and highly addictive.

Scientific conception

An everyday interpretation of the word 'drug' in the English language corresponds to the meaning reflected in the misconception statement above – something that is taken to achieve a 'high' that is not legally available, is harmful to the body (especially in excessive amounts) and is addictive. This meaning is also reflected in terms such a 'being on drugs', drug dealers and drug education. The scientific definition of 'drug' is more wide-ranging and includes any chemical that has an effect on living cells, whether that effect is helpful or harmful to an organism. Drugs include medicines available from a pharmacy and elsewhere, the recreational drugs alcohol, nicotine and caffeine, and illicit drugs such as tetrahydrocannabinol (found in cannabis), cocaine and heroin. Herbal medicines are also drugs, as are the so-called 'legal highs', e.g. mephedrone. Therefore the majority of drugs that are available are beneficial, legal to own (although sometimes a prescription is needed), and non-addictive.

A medicine, on the other hand, has a more specific meaning, being a substance used for the prevention, diagnosis or treatment of disease. All medicines are drugs, but not all drugs are medicines. This meaning is generally well understood and people typically have a positive image of anything that is called a medicine, though have a negative image of anything they perceive to be a drug.

Reconstruction

With older pupils drugs education is usually part of their Personal, Social and Health Education curriculum (PSHE), and so may have been introduced to the idea of illicit drugs outside of science lessons. In Year 6 the Science Programme of Study has a topic on healthy lifestyles, including diet and exercise, and so you may decide that it is more appropriate to teach about drugs and medicines during science lessons. With KS1 children, teachers could bring in a table display of things around the home that are harmful to the human body and things that are safe. The harmful things could include motor oil, oven cleaner, paint, a laser pen and white spirit. Remind children that medicines can be very dangerous unless a doctor or parent has given permission for them to be taken.

Sources: Bjornsdottir *et al.* (2009); Cruikshank (2012).

Notes

1. Note that discretion and sensitivity should be exercised, bearing in mind that many primary-aged children are within obesity limits.
2. With older, more sensible classes, and only after appropriate risk assessment, you could consider allowing pupils to carry out this experiment themselves.

6

Feeding relationships

6.1 Food chain rules

Misconception

The arrow in a food chain means 'eats'.

Scientific conception

As shown in Figure 6.1a, pupils will frequently draw a food chain with the arrows reversed that incorrectly implies that a rabbit is a **predator** of a fox, although when questioned they will tell you that the opposite is true. The error is due to the widely accepted meaning of an arrow in any diagram to show *direction of action*; the thing having the action done to it is placed at the pointed end of the arrow. For instance, in physics a force arrow is drawn away from the source of the force and towards the thing being pushed; in cartoons, arrows represent the movement of a character or object from one place to another.

With food chain and food web diagrams we are actually asking pupils to mentally reverse this familiar association and remember that an arrow means 'is eaten by'. Thus, a correct food chain would be as depicted in Figure 6.1b.

Pupils will usually spot their mistake if they are made to think about whether the food chain they have just depicted makes any sense: can rabbits actually eat foxes?

Grass ◄——————— Rabbit ◄——————— Fox

Figure 6.1a Reversed arrow food chain (misconception)

Grass ——————► Rabbit ——————► Fox

Figure 6.1b Food chain with correctly oriented arrows

However, if at least one of the organisms is unfamiliar then errors go uncorrected; for instance, although commonly cited in food chains, many pupils do not know what a thrush or an aphid are.

Reconstruction

This issue is sometimes difficult to address since it requires rote learning that is at odds with familiar associations of the pictorial meaning of an arrow, and pupils tend to remember its correct usage with food chains one day but forget it the next, reverting back to the misconception. As with all rote learning, repetition and drill will help.

One tip is to use the 'Pacman rule', referring to a well-known video-game character (Figure 6.1c). Get pupils into the habit of using a pencil to lightly draw 'Pacmen' on the ends of their food chain arrows and imagine the character is moving – he only munches in one direction, where the 'mouth' is facing. Therefore the organisms in the food chain eat in the same direction as that in which 'Pacman' munches. Tell pupils not to forget to rub out their 'Pacmen' before handing in a piece of work.

Figure 6.1c Pacman rule

It is a good idea when possible to use photographs or diagrams of organisms when constructing food chains, and not just words, as some organisms may be unfamiliar to pupils (Figure 6.1d). When each organism is visualized in this way it is sometimes obvious which is the predator and which is the **prey**. The same pictures that are used for classification exercises (e.g. 2.2) can double up as useful food chain elements.

Source: Schollum (1983).

Figure 6.1d Using pictures to illustrate a food chain

6.2 Food chains and population numbers

Misconception

If lots of caterpillars die, this has no effect on the numbers of nettles or hedgehogs.

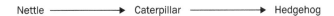

Nettle ⟶ Caterpillar ⟶ Hedgehog

Figure 6.2 A simple food chain

Scientific conception

Learners can misunderstand the wider effects of population changes within an ecosystem in a number of ways. The statement above suggests that a decrease in numbers of one organism has no effect on the others in the food chain. In the example given, if the number of caterpillars decreases, because they act as a food supply for the hedgehog population the number of hedgehogs would be expected to decrease in turn as some die due to starvation. In addition, surviving hedgehogs will tend to reproduce at a reduced rate in reaction to the scant food supply (Figure 6.2). A second effect of fewer caterpillars in the ecosystem would be that nettles would tend to thrive as there are fewer caterpillars around to eat them.

In reality a more complex situation would ensue where perhaps another organism in competition with caterpillars would flourish and start to eat more nettles, keeping the nettle population constant. Also, hedgehogs would have a varied diet and, after the caterpillars' demise, would perhaps start to hunt a different prey, so avoid starvation. However, since the only evidence put before us is the single food chain, we need to explain the predictions in population changes only in terms of these organisms.

Other misconceptions involve a failure to consider the food chain as a holistic system where a change in the numbers of one organism affects all of the rest. Pupils who successfully predict an effect of a population change on a predator–prey relationship sometimes forget to include the **producer** (the plant), whose numbers are commonly predicted to remain constant. Alternatively, they think changes in predator numbers will affect prey numbers, but not vice versa, e.g. if hedgehogs die then caterpillars thrive, but if caterpillars die this will not affect hedgehog numbers. A different misconception is the idea that when the population of an organism changes this only affects other organisms adjacent to it in the chain, e.g. fewer nettles would affect the numbers of caterpillars, but not the hedgehog population. Anyone who is not able to fully appreciate the far-reaching impacts of changes to a single population may trivialize a media report about an endangered species, only believing that species alone is under threat, when the likelihood is that many members of an ecosystem will be adversely affected.

Reconstruction

More practice with food chain population change exercises would help learners understand that a food chain represents an interdependent system, and not just a series of isolated predator–prey, or **consumer**–producer relationships.

Talking to the class about real-world examples of population changes within food chains/webs could include pest control, e.g. introducing ladybirds into an ecosystem to reduce the population of aphids that are destroying crops.

Making the jump from simple linear food chains to more complex food webs can be problematic. Using an ecosystem that contains familiar organisms such as African grassland can facilitate this process. Lion, zebra, crocodile, locust, antelope, acacia tree, grass, leopard, etc. can be first arranged into sensible linear food chains that can later be converted into food webs by joining the chains together with further, offshooting arrows. A food web wall display in the classroom utilizing pictures can be useful, using lengths of coloured string for the arrows.

Sources: Gotwals and Songer (2010); Griffiths and Grant (1985); Leach *et al.* (1992).

6.3 Predators within food chains

Misconception

A sparrowhawk is a predator of thrushes, ladybirds and aphids.

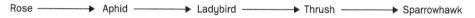

Figure 6.3 A food chain comprising multiple predators

Scientific conception

The pupil thinks an animal placed higher in a food chain is a predator of all others placed below it. This may be due to thinking the food chain symbolizes a power hierarchy, similar to roles in human organizations; for instance, with the army ranks of private, corporal, sergeant, staff sergeant, etc., each rank holder has authority over all those lower in the chain of command. It cannot help when we tell pupils that the sparrowhawk is the **top predator**, a term which has connotations of overarching dominance.

Each arrow in a food chain represents a single feeding relationship. From Figure 6.3 we can deduce that sparrowhawks eat thrushes, thrushes eat ladybirds, and so on. Note that food chains are linear representations showing only a single pathway, and thus are simplifications that do not tell the whole story. Within an ecosystem a sparrowhawk may indeed eat ladybirds as well as thrushes, which could be represented by drawing an additional arrow from ladybird to sparrowhawk. However, the diagram could no longer be called a simple food *chain*, and instead is the beginnings of a more complex food *web*.

Reconstruction

It needs to be made clear to pupils that within a food chain only organisms immediately next to each other have a feeding relationship. These relationships cannot 'skip' over **trophic levels**. Remind pupils that when an animal is the top predator this simply means that it is not the prey of any other animal, and has nothing to do with overall dominance over the other organisms in a food chain.

Day trips to woodland centres provide a useful context for teaching the ideas that underpin food chains and webs, providing a natural setting with direct access to organisms that make up the food chains/webs.

Sources: Barman *et al.* (1995); Griffiths and Grant (1985).

6.4 What is interdependence?

> **Misconception**
> *Wild animals never go short of food.*

Scientific conception

Young children tend to think that food is always plentiful for wild animals, which co-exist peacefully because they have similar needs – they do their best to get along with each other. They think of plants and animals as individual, isolated entities instead of understanding that species live as members of populations in a community that are dependent upon each other for survival. In any ecosystem there is always life and death competition between organisms for scarce resources; some species triumph over others in these competitions which can end up with the out-competed species disappearing from an ecosystem. The idea that organisms do not exist in isolation but are vitally dependent upon each other is important in ecology. This **interdependence** usually takes the form of one organism being food for another. However, a dependence can also be non-feeding related, as in the sparrow who needs the oak tree to nest in, or can involve interactions with non-living features of the environment, as in mineral uptake by plants from the soil. This idea of infinite resources within an ecosystem is problematic as it will impact on a correct understanding of sustainability.

Related misconceptions include the idea that wild animals are cared for and fed by humans so never go hungry, and that a food chain exists purely to provide food for humans.

Reconstruction

When children consider linear food chains the true situation of different organisms competing with each other for the same resources is not always apparent. The presentation of food *webs* would help them understand how food chains are really interlinked, and that populations can rise or fall depending on whether one organism outcompetes another (see 6.2). It would be better to start children off thinking about carnivore/herbivore and not herbivore/producer relationships, since it is easier for them to comprehend a lion competing with a leopard for antelope, instead of an antelope competing with a wildebeest for grass. Basic ideas relating to supply and demand would be necessary for children to fully appreciate interdependence – the fact that globally, resources are finite and so can become scarce within an ecosystem, therefore demand increases, and to satisfy demand the number of competitors must be reduced.

Sources: Leach *et al.* (1992, 1996); Munson (1994).

7
Microbes and disease

7.1 Are all microbes harmful?

> **Misconception**
>
> *All microbes are detrimental to human life.*

Scientific conception

The automatic association of bacteria and viruses with illness is notable. They are seen as 'germs' or 'bugs', something to guard against; in addition, pupils learn that **microbes** are partly responsible for food spoilage. While these viewpoints are valid, and rein-forced by that part of the primary science curriculum which is devoted to the ideas of infective disease and vaccination, the useful roles that microbes play in our lives can be overlooked or forgotten by pupils. Bacteria and fungi have widespread uses in the food and pharmaceutical industries as well as helping rid the environment of dead plant and animal material through decomposition. Bacteria living inside the human gut have vital functions including the digestion of food and the production of vitamins.

Reconstruction

Remind pupils of the things we would not have if it were not for microbes, e.g. cheese, bread, yoghurt, alcoholic drinks, antibiotics, biotechnology and genetic engineering (which includes genetically modified crops). Also, microbes play a vital role as 'nature's cleaners' through the process of decay; a related use is the treatment of sewage. There is a current trend for taking fermented 'biotic' health drinks and live yoghurts for purported health benefits, and pupils can be reminded that these actually contain living bacteria. Traditional practical activities such as making bread or yoghurt can underline the idea of microbial usefulness.

Sources: Barenholz and Tamir (1987); Byrne and Sharp (2006).

7.2 Bugs

Misconception

Bacteria and insects belong in the same animal group because they are bugs.

Scientific conception

The colloquial use of the term 'bugs' to describe both microbes and arthropods can act as a source of confusion for children. This misconception has been known to materialize when pupils are asked to draw bacteria and end up drawing insect/spider-like creatures. During the early years many children are taught to simplify the categorization of arthropods they experience around the home such as insects, spiders or woodlice by calling them creepy crawlies, minibeasts or bugs. At KS2 when the concept of microbes is first introduced they may also pick up on the informal use of the word bugs to describe bacteria particularly; possible prompts include TV programmes that are centred around the life sciences such as the popular *CSI* and hospital dramas, where health professionals are overheard using the term.

A related problem is connected to the use of the colloquialism 'germ' as meaning something small and harmful to humans; when asked to draw germs children have depicted insects and spiders, as well as microbes.

Reconstruction

Teachers can initially elicit misconceptions by asking pupils to 'draw some bugs'. Referring children to the results of this activity, it is advised to discourage any further use of the word *bug* in the classroom, explaining why it is confusing and instead insisting on the more scientific terms *microbe*, *insect*, *spider*, etc. Reminding pupils of the rules of biological classification should help make it clear to learners that microbes and arthropods are very different kinds of living things, the former being **microscopic** single-celled creatures, and the latter much larger, having a number of body sections and pairs of jointed legs.

Source: Nagy (1953).

7.3 What is inside a bacterium?

Misconception

Bacteria have intestines and lungs.

Scientific conception

When learners realize that microbes are tiny independent living entities they may begin to attribute a number of features to them that multicellular organisms possess

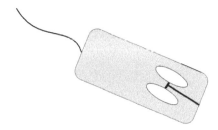

Figure 7.3 A bacterium depicted with lungs (misconception)

(Figure 7.3). They reason that since larger animals have organs that are vital to life then so must microbes, and may include the heart, a mouth, and respiratory and digestive systems in their drawings.

Organs such as lungs found in larger animals are a sophisticated collection of tissues made up of millions of cells. Thus, it is not possible for a living thing such as a bacterium to be able to house such an organ because the bacterium is itself only one cell. Indeed, microbes do share all of the same life processes as larger organisms[1] such as respiration and nutrition, but because they are so tiny they have found simpler mechanisms by which to carry these out. For instance, aerobic bacteria do not breathe; instead, oxygen that is needed for respiration simply drifts (**diffuses**) into a bacterium across its outer layers (cell wall and cell membrane), as do molecules such as glucose that are required for nutrition.

This misconception has similarities to the way that children often include human facial features on their drawings of animals in order to give them a personality (anthropomorphism).

Reconstruction

A detailed treatment of the interior physiology of microbes is well beyond KS2, although classes with more able children should be able to partly or wholly assimilate a simplified scientific explanation, as described above.

Sources: Dreyfus and Jungwirth (1988, 1989).

7.4 Are all microbes living things?

Misconception

Microbes inside our bodies are alive, while microbes in the environment are not.

Scientific conception

Pupils are able to appreciate that microbes such as bacteria that are infecting a human body and causing a disease are living things because of ideas such as the 'battle' between the immune system and the invading microbes. However, although they may understand that microbes are a constant presence in the external environment and that we need to guard against infection, e.g. by cleaning wounds, they do not necessarily see these freely existing microbes as being living things, and instead imagine some abstract agent with the potential to infect whose appearance and behaviour they find difficult to describe. A similar misconception is that mouldy bread comes about due to non-living environmental factors, analogous to rusty iron.

Whether microbes are present inside or outside the body does not make any difference to their status as living things. Confusion might develop from the knowledge that some bacteria and fungi in the environment produce spores. Although spores are inactive and dormant ('sleeping') they are still alive and when reactivated become microbial cells, similar to how a germinating seed becomes an active plant when favourable conditions are present (see 1.2).

Reconstruction

As with 7.5, remind pupils that microbes that are currently infecting a human body may have once been present outside that body, in the environment. When the microbes were living in the environment they must have been alive because the chain of life can never be broken unless the microbes die; microbes are alive regardless of whether or not they are presently causing an infection.[2] Showing pictures of the same microbe both in the body and in the environment would help this, particularly time-lapse sequences of environmental bacteria dividing, e.g. *E. coli* (try the internet). If your school is lucky enough to have access to a decent microscope there are prepared slides available of real bacteria and fungi that will help foster further interest.

An experiment to study the activity of yeast under different conditions (temperature, acidity, sugar/no sugar, light, etc.) would serve as a reminder that microbes are able to live outside the human body. The yeast is placed together with a little water into a test tube or small bottle and then covered by a balloon. As the yeast cells become active they produce carbon dioxide gas making the balloon slowly inflate.

Sources: Maxted (1984); Sequeria and Freitas (1987).

7.5 Can microbes exist inside the human body?

Misconception

Microbes are never found inside the human body, even though they are plentiful in the environment.

Scientific conception

Older primary-aged children are able to understand that an illness either may be infective, i.e. can be caught (e.g. chickenpox, AIDS), or appears for other reasons (e.g. lung cancer, depression). Some may believe that in both of these instances microbes are not involved; instead, in the case of infective disease, some poorly defined abstract 'thing' is passed from person to person.

Pupils with this erroneous idea are fully aware of taking precautions against infection by environmental microbes, e.g. by washing hands, but do not make the conceptual jump to bodily invasion by microbial **pathogenic** organisms. They are able to give a name to the environmental danger ('bacteria' or 'virus'), although further description of the appearance and behaviour of these microbes is often scant. Similarly, they apply a degree of abstraction to the nature of the disease itself, although they are able to describe symptoms. They can also associate cause with effect in the sense of it being *these* microbes that are responsible for *that* subsequent infection, but do not imagine them living inside a human body, multiplying, and using it as a host. Because of this, these pupils would be unable to fully appreciate how the immune system works by eliminating invading microbes or the ideas underpinning vaccination.

There are echoes here of the misconceptions described in 7.4, where microbes inside and outside the body are considered to be very different things. There is also resonance with the idea that just one type of microbe exists that is responsible for all infective diseases; this omnipotent microbe acts as a kind of metaphor for the poorly understood abstract infective agent described above. Another related misconception is that all diseases are infective.

Reconstruction

The story of Edward Jenner's development of vaccination is commonly taught as part of a Year 6 microbes topic and can be used as a vehicle by which to explain exactly how microbes infect, multiply and then are destroyed (see box). The pedagogies described in 7.4 are also relevant here.

> **Famous scientists**
>
> **Dr Edward Jenner.** In the late eighteenth century smallpox ravaged much of Europe, carrying with it high levels of mortality. Jenner, an English country doctor, noticed that milkmaids who had caught the similar but far less dangerous disease *cowpox* from cows did not subsequently contract smallpox. Understanding that cowpox must be carrying some agent that conferred immunity, he infected a young boy called James Phipps with cowpox. He later purposely infected the boy with smallpox – fortunately, and as Jenner had predicted, James did not develop smallpox. This experiment laid the foundations for modern immunology and today we routinely inoculate young children with inactive or less virulent strains of serious diseases such as polio and tetanus. Jenner's apparently ruthless methods have been challenged on ethical grounds. However, the practice of introducing a small amount of infected material to people with a view to their contracting a lesser form of the disease and building up immunity was an accepted practice of the day.

Sources: Maxted (1984); Nagy (1953).

7.6 Spreading disease

Misconception

Having close contact with someone with an infective disease means that you automatically and immediately catch that disease.

Scientific conception

Whether an infection spreads from one person to another is not automatic, and depends on a number of factors. Some conditions are easier to catch than others: for instance the common cold is extremely contagious, the virus being able to pass from person to person via exhaled air without the need for physical contact; on the other hand, leprosy is extremely difficult to catch even after prolonged contact. Microbes that cause disease (pathogens) can enter a person's bloodstream (infection) without causing a full-blown disease because either insufficient organisms are transmitted in order to cause the onset of symptoms, or the immune system is rapidly mobilized to fight and destroy the invaders. If pathogens are not given the opportunity to multiply to sufficient numbers inside the host's body then symptoms will not appear. Thus, a person can come into very close contact with an infected patient and not necessarily catch what they have, although with extremely infectious or potentially harmful diseases such as mumps isolation from others is usually recommended.

Even if disease does occur after infection it is rarely an immediate event as pathogens need time to multiply and overcome the host's immune defences. Different conditions have different incubation periods: with the common cold, symptoms can appear within 24 hours of infection by the virus; rabies can take up to two years to materialize.

Reconstruction

Remind pupils of the scientific ideas as presented in this section. A contemporary example is the shunning of HIV carriers by society due to a fear of infection through everyday physical contact, despite the fact that HIV can only be transmitted via sexual contact or infected blood.

Simple ideas about the nature and transmission of contagious disease can be explained to KS1 children by reading the story book *Germs* by Ross Collins. An activity suitable for younger primary children first involves rolling a small foam ball in multi-coloured glitter. Pass the ball around the class until all children have touched it and glitter has been transferred onto their hands. Explain that some microbes are passed from person to person in a similar way, but because they are tiny they are invisible and a person would not know that they were carrying microbes. Ask the children to wash their hands and then check to see if all glitter has been removed – this can be linked to the importance of regular handwashing, and correct washing techniques. An example of a microbe that can be transmitted by touch is the rhino-virus (common cold), although the virus is more commonly spread via airborne drop-lets created during sneezing.

Sources: Collins (2005); Keselman *et al.* (2007); Nagy (1953).

7.7 How do you catch a cold?

Misconception

You can only catch a cold if you are exposed to wet and cold conditions.

Scientific conception

Concerned parents sometimes warn children who venture out on a winter's night inadequately dressed, 'put something on or you'll catch your death of cold . . .'. This statement reflects a very widespread though erroneous belief that neglects the fact that the common cold is caused by a virus that can only be caught via contact with an infected person.

It is true that people catch colds more frequently during the late autumn, winter and early spring months. It is thought that this might be due to several factors: for instance, people tend to crowd together more indoors during spells of cold weather so increasing the likelihood of the virus spreading through a population. This pattern has also been attributed to the start of the school year in September when children suddenly come into contact with large numbers of other people. There is a plethora of folk remedies and pseudoscientific recommendations for evading the common cold virus, including regular doses of vitamin C – a strategy that has not been medically shown to have any significant effect.

To summarize, keeping out of cold and wet weather or wearing more clothing will have no influence on the probability of a person catching a cold. The only way to avoid contagion is to keep away from infected people; of course, given the frequency of this condition in the general population ('common' cold) this is an impractical policy.

Reconstruction

Make pupils aware of the scientific ideas given in this section. Remind them that some diseases are due to infections caused by microbes, and others are not (see 7.5); the common cold lies within the former category, so in order to spread, the virus needs to pass from an infected person to somebody else during close contact.

Sources: Byrne (2011); Maxted (1984).

7.8 Are antibiotics a cure-all?

Misconception

Antibiotics work on both bacteria and viruses.

Scientific conception

This statement implies that the pupil might have constructed the idea that bacteria and viruses can be classified as being the same kind of organism. In fact, these two types of microbe are very different. A bacterium consists of a single cell and although more closely related to an animal or plant cell than a virus is, bacteria are classified under a different kingdom (2.1). A virus, on the other hand, is not cellular, instead being a very simple arrangement of a nucleic acid (such as **DNA**) covered by a coat of protein. In fact, some scientists think that viruses should not be classified as living things at all. Figures 7.8a and 7.8b compare the basic morphologies of a clump of *E. coli* bacteria and a phage virus; note that the diagrams are not to scale – each bacterial cell would be about 20 times larger than the virus.

Antibiotics such as tetracycline kill bacteria by preventing some of their internal chemical reactions taking place, so upsetting the balance of processes within the cell. Viruses have no internal chemistry so cannot be affected by antibiotics and are very difficult to treat with any medicine that is currently available; for instance, there is no cure for viral diseases such as influenza, chickenpox, measles, HIV or the common cold.

Reconstruction

Although beyond KS2 level, an awareness of the classification rubric for microbes that differentiates bacteria, viruses and fungi would help remind pupils that these groups of organisms differ greatly from each other. A common KS3 activity is to ask pairs of pupils to research a different microbe in the library and then produce a poster or PowerPoint show.

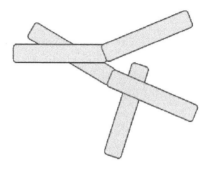

Figure 7.8a *E. coli* bacteria

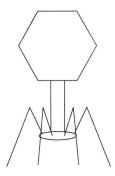

Figure 7.8b A phage virus

The teacher could prompt pupils to recall their own experiences of illnesses such as the common cold to demonstrate that viral diseases are often medicinally incurable and only the symptoms can be treated, e.g. paracetamol tablets to reduce fever. The most frequent medical advice offered with viral disease is to let the condition run its course, thus allowing the body's natural immune mechanisms to deal with the infecting viruses in their own time.

Sources: Barenholz and Tamir (1987); Prout (1985).

7.9 How does vaccination work?

> **Misconception**
> *The doctor gives my grandmother a jab when she catches the flu.*

Scientific conception

This statement implies a belief that a vaccination is able to effectively treat a disease. Children may not differentiate between the prevention and treatment of an illness, and lump all medical procedures into one single category. Another example is that if people with lung cancer stop smoking they can be cured.

The belief that an influenza vaccine works by treating the illness is incorrect. Vaccinations are given to healthy people to help prevent future infections by stimulating part of the immune system (white blood cells) to produce **antibodies**. When those people are subsequently exposed to the disease they are able to fight it immediately because they can produce the antibodies very quickly.

A related misconception is that medical treatment will always lead to a permanent cure.

Reconstruction

Inform pupils that prevention and treatment are two different ways to deal with illness, each being carried out sequentially, at different times. Once a disease has taken hold then preventative measures are abandoned and treatments become important. Refer to examples that will be familiar such as influenza (prevention = vaccination/avoiding contact with infected persons; treatment = bed rest/drink plenty of fluids) or heart disease (prevention = diet/exercise; treatment = drugs/surgery).

Address the related misconception by stating that treatment does not always lead to a cure; under certain conditions some illnesses are nearly always incurable even though symptoms can be treated to a degree, e.g. lung cancer.

Did you know?

Vaccines that can cure. In a small number of recent cases involving frontier medicine the distinction between prevention and cure has been blurred as some vaccines are administered once the patient has already contracted the disease. Some experimental AIDS vaccines work in this way.

Sources: Barenholz and Tamir (1987); Nagy (1953).

7.10 Can someone be healthy and ill at the same time?

Misconception

You can be either healthy or ill, never anything in between.

Scientific conception

This statement reflects the belief that health and illness are two discrete conditions instead of being a continuum. When people are infected by the influenza virus the first symptoms may be similar to those of the common cold (e.g. mild fever, runny nose), and at this early stage they are able to continue to pursue their lives normally. Later symptoms may be more severe and commonly require bed rest for a number of days. Eventually the symptoms subside and sufferers feel able to begin to return to their usual routines. At what point in this sequence of events does health cease and illness begin … and vice versa? Can a person be called healthy when they return to work even though they carry residual symptoms, or only when they are completely symptom-free? If the influenza bout has been complicated with, say, a chest infection, feelings of mild wheeziness may linger for weeks after recovery from the symptoms of the flu itself, although otherwise the person functions quite normally – would such a person be classified as still being ill? How about people with chronic lower back pain that comes and goes – are they ill only when symptoms appear and healthy at other times, or ill all of the time because they suffer from a chronic condition?

Instead of using the dichotomous and mutually exclusive labels of 'healthy' and 'ill' it is preferable to look at the issue using the concept of the *degree of healthiness*

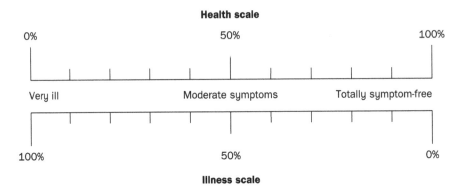

Figure 7.10 Health and illness as continua

(Figure 7.10). Thus, a person can enjoy some degree of health even though they are experiencing the symptoms of an illness.

Reconstruction

It is easy to see how this misconception can arise when one considers common and acute illnesses such as chickenpox where symptoms appear and disappear abruptly. Using examples of chronic illnesses such as lower back pain with pupils would serve as a good illustration of the concept of having a degree of healthiness. Most people with this condition would probably not regard themselves as being either healthy or ill; instead, they would comment that some days are better than others, reflecting the idea of a continuum of health/illness.

Source: Natapoff (1978).

7.11 What happens to make food decay?

Misconception

An apple goes rotten all by itself.

Scientific conception

This statement implies the belief that when material naturally decays it has disappeared of its own accord with no action from any external agent. In fact, this view is only partly true as, during the processes of decay, **matter** does not merely self-destruct in this way.

Any piece of dead material will decay due to the activity of microbes such as bacteria and fungi that were present inside the organism when it was alive, and also via microbe contamination from the surrounding environment after death. Larger organisms that feed on the decaying matter such as insects and rats will facilitate these microbial processes. For instance, a rotten apple in a fruit bowl has been partly acted upon by microbes in the surrounding environment that have drifted through the air and landed on the surface of the apple. The microbes break down the fruit and use it as food, so given enough time the apple will rot down to nearly nothing as it is consumed by the microbes bit by bit. For this reason if we cover food in the kitchen we can slow down these processes by keeping out microbes, insects and other external agents of decomposition.

The view that an apple can go rotten of its own accord would be reinforced by the well-known food spoiling phenomenon of *apple browning*, which can be seen a few minutes after the inside flesh of an apple is exposed to the air. This occurs due to an already present **enzyme** within the apple cells reacting with oxygen in the air, and not microbial activity. Note that with animal matter particularly, during the early stages of decomposition, cells *do* begin to break down of their own accord and destroy themselves using their own enzymes (autolysis) without any microbial assistance, although simultaneously, contaminating microbes will start to act on the tissues.

A related misconception is that only larger organisms such as insects and worms are responsible for the decomposition of dead matter. Pupils may have difficulties remembering that microbes, although invisible, are a constant presence in the environment and are causative agents in decay. In addition, they may think that bacteria have nothing to do with decay because they only act on living organisms, particularly people, causing disease. Pupils commonly refer to the problems of food spoilage and conclude that the process of decay is wholly unhelpful instead of appreciating that decay is a vital part of the natural breakdown of dead material in an ecosystem, recycling substances that are useful to living plants such as minerals.

Reconstruction

The expression 'one bad apple spoils the whole barrel', although usually used in a social sense to signify the negative influence of a 'bad' person within a group of people, can be referred to in order to show that if one piece of fruit in a bowl shows early signs of decay it is best to remove it to prevent the spread of contaminating microbes to other pieces of fruit. This explanation can be linked to familiar primary school practical activities such as the investigation of the decay of bread placed in different locations in the classroom. There are engaging time-lapse videos available on the internet that show food decaying over a period of time and can be used to reinforce the ideas.

Sources: Leach *et al.* (1992); Smith and Anderson (1986).

Notes

1. But see the box on p. 20 for a discussion of viruses.
2. The debate as to whether viruses are living or otherwise notwithstanding (see the box on p. 20).

8

Heredity and variation

8.1 Same-sex-only inheritance

Misconception

Sons take after their fathers, and daughters take after their mothers.

Scientific conception

Pupils may believe that they have inherited characteristics from only a single parent – the one who is of their gender. All organisms produced by sexual reproduction, from grass plants to humans, contain genetic material from both parents in the form of equal numbers of chromosomes from each (Figure 8.1a). Thus, children may display outward, inherited characteristics (**phenotypes**) from both mother and father, including hair and eye colour, body size and shape, as well as the propensity to develop certain diseases later in life. Pupils notice, for instance, that boys share more obvious gender-related attributes such as a reproductive system with their fathers, and assume that their whole body is totally derived solely from that parent. In a similar vein, pupils who correctly infer that traits can be inherited from both parents mistakenly conclude that boys inherit the majority of traits from their fathers, and girls from their mothers.

A related misconception is the belief that children of both genders inherit most of their characteristics from their mothers, since the process of gestation (pregnancy) occurs entirely within the mother's body.

Reconstruction

Ask pupils to complete a table (Figure 8.1b) that lists physical characteristics they think they may have inherited from their fathers and mothers. If children bring in photographs of their parents this can help others in the class appreciate their peers' observations. If there are sensitivity issues related to pupils not knowing/living with

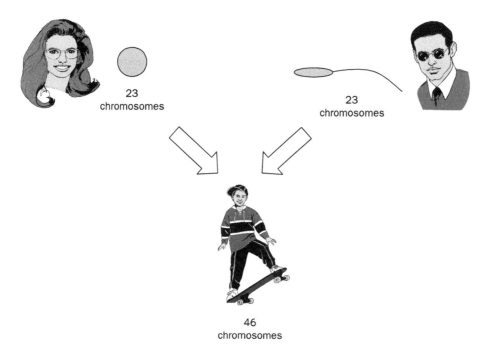

Figure 8.1a Children inherit an equal number of chromosomes from each parent

Physical feature	From father	From mother	Not sure who from

Figure 8.1b Recording physical characteristics

one or both biological parents then this activity could instead be carried out by using photographs of celebrity couples and their children.

Similarly, pupils can construct their own family trees going back a couple of generations to see physical traits being passed down, or even skipping generations to appear only in grandchildren.

Simple ideas about inheritance can be taught to KS1 children by referring to experiences set in familiar contexts, such as a ginger cat usually has ginger kittens, and the puppies of pure-bred parents will be the same breed as their parents; e.g. if two labradors mate then they do not produce bulldog puppies.

Sources: Engel-Clough and Wood-Robinson (1985); Kargbo *et al.* (1980).

8.2 Why do giraffes have long necks?

Misconception

Modern giraffes have long necks because their ancestors' necks became longer as they stretched to reach leaves high in trees.

Scientific conception

It is commonly believed by children and adults alike that adaptations arise because of changes that occur during the lifetime of an organism. For instance, early giraffes had short necks and could only reach leaves at a certain height on the tree; as they strained to reach the higher branches their necks became slightly longer. This adaptation was passed to the next generation, where the process was repeated, and after several generations giraffes ended up with very long necks.

This commonly held idea is *Lamarckian*, named after Jean-Baptiste Lamarck, the founder of a now defunct theory of evolution. Scientists instead now accept *Darwinian* evolution, which is based on the idea of natural selection. Charles Darwin proposed that instead of the giraffe ancestor having a short neck, there was a variety of giraffes with different neck lengths living together during the same time period. Due to some event such as a drought that caused a reduction of all **flora**, plants that lived close to the ground became scarce due to overfeeding and the shorter-necked giraffes died out due to starvation, while their longer-necked competitors were able to reach the higher, untouched vegetation. This is the basic principle behind Darwinian evolution, that modern organisms have a particular adaptation because at some time in the past that adaptation has conferred some advantage to an ancestor over its competitors, or *survival of the fittest*.

Of course, body changes can occur in individual organisms due to lifetime events, including changes in bone length in response to physical stress. However, as is the case with the related misconceptions in this series, these changes cannot be passed to the next generation because the information is not encoded in **genes**.

Reconstruction

Evolution is a new topic in the Year 6 Programme of Study, and children will need to understand the fundamental concepts that underpin Darwinian theory. This particular misconception can also surface during lessons that deal with plant and animal adaptations. A typical teaching sequence is to ask pupils to note the physical characteristics of different organisms and then link those characteristics with each organism's habitat, explaining why they might be suited to living in that environment. This provides an ideal juncture at which to feed in the idea of natural selection, describing how an organism's characteristics appear to have been purposely 'sculpted' to fit their habitat, when in fact their adaptations are the consequence of chance events long in the past.

Lamarckian ideas can be refuted by encouraging the understanding that information will only cross from parent to child if it is present within the genes, and that genetic information cannot change in response to life events (8.3). Thus, it did not matter how much the ancestor giraffes stretched their necks because this stretching could not have entered the genes and so not be passed on to their offspring.

There are commercially available computer simulations of natural selection available for use in schools. Although they tend to go well beyond the primary curriculum they include some relevant games and activities that would be useful for younger pupils.

Did you know?

Creationism in schools. Recently there have been attempts by creationist religious groups to raise the profile of the pseudoscientific idea of intelligent design (ID), promoting its inclusion within the curriculum alongside *bona fide* science theories. ID takes a position that opposes Darwinian natural selection, suggesting that organisms' adaptations arose because of the intervention of a Creator, and some pupils may argue the case for ID in the classroom, motivated by religious belief or innocent curiosity. As teachers of science we must make it clear to pupils that ID is not a scientific theory, i.e. something that is backed by convincing evidence, and as such is inappropriate for discussion during science lessons, although as a religious viewpoint it can be considered alongside other belief systems.

Sources: Adeniyi (1985); Jensen and Finley (1995).

8.3 The bodybuilder's son

Misconception

The son of a bodybuilder always has big muscles.

Scientific conception

Pupils can be aware from an early age that they inherit certain characteristics from their parents, informed by comments such as 'hasn't he got his father's eyes!' Some children assume that almost any characteristic is inheritable, even if that characteristic is the result of lifetime events such as a haircut, a limb amputation or, as in the case of the example given in the above statement, exercise-induced muscle growth.

To be inheritable a characteristic needs to be encoded genetically, i.e. be present in the genes. Attributes such as eye colour and facial features are examples of such *genetic variation*. Physical changes that occur solely as a consequence of exposure to one's surroundings, such as developing a suntan, undergoing cosmetic surgery or breaking a bone, are termed *environmental variation*, and are not passed on to children. Traditionally, discussions related to these ideas have been called nature vs.

nurture debates, though pupils sometimes merge the two and lump all characteristics as being inheritable. Note that some characteristics occur due to a combination of environmental and genetic factors, such as height and body weight.

Reconstruction

Pupils need to be able to differentiate between changes that happen solely due to life events and those that they have no control over because of parental genetic heritage. Explain that for something to be passed on to a child it needs to be already there within the parents' genetic make-up; more specifically, it needs to be present in the genes within the **sperm cell** or **ovum** that combine to make a new individual. They cannot change, add to or take away information that is already in their genes, so it does not matter what you do to your body during your lifetime, this will not affect your offspring.[1]

Asking pupils to make a simple family tree going back a couple of generations will help show how some characteristics such as hair and eye colour are inheritable. If there are sensitivity issues related to any pupils not knowing the family history of one or both of their biological parents then the teacher can create a 'model' family tree that the whole class can refer to, based on members of a family the teacher knows.

Although it is beyond KS2, drawing a simple representation of a chromosome will help children visualize what a gene actually is, that it is made from DNA and that it duplicates itself, with one copy being given to offspring (Figure 8.3). Say that we are born with these genes and pass them on to our children. During our lifetime they do not change, we are merely custodians. If we build up our bodies in the gym this does not change the genes, so we cannot pass on this characteristic to our children.

As is sometimes the case in school science, reality is at odds with the simplified concepts we teach to primary children because notable exceptions to the rule exist. Genes *are* able to change due to exposure to environmental effects such as UV light, X-rays and certain very toxic chemicals. These changes are *mutations* and nearly always have devastating consequences, for instance excessive exposure to UV light causes mutations in epidermal cells that trigger skin cancer. However, only mutations in sperm cell or ovum DNA would be inheritable.

A gene

Figure 8.3 Locating a gene on a chromosome

Did you know?

Epigenetic inheritance. There have been recent advances with theories of **epigenetics**, where changes in chromosomes can occur during an individual's life in response to environmental stimuli and be passed to offspring. The changes mean that genes are expressed differently, so changing the characteristics of children. For example, male mice given doses of morphine fathered offspring with hormonal abnormalities, showing that life events could indeed have consequences for later generations. It is important to note that with epigenetic alteration the genes themselves do not change, merely the chromosomes where the genes are located, which causes genes to either 'switch on' or 'switch off'.

Source: Nehm and Schonfeld (2008).

8.4 Are certain human characteristics dying out?

Misconception

Our little fingers are getting smaller because we no longer use them.

Scientific conception

The idea that the use or non-use of a characteristic affects whether that characteristic disappears in a population is another variant of the Lamarckian misconception (8.2); that is to say, life events can have an effect on genetic inheritance.

If having a smaller little finger confers an evolutionary advantage then humans with this trait would out-compete others with larger little fingers and through natural selection the proportion of people in the population with smaller little fingers would increase (8.2). However, since there appears to be no significant disadvantage to having a larger little finger this is unlikely to happen.

The human body has remnants of traits we no longer find useful that we have inherited from distant ancestors, called vestiges (see box). We still have the genes for these characteristics even though their use is now redundant. Having thick body fur is important for hairy apes such as gorillas, serving an insulation function in cold temperatures similar to the human use of clothing. The common ancestor of humans and other apes was probably hairy like modern gorillas, but at some point in history along the human evolutionary branch of this tree of life it must have been advantageous *not* to be hairy, since hominids (human-like species) lost their hair, and evolved into the nearly hairless modern human. It has been speculated that our ancestors took to living in coastal marine or fresh-water environments where thick fur would produce significant water drag (the aquatic ape hypothesis).

> **Did you know?**
>
> **Vestiges.** The human body has leftover signs that imply that we share common ancestry with a variety of creatures. The human coccyx is a short, redundant tail. The vestigial presence of human hair has been discussed in the main text, and a related vestige is piloerection (goose bumps) in reaction to cold, which serves a useful function in hairy animals by temporarily increasing the thickness of their fur, thus enhancing heat insulation. Another fur-related vestige is how the hair on the back of our hands and wrists always grows away from the thumb and towards the little finger, supposedly because when our ancestors walked on all fours the thumb formed the leading edge of the forelimb, so that grass brushed their hands 'with the grain' of the hair.

Thus, human ancestors' loss of fur was not due to non-use, but instead having fur must have conferred some evolutionary disadvantage that caused hairy hominids to die out. Similarly, human little fingers could not shrink over generations just because they are not used very much. Conversely, in the developed world the little finger plays an increasingly vital role – the IT explosion that began in the 1980s has made most of us into keyboard operators to some degree, and a proportion of us are touch typists who use all of our fingers.

Reconstruction

If learners think that with each new generation the little finger is becoming incrementally smaller, then similar interventions as detailed in 8.2 and 8.3 are necessary that help them construct the scientifically acceptable idea that only information passed in genes is inherited, including the shape or size of body parts. This information is with us from the time of our conception and does not change before we pass it on to our own offspring, no matter how often we may use a specific body part during our lives.

Source: Bishop and Anderson (1990).

8.5 Why are organisms adapted to living successfully in their habitats?

> **Misconception**
>
> *Polar bears grow thick warm coats because they live in a very cold environment.*

Scientific conception

Some learners believe that an organism reacts to its immediate environment by generating an adaptation during its lifetime. Thus, polar bear cubs sense the cold at a very young age and in response grow thick coats. This is similar to the giraffe neck misconception covered in 8.2, but differs as the polar bear's adaptation is not inheritable, with each new generation of polar bears reacting similarly and producing its own adaptations in response to environmental conditions. Another example of this misconception is the belief that cheetahs run fast merely because they have learned how to do so; if they ran slowly they would not catch any prey and starve.

As discussed in 8.2, adaptations such as a polar bear's thick fur exist because there was once variation within the population of an ancestor of polar bears where different individuals had a variety of fur thicknesses. The climate turned colder, so the bears with thicker fur had an advantage over others in the population and the disadvantaged shorter-haired bears either migrated to warmer regions or died of cold. Thus in the region we now call the Arctic, polar bears have thick fur because their ancestors were the only individuals equipped to survive, with this adaptation being passed down the generations via the genes.

A similar misconception is that all variation arises only due to an organism reacting to its immediate environment (environmental variation), such as overeating results in an increased body mass. It must be remembered that some variation is inheritable and is caused by differences in the genetic make-up of organisms (genetic variation), which is due to the mixing of genes during sexual reproduction producing a variety of offspring. Different children in the same family are never absolutely alike despite the fact they may have the same parents (as long as they are not identical twins); these differences are due mainly to gene crossover and chromosome mixing when sperm and egg cells are made. Polar bear cubs born in zoos in hot countries will still grow thick fur despite the warmer weather because they are genetically predisposed to do so.

Reconstruction

Since the misconception is to some degree a Lamarckian variant, the pedagogies that encourage the construction of concepts that align with natural selection as described in 8.2 and 8.3 are appropriate.

Source: Deadman and Kelly (1978).

8.6 Biological variation

Misconception

A dog looks different to a cat – this is an example of variation.

Scientific conception

The statement implies an understanding that variation between organisms means dissimilarities between different species. In fact, the school science definition states that only differences between individuals of the *same species* count as 'variation'. There is great variation in size, coat colour and other physical characteristics between different breeds of dog, but all belong to the same species because they can interbreed successfully to produce fertile offspring (Figure 8.6). It is common for learners to turn to the everyday meaning of variation which is more all-encompassing, being any

Figure 8.6 Noticeable variation exists within the species *Canis familiaris* (domestic dog)

differences between cases. Thus they believe any differences between living things can be called variation.

Reconstruction

The comparison of human physical characteristics has been traditionally used to help pupils appreciate what variation means. Ask pupils to compare themselves with the person sitting next to them and write down five examples of variation, i.e. how they look different. Tell the class not to make personal or nasty comments about their partners. Taken further, surveys that involve measuring heights, shoe sizes or hand spans to create bar charts or frequency charts will draw in numeracy skills.

This work can be linked to discussions about adaptations. The fact that individuals within the same species are different means that if their environment changes, some individuals will be more suited than others and survive, so the adaptation becomes more common within the whole population (see 8.2).

All of the above can help pupils understand variation, but it may not prevent them from over-categorizing and believing that diversity in different species can also be called variation. In the end it will merely be a case of pupils remembering by rote learning that variation is only intra-species. A deeper discussion involving genetic and environmental variation will facilitate their understanding and recall (8.3).

Source: Hackling and Treagust (1982).

8.7 If we evolved from apes, why are there still apes?

Misconception

Humans evolved from chimpanzees.

Scientific conception

This common idea reflects a linear model of evolution where at some point in history chimpanzees evolved directly into humans. The misconception is essentially Lamarckian, with species physically transforming during the period of their lifetimes and then giving birth to offspring that inherit these physical transformations. Therefore, ancestors change directly into descendants, and the two cannot co-exist.

Although *Homo sapiens* and chimpanzees are very closely related in a genetic sense there is no direct lineage between the two species. Both species did, however, evolve from a common ape-like ancestor that lived approximately 15 million years ago. It is true that chimpanzees did evolve before humans – the first chimp appeared around 4 million years ago while humans are a very young species, with the first anatomically modern *Homo sapiens* appearing only about a quarter of a million years ago. Nevertheless, chimpanzees were not our great, great (etc.)-grandparents; they are more like our evolutionary cousins (see 'Reconstruction' below).

Even if humans were directly descended from chimpanzees the two species could still potentially co-exist together today. Just because one species has evolved from another does not mean that the ancestor species will automatically die out and be replaced by the descendent species. For instance, the domestic dog evolved from the grey wolf around 20 000 years ago and both species are still in existence. The question *if we evolved from apes, then why are there still apes* has been used erroneously by Creationists in attempts to refute Darwinism and make the case for Intelligent Design (see Box 8.2).

Reconstruction

Meikle and Scott (2010) suggest using the idea of cousins to address this misconception. We are related to our cousin but we are not directly descended from them in a linear way; instead we share common ancestors, our grandparents. If we consider chimpanzees as evolutionary cousins then the situation is the same, both species had a common ancestor who lived many millions of years ago, which means humans and chimpanzees are distantly related. Just as we could not have evolved from our familial cousin, humans could not have evolved from chimpanzees (Figure 8.7a).

This could be taught as part of a general topic or discussion on human evolution in Year 6. To help illustrate this, introduce the theme of how the human skeleton has adapted from the time our species diverged from other primates. One main feature to account for would be the move to bipedalism, i.e. when our ape-like ancestors first began to walk on two legs instead of four. In order to walk efficiently on two legs certain adaptations to the skeleton were necessary (Figure 8.7b). Feet developed an arch, and toes, no longer necessary for grasping trees during arboreal movement through the forest, became smaller to aid bipedal walking. The shape of the backbone altered to allow a more upright stance. Knee joints became bigger to support the entire weight of the body during upright walking and running. The upper leg (femur) turned inwards from the hip to the knee to allow comfortable standing for prolonged periods. Legs became longer, and arms, no longer needed for locomotion, became shorter. These adaptations allowed our bipedal ancestors to stand erect and so have their hands free to manipulate tools, thought to be vital in allowing the development of human technology. These discussions can be part of a more general treatment of evolution, with fossils of human ancestors comprising evidence to support Darwinian theory.

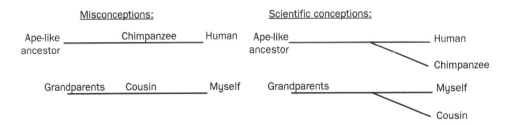

Figure 8.7a Using cousins as an analogy.[2]

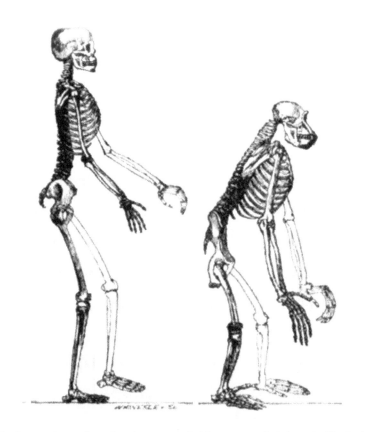

Figure 8.7b Comparison of modern human and chimpanzee skeletons to illustrate skeletal changes necessary for bipedalism

A useful story book for introducing KS1 children to fossils and simple ideas about evolution is *Gumdrop and the Dinosaur* by Val Biro. Similarly, *Dinosaur* by Meredith Hooper is a good text for upper KS1/lower KS2 children.

Famous scientists

Mary Anning. Although celebrated in her day, in recent times Mary has been little known outside of the fields of palaeontology and fossil collecting. Born into a poor working-class family in 1799 she had only a rudimentary education and did not become qualified as a professional geologist, instead being entirely self-taught. She is credited for unearthing many fossils of note from the sea cliffs around Lyme Regis, Dorset, including the first ever plesiosaur (an extinct sea lizard). Her work led directly to the development of important scientific theories such as the extinction of species, which provided a foundation for the later claim that there was a prehistory before humans when dinosaurs roamed the Earth, an idea contrary to biblical teachings of the time. Mary achieved all of this despite the social barriers of her humble background and the fact that she was a woman, both of which at the time precluded her from following a career in academia. In 2010 the Royal Society recognized her as amongst the ten most influential women in the history of British science.

Sources: Biro (2004); Hooper (1996); Meikle and Scott (2010).

Notes

1. An exception to this is exposure of a pregnant mother to environmental influences that may affect a foetus, such as drugs or pollutants; however, this is not genetic inheritance.
2. Adapted from Meikle and Scott (2010).

PART THREE
Chemistry

9
Chemical changes in materials

9.1 What is a material?

> **Misconception**
> *A material is something used for building, clothing or stationery.*

Scientific conception

Pupils can use the word *material* purely in its everyday sense, e.g. bricks are building material, fabrics are clothing material, and stationery is writing material. Other familiar non-scientific meanings include information (research material), and something solid, worldly and corporeal ('Jesus appeared in material form'). Pupils might classify anything outside these categories as being a non-material.

In science a material is something that is made from matter, i.e. from atoms, molecules or **ions**. Gases are included within this category, though pupils often do not consider them to be materials due to overlap with the everyday 'solid' meaning considered above. Non-material entities are those not consisting of matter, e.g. energy.

The term *raw materials*, meaning the starting substances for an industrial process, may also act as a source of confusion, even though all raw materials are *materials* in the scientific sense.

Reconstruction

This misconception may crop up when the term 'material' is first introduced to pupils in primary science in Year 1. During this and other primary chemistry topics that pupils experience, the word 'material' would be used extensively by the teacher in many classroom contexts, including activities that involve liquids and gases. It would be hoped therefore that pupils implicitly construct a scientifically all-encompassing understanding of the word and understand that this is different from any everyday meaning that they know. This process can be facilitated during classification exercises, such as the placing of objects into exclusive solid, liquid and gas sets, by repeatedly referring to all of the objects as materials.

Source: Bouma *et al.* (1990).

9.2 When something burns why does it disappear?

Misconception

When an object burns, parts of it disappear and no longer exist.

Scientific conception

When a piece of wood burns, flames appear to eat away at the wood which turns into something different that is much smaller, i.e. ash. Some pupils are unable to explain why this size reduction takes place, and are at a loss when asked what has happened to the original wood. They may think that through the action of burning the flames convert some of the wood into ash, with the rest of the wood being completely destroyed, no longer existing in any form. Others might conclude that the missing wood becomes smoke, which is nearer to the truth, although when pressed they insist the smoke then 'disappears into the air', likewise ceasing to exist.

As with any **chemical change**, during **combustion** the mass of materials is always conserved. That is to say, if you weigh what you start with and what you end up with, these values will be identical because matter can be neither lost nor created. The particles that make up wood and oxygen have been rearranged during combustion to make new materials, carbon dioxide and water (Figure 9.2).

wood + oxygen ⟶ carbon dioxide + water

Figure 9.2 Simple word equation for the complete combustion of wood

If a piece of wood is observed whilst burning it might appear that there is a quite obvious disappearance of mass as the wood shrinks and turns to ash. But since combustion produces carbon dioxide gas and water (as **steam**), these gaseous products invisibly rise up in **heat** currents and spread out into the surrounding air – they have not ceased to exist, they are merely difficult to detect. To complicate matters slightly, often not all of the wood burns completely and so other products are usually made such as gaseous carbon monoxide and solid carbon. Some of this carbon is lost as smoke (soot) and the rest becomes part of ash, which also includes minerals in the wood that are incombustible. If burning takes place within a sealed container then all of these products of combustion cannot escape; if the container and its contents are weighed before and after combustion, there will be no reduction in mass.

A related misconception is that during combustion the wood disappears because it turns into heat energy.

Reconstruction

While burning a candle on a tabletop, ask pupils *why does the candle become smaller? What has happened to all of the wax?* This will help elicit some of the misconceptions discussed above. Then, place a candle into a sealable transparent container such as a large jam jar, preserve jar or similar. Weigh the candle plus container. Light the candle, being sure to quickly seal the top and leave it to burn until it extinguishes itself – this will take less than half a minute with a large jam jar. Keeping the jar sealed, reweigh the contents, explaining that although it might be surprising that the weight has not changed, this conservation of mass occurs because the gases produced by burning have been trapped within the jar. These products normally drift away from the flame and escape into the surrounding air. Conclude by saying that burning does not destroy the wax, which then ceases to exist; it merely changes it into something else, mostly carbon dioxide and water.

Although some pupils may predict a loss of mass within the closed container, others might believe the burning will result in an increase in mass, possibly because the smoke being produced is thought to add its mass to the final value. Like the main misconception, this type of thinking belies the error of failing to conserve mass during a chemical change.

Source: Watson *et al.* (1997).

9.3 What happens when a candle burns?

Misconception

Candle wax does not burn, it just melts.

Scientific conception

A lighted candle will melt the wax around the wick and also burn the wax as a fuel. Excess melted wax that does not burn runs down the outside of the candle and re-solidifies, which may give the impression that the flame merely melts the wax. A chemical change has taken place because something new has been produced – the products of combustion – which include carbon dioxide, carbon monoxide and water, all of which escape as gas (9.2).

Reconstruction

Burning a candle on a balance will show a slow and steady decrease in mass as the gaseous products of combustion escape. If the candle were merely **melting**, then the mass would remain the same.

Periodically watching a tea light candle burn over the course of an hour or so will show the wax first melting, becoming completely liquefied. As the candle continues to burn the liquid wax gradually disappears completely, which can be linked to the wax being converted to invisible gaseous products during combustion that escape into the surrounding air. Be aware that because of its similar appearance some pupils may think this melted wax is water.

Some pupils may also believe that liquids are automatically lighter than solids (11.3) so the decrease in mass of a burning candle is to be expected because the wax melts. If you weigh a burning tea light candle while the wax is completely liquefied and immediately blow out the flame, then reweigh it after the wax has resolidified, it can be shown that wax weighs the same whether it is in solid or liquid form.

Source: Meheut *et al.* (1985).

9.4 Some confusing terminology surrounding chemical and state changes

Misconception

When burning paper shrinks to leave ash, part of it has evaporated.

Scientific conception

A Year 6 practical lesson that would be familiar to primary teachers involves pupils observing the changes that take place when a variety of everyday materials such as paper, twigs and fabric are carefully burned over a candle flame. These observations are then used as a basis for discussions about the comparative natures of **reversible** and **irreversible changes** in materials, with combustion being held up as an example of a process that is irreversible. A pupil making the misconception statement above has grasped the correct notion that the paper has undergone change, and bits of what the paper changes into (ash) have drifted away during the burning event. As with many related instances in school science (e.g. 9.1), the pupil has erred in the choice of word for the escaping process, and has elected to use the literary and not the scientific meaning of 'evaporate'. The everyday definition is to disperse or disappear, e.g. 'on the arrival of the police the crowd evaporated', therefore in this sense the ash has indeed evaporated. In science, **evaporation** has a more specific meaning: the change of a liquid into a gas below the boiling point, as in 'during the course of the day the puddle evaporated'. When the paper burns it does not evaporate because it is not a liquid.

Many people find it surprising that one of the substances made when most things burn is water (9.2), which is usually associated with extinguishing flames. When paper burns water is produced, although as soon as the water appears it immediately boils due to the high temperature of the burning reaction and escapes into the air as gaseous steam. However, strictly speaking this is still not evaporation because the change into gas takes place above the boiling point of water, which is 100°C; scientifically, the change is **boiling**. Note that the process of melting (see the next paragraph) and evaporation may indeed occur when some substances burn, e.g. burning chocolate melts; burning wax melts then evaporates. Clearly, this is not the case for all instances of combustion.

Pupils have been known to substitute the word 'melt' in a similar fashion, confusing it with its everyday meaning of mysterious disappearance, as in 'she melted away into the night'; thus a burning piece of wood in a campfire slowly melts to become ash. As with evaporation, the scientific meaning of melting is quite precise: the changing of a solid into a liquid. Another reason why pupils might use an inappropriate word is that there is uncertainty with the scientific definitions of words that are involved in similar contexts. For instance, during a **state changes** topic the words melting/**freezing** are confused with each other and then used interchangeably, as are evaporation/**condensation**, because the pupil has not yet fully assimilated exactly what these words mean, and merely attempted to rote-learn them.

Related misconceptions include that a candle melts but does not burn (9.3), and confusing **physical** and chemical changes (pupils may lump all changes into the same category without any differentiation).

Reconstruction

Frequent teacher use of scientific terminology helps pupils to successfully rote-learn correct definitions of words. If words such as burning, evaporation and melting are presented in a variety of scientific contexts, including practical work, then their definitions would be reinforced and their correct usage by pupils facilitated. Referring to the differences between physical and chemical changes will help to remind pupils that burning, evaporation and melting are quite different processes.

The concept of irreversible chemical change can be introduced to KS1 children through the simple activity of baking bread. Make up a simple dough and give out a handful to children to knead and then shape as desired. Place in an oven for 20 minutes at 150°C to produce little parcels of bread.

Source: Papageorgiou *et al.* (2010).

9.5 Are some acids 'safe'?

Misconception

All acids are corrosive.

Scientific conception

The word *acid* frequently conjures up associations with danger, burning, and science laboratories. Although lab acids such as hydrochloric, sulphuric or nitric are rarely utilized during science teaching at the primary level, and so the term *acid* may never be formally referred to by teachers, older pupils would still be familiar with the word and its associated descriptors. Acids are not only found in the science lab, many have a use around the home; in fact quite a few acids are common foodstuffs so are not corrosive or otherwise harmful.

Reconstruction

Pupils need to be aware that many familiar, everyday substances are acids. Some are capable of causing harm (e.g. car **battery** acid, drain cleaner) while others are safe (citric acid in lemon juice, tannic acid in tea). These examples serve to show that acids are not restricted to the science laboratory and are not all dangerous. Having physical examples on show in the classroom would help during these discussions.[1]

A familiar pedagogical demonstration tool in the primary classroom is the mixing of vinegar with bicarbonate of soda, which produces profuse fizzing. This chemical reaction is used to illustrate different phenomena, from the behaviour of gases in Year 5 to making a model volcano as part of a geography project. In contexts such as these, teachers can take the opportunity to introduce the fact that scientists call vinegar *ethanoic acid*, and that this is an example of an everyday, safe acid.

Did you know?

The most powerful acid. Through curiosity pupils may ask you *what is the world's strongest acid?* Sources vary as to the most *corrosive* acid (technically corrosion is different from strength), although one contender is hydrofluoric acid, which is able to dissolve glass easily and when in contact with human skin readily liquefies flesh. In lower concentrations skin remains undamaged but the acid permeates through and begins to dissolve the bones. At the other end of the spectrum are non-corrosive acids such as carbonic acid, found in acid rain. Pupils sometimes mistakenly consider acid rain as being able to cause immediate corrosion to exposed areas of their skin.

Source: Hand and Treagust (1988).

9.6 What is rust made of?

Misconception
Rust is a type of decay caused by a fungus.

Scientific conception

Pupils may be aware that iron or steel objects left outdoors during periods of wet weather can develop rust. A familiar example would be the rusty chain on a little-used bicycle that has been left uncovered in the garden over winter. This association of rusting with wet conditions is sometimes merged with the understanding that organic materials can decay when left in damp areas; examples include the underside of a log, the mouldy contents of a compost bin, fallen apples left to decompose on the lawn, and a rotten wooden shed or fence that has not been sufficiently damp-proofed. In these instances the materials decay due to the action of living organisms such as fungi (mould), bacteria and insects, and pupils sometimes incorrectly attribute these same living causes to the seemingly similar case of rusting metal.

When iron or steel is exposed to prolonged moist conditions it takes part in a chemical change. The iron combines with oxygen from the air and/or in the water to become brown/orange iron oxide, what we commonly call 'rust'. This is wholly a chemical change and does not require the action of any living organisms such as fungi or bacteria.

A related misconception is that rust is simply an impurity from within the metal that works its way to the surface over time. Another common misunderstanding is the idea that when iron becomes rusty it also becomes lower in mass because it is flakier, weaker and more insubstantial. In fact, rusted iron has a greater mass than the non-rusted iron because rusting involves capture of oxygen atoms from the air, which add their own mass to the system (see 9.2).

Reconstruction

The physical appearances of rusty iron and decayed organic matter can be very similar, acting as source of the misconception. Also, young children realize that both rusting and decay are 'bad' or unwanted outcomes, for instance through exposure to curricula focusing on healthy lifestyles that deal with ways to avoid food becoming rotten. This association may further enhance the possibility that children attribute both rusting and organic decay to the same living causative agents, e.g. fungi.

It is difficult at the primary level to adequately explain the difference between decay and rusting without using concepts rooted in secondary science, such as the nature of oxidation reactions. It would be necessary to correct the misconception on a simple level by stating that rusting is a purely chemical change unlike organic decay, which requires the presence of living organisms such as bacteria or fungi. One way to underline this difference is to demonstrate that rusting will still take place at low temperatures inside a fridge, while the decay of many foodstuffs is slowed to a large extent because the growth of microbes is inhibited. This can be done by placing an iron nail in a jam jar of tap water with the lid screwed on in the fridge for a couple of weeks. The discussion of rusting alongside other chemical changes such as combustion will also facilitate its correct categorization.

Source: DES (1984).

Note

1. Since acids are only introduced properly in Year 7, at the primary level there is no immediate necessity to spend too much time dealing in detail with their chemical behaviour or everyday uses.

10
Particles

10.1 Particles within solids and liquids

Misconception

Particles in a liquid are further apart than particles in a solid.

Scientific conception

Although not part of the primary curriculum, many schools introduce elementary particle theory as part of topics that deal with **states of matter**. After teaching, pupils are normally able to correctly depict the particles as arranged in a 'typical' solid (Figure 10.1a). However, particles in a liquid are often inaccurately drawn as being further apart than those in a solid (Figure 10.1b), as a kind of intermediate between solid and gas particle arrangements.

A reason for this may be confusion with how particles behave when a material boils or evaporates. Pupils learn that when a liquid becomes a gas the liquid particles are heated to such an extent that they become excited enough to escape from the surface of the liquid and spread out into the room. A common illustration of this process is boiling a kettle, with pupils tending to remember that particles of a gas are much further apart than they were when in the liquid state (Figure 10.1c). They are told that a cupful of water inside a boiling kettle becomes steam/water vapour that can fill an entire room. Learners may generalize this explanation to melting, and assume that when a solid becomes a liquid the solid particles similarly become excited and break apart (correct) and then move slightly further away from each other to form a liquid (incorrect).

Figure 10.1d gives a more accurate depiction of the arrangement of particles in the liquid phase. The particles remain touching as in a solid but have lost their regular arrangement and exist in a random and overlapping pattern in three dimensions. Since liquid particles are no longer fixed in position they can roll over each other, giving a liquid its characteristic abilities to flow, be spilled, and take the shape of the bottom of

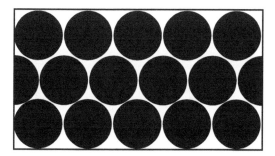

Figure 10.1a Particles in a solid

Figure 10.1b Particles in a liquid (misconception)

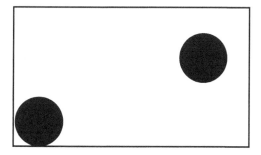

Figure 10.1c Scientific depiction of particles in a gas (inter-particle distance not to scale)

its container. Solids on the other hand have a fixed shape because their particles are stuck into position like bricks in a wall, although they do vibrate around a fixed point. Thus it does not matter whether particles are in the liquid or solid state, they remain the same distance apart, in close contact with each other (but see the unusual case of water, next paragraph).

Figure 10.1d Scientific depiction of particles in a liquid

The assumption that liquid particles are further apart can also lead to the idea that a liquid therefore takes up more space than a solid – it does not. In fact with water the opposite happens, with solid particles taking up more space than corresponding liquid particles; this is why it is sometimes difficult to remove ice cubes from a freezer tray – the particles in ice are further apart than in water so the ice expands when it freezes. This is also the cause of burst water pipes in sub-zero temperatures, and the reason why we mix antifreeze into the water inside a car radiator/cooling system.

Did you know?

Thermal expansion. Although it is correct to say that the distance between particles in a material remains constant when a solid becomes a liquid or vice versa (water excepted), this idea must not be confused with the fact that heating a substance in the same phase can cause the material to expand because the particles do actually move further apart. For instance, if a steel key is heated strongly in a flame it will expand to such an extent that it will be too large to fit its lock. If the steel were to be heated until it melts (around 1400°C), then the liquid steel further heated to (say) 2000°C, the liquid would continue to expand directly in response to the input of extra heat.

Reconstruction

This is a difficult misconception to deal with as the (correct) idea of liquids being an intermediate stage between solids and gases makes perfect sense to learners who may then go on to assume that the spreading out of particles in boiling or evaporation also occurs at melting. Physical models are a useful way to introduce the concepts of particle arrangements, particularly *Molymod* and similar products. Using such models as props, emphasize that when a solid melts, the particles do become more excited and break free of their physical bonds but they tend not to move any further apart. A good analogy for liquid particles that would be familiar to children is the colourful plastic ball pools that are found in public indoor play areas, where the balls are touching one another, are free to move singly (so can flow), and settle into the bottom of their containing tank. A further example that would be familiar to KS1 children is how breakfast cereals such as Rice Crispies settle into the bottom of their box, and can be spilled, poured, etc.

In one way water is a poor example to use because of its anomalous expansion on freezing, as mentioned above. A better material would be candle wax, which can be carefully melted in a test tube (or similar small, glass, heat-resistant container), using another candle as a source of heat. Once melted, the height of the liquid wax is marked off on the side of the container using a marker and the wax then allowed to cool. The solid wax should not contract to below this mark, showing that both solid and liquid wax occupy an equivalent volume, suggesting that the solid and liquid particles are similar distances apart.

In a different way water is useful to show that there are no gaps in between the particles of a liquid because a plugged syringe containing water is incompressible.

Sources: Novick and Nussbaum (1978); Papageorgiou *et al.* (2010).

10.2 How can we best draw 'particles'?

Misconception

The macroscopic nature of materials persists at the particle level.

Scientific conception

The diagrams in Figure 10.2a show the kinds of imaginative though inaccurate illustrations pupils may produce when asked to draw 'particles'. These drawings indicate that the **macroscopic** identity of the whole material (copper, aluminium or air) has persisted at the atomic level.

The copper depiction has been called the 'currant bun' model, where copper particles (or atoms) exist within a bed of copper. In reality, copper atoms are not embedded in a physical material, instead being tightly linked to each other in a regular pattern (Figure 10.2b). The gaps between the atoms are filled with nothing, i.e. a **vacuum**.

In Figure 10.2a the pupil has drawn an aluminium **atom** as being made from different types of aluminium material (foil and powder), which is at odds with what scientists believe is actually inside an atom. As with all atoms, a single aluminium atom is made up of even smaller building blocks, or **subatomic** units, called neutrons, protons and **electrons** (Figure 10.2c). Each of these units is thought to similarly consist of still smaller subatomic pieces such as quarks, leptons and gluons; one theory proposes these smaller pieces are made from entities called *superstrings*. Thus, atoms of every material are built from these same kinds of fundamental building blocks, whether that material is aluminium, copper, oxygen, carbon, or something else. It is rather like how the same Lego bricks can be arranged in different ways and

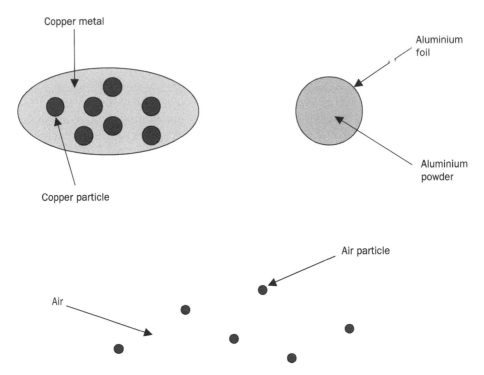

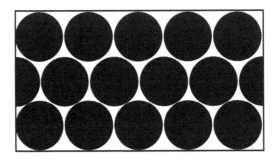

Figure 10.2a Some pupil depictions of particles (misconceptions)

Figure 10.2b Atoms in a typical solid, e.g. copper

used in different quantities to build different objects. To say that an aluminium atom is made from aluminium is not reasonable and is analogous to saying that the clay bricks that make up a house are house-shaped.

In Figure 10.2a the air depiction is a variant of the currant bun model, where particles exist within a continuous medium made from the same material. As with the

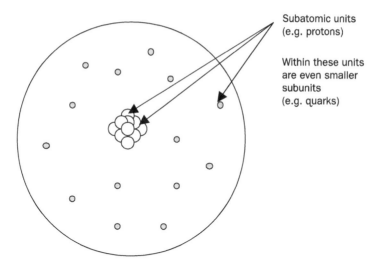

Subatomic units
(e.g. protons)

Within these units
are even smaller
subunits
(e.g. quarks)

Figure 10.2c A simplified diagram of a whole atom

copper depiction, the space between the 'air particles' is actually a vacuum and contains no matter.

There are several similar and very common misconceptions where pupils apply macroscopic qualities to particles, describing them as hard, able to melt, expand, contract, get hot, etc., where in fact the physical structure of a particle cannot change in any of these ways even though macroscopic samples of the material can. For instance, if an ice cube melts then its particles do not melt as well, they merely rearrange themselves to become less loosely held together, and form liquid water.

Reconstruction

If pupils have constructed misconceptions where the macroscopic nature of the whole material persists at the particle level as in Figure 10.2a, challenge their thinking by asking questions such as *what is the aluminium foil/powder made from? What is the copper metal into which the copper atoms sit made from?* An aluminium atom is the smallest piece of aluminium that can exist, so it does not make sense to say that the foil/powder in the pupil's drawing must itself be composed of aluminium atoms. A parallel argument can be made with reference to the copper bed and the continuous air medium.

At primary school level a detailed discussion of subatomic particles would probably not be useful as it is a long way beyond the curriculum; that said, the simple knowledge that particles are made of even smaller particles may help pupils visualize a more scientific model. Use of the Lego analogy as mentioned above would be likely to help this process.

Sources: Brook *et al.* (1984); Nussbaum (1985); Renstrom *et al.* (1990).

10.3 How much air is in a flat tyre?

Scientific conception

If a bicycle tyre or a football deflates due to a puncture it is colloquially acceptable to say that *all the air has been let out*. Once the puncture has been repaired, to reinflate the tyre we then need to *put some air in*. To state that a containing vessel such as a tyre does not have any air inside implies that there is nothing at all present, i.e. a vacuum exists within the tyre, which scientifically is incorrect. Consider Figure 10.3.

The air particles inside an inflated tyre are more concentrated than the surrounding air particles outside the tyre (Figure 10.3, left diagram). This is because during inflation air has been pumped into the tyre under pressure, so becoming **compressed air** inside the tyre. This is why when we press an inflated tyre with our fingers it feels springy and firm – the air particles at high concentration inside push out against the tyre wall. It is as if the particles are pushing outwards because they want to escape into the surrounding atmospheric air as inside the tyre they are too crowded. Indeed, if the tyre becomes punctured the particles rush out through the hole, causing the pressure to drop inside, and the tyre deflates (Figure 10.3, right). With the totally deflated tyre note that not all of the air particles have escaped; some of them remain inside the tyre. This is because when the tyre is punctured, air only continues to escape until the concentration of particles inside the tyre is exactly the same as the concentration of particles in the surrounding air (Figure 10.3, right). When we press a deflated tyre there is no firm springiness because it does not contain air under pressure, merely air at normal atmospheric pressure. Thus, a deflated tyre may appear at first reckoning to be devoid of air when in fact it contains plenty, whose particles are at the same concentration as the surrounding air.

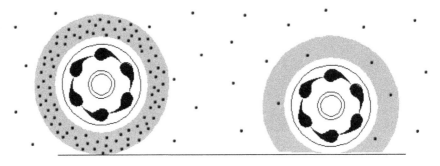

Figure 10.3 The concentrations of air particles inside and outside an inflated (left) and a totally deflated (right) tyre

Reconstruction

Air is invisible and in everyday situations its presence is not usually acknowledged, e.g. the air that exists in an 'empty' cup. When we can sense air then we tend to acknowledge it, as in the air in an inflated balloon because we can feel its pressure pushing outwards, or being aware of a draught of cold air coming in through the open door of a house, or when we hear air escaping from a punctured tyre. Informing pupils of these instances will help to remind them that air is a constant presence around us that we normally hardly ever notice. Although beyond the primary curriculum, an explanatory model that includes particles would be helpful, and be within the grasp of bright upper KS2 pupils, laying the foundations for later work in Year 7.

Source: Sere (1985).

10.4 Lighter than air?

Misconception

When a party balloon is inflated with air, the balloon becomes lighter.

Scientific conception

An inflated party balloon appears to have little or no **weight**, capable of being effort-lessly bounced around a room, and **sinks** slowly to the ground when released. In contrast, a deflated balloon behaves like a thin piece of rubber, falling quickly to the floor when dropped. These phenomena can lead to the mistaken belief that once a balloon is blown up it now contains air and it becomes lighter in weight (see 10.3).

Unexpectedly for many pupils, the inflated balloon is actually heavier than the deflated one. This is because the act of blowing up a balloon forces air in under pres-sure, which makes the air particles inside the balloon more concentrated than in the surrounding air (Figure 10.4a, left). Each individual air particle has a mass of its own, so air is not massless or weightless, and the greater concentration of air particles inside the inflated balloon means it will be heavier than if it were deflated. This is colloquially termed a *heavier than air* situation. It is for this reason that scuba divers know that a full air cylinder will become noticeably lighter once empty. The concen-tration of air particles inside a deflated balloon[1] is the same as that in the surrounding air (Figure 10.4a, right), therefore it contains fewer air particles and weighs less than an identical inflated balloon.

These phenomena can also be explained in terms of **density** (see 14.1 for more about density). Imagine the Earth's atmosphere as a 'sea of air'. An inflated balloon weighs more than an identical volume of surrounding air, so is more dense; therefore, if released it sinks to the floor of the sea of air, as would a piece of solid metal when released in water. A balloon full of helium, however, weighs less than the surrounding sea of air because of the very light weight of individual helium particles, so is less dense. A released helium balloon therefore rises in an attempt to float on the surface

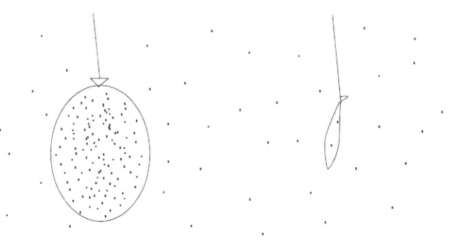

Figure 10.4a The concentration of air particles in an inflated (left) and deflated (right) balloon

of the sea of air, as would a piece of expanded polystyrene released under water. Colloquially, this is a *lighter than air* situation.

Hot air balloons can act as a source of further confusion. The reason why they rise is because the air inside has expanded in response to the addition of heat, so the air particles inside are less concentrated than those in the surrounding air, thus the parcel of air within the balloon is less dense, or lighter than air (Figure 10.4b).

Reconstruction

Children may have heard the story *Winnie the Pooh and the Honey Tree*, where Pooh borrows a party balloon from Christopher Robin and uses it to float up a tree to steal honey. The story can be used as an introduction to an investigation where the aim is to make an object rise by using balloons inflated with air. Of course, pupils soon realize that this is impossible, which refutes the misconception that balloons inflated with air are lighter than air. Air balloons can be compared to helium balloons, which are lighter than air.

Carbon dioxide balloons can be prepared by stretching a party balloon over a small bottle that contains vinegar and bicarbonate of soda. This is best done by first pouring the vinegar into the bottle, spooning some bicarbonate inside the deflated balloon, then sealing the balloon over the neck of the bottle, causing mixing. The liberated gas will be collected in the balloon which can then be removed and tied off. Released carbon dioxide balloons fall to the floor quite quickly, demonstrating clearly that not every gas is lighter than air.

Ask pupils to predict what would happen to the mass of a party balloon when it is inflated, then get them to test their hypotheses by using a fairly sensitive balance to compare the masses of a deflated and an inflated balloon.

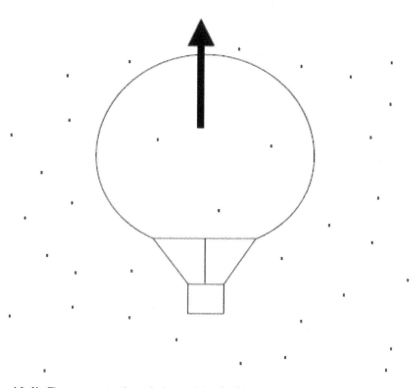

Figure 10.4b The concentration of air particles inside and outside a hot air balloon

> **Be safe!**
>
> **Safety with balloons.** It is advised that adults supervise the inflation of party balloons due to a (slight) risk of choking. Balloon hand pumps are commercially available to help with the quick inflation of large numbers of balloons. Also consider any children who might have an allergy to latex rubber.

Source: Sere (1985).

10.5 When you stir sugar into a cup of tea does it become heavier?

> **Misconception**
>
> *When a solid dissolves in water it does not contribute to the mass of the solution.*

Scientific conception

If 3 g of salt is completely dissolved into 100 g of water, pupils tend to predict that the mass of the resulting mixture would be 100 g. When a material such as salt dissolves it does not cease to exist, regardless of the fact that it has disappeared from view. During the dissolving process the sodium and chloride particles that make up salt become detached from each other and spread out within the water to such an extent that the white bulk of solid salt is no longer visible. Imagine if you sprinkled a quantity of black pepper while running across a sandy beach – it would be very difficult to go back and find individual pepper particles in the sand. Each sodium and chloride particle has its own mass, which contributes to the overall mass of the solution it eventually becomes part of. Thus, when 3 g of salt is dissolved into 100 g of water the solution would weigh 103 g precisely.

Alternatively, some pupils may believe that when salt dissolves in water the total mass of solution *decreases* due to the salt acting like a sponge and absorbing some of the water's mass.

Reconstruction

The misconception can be elicited by asking the class what would happen to the mass of a sample of water if some salt were to be thoroughly dissolved. An alternative and more familiar scenario is dissolving sugar into a cup of tea, although if this is done practically in the classroom things tend to get sticky and messy so salt is usually preferred. Pupils could then test their predictions by weighing salt, water, mixing the two and then finally weighing the solution. Note that there will be plenty of room for experimental error with this practical as mass can be easily lost during the mixing process due to spillage, and so a final demonstration may be necessary with the teacher repeating the procedure in a controlled manner. Support your argument by saying that since the solution tastes salty then the salt must still be there somewhere, and so must also contribute to the overall mass. Do not ask pupils to taste the salt water unless conditions are appropriately hygienic. A demonstration using a coloured solid such as copper sulphate in place of salt would help learners appreciate that when something becomes part of a solution its particles are still present.

To underline the point, dissolve 40 spatulafuls of salt into 100 ml of hot water. The increase in mass is obvious as the solution becomes noticeably heavier than before when weighed by hand.

Source: Piaget and Inhelder (1974).

Note

1. As is the case with 10.3, a deflated balloon still contains air inside.

11

States of matter

11.1 Can something be hollow and solid at the same time?

Misconception

A football is not a solid.

[Talcum powder] is a kind of liquid, but it isn't liquid . . . It's a bit solid, but it isn't. (Pupil, reception class; Russell *et al.*, 1991, p120)

Scientific conception

During the primary years pupils are taught to use the observed properties of materials to sort them into the familiar sets of solid, liquid and gas. These sets are mutually exclusive in the sense that pupils are taught that any material cannot belong in more than one set. There are sometimes difficulties when deciding precisely which set some objects should fall into, such as a football, which pupils often consider to be a non-solid because it is hollow. With this particular example there has been a clash of meanings with the everyday definition that states an object that is non-hollow is 'solid', as in 'the castle wall was solid'. Other objects that can be improperly categorized by pupils as non-solids for the same reason are a feather, cotton wool, articles of clothing/fabric, items made using a wire frame, a bathroom sponge, and powders.

With hollow objects such as a football the interior is gaseous, containing air, but the football is made from a material such as plastic, leather or rubber, so although there are areas inside the object that are gas the football itself is a solid. Similar examples are metal scuba-diving cylinders and inflated balloons, which are solid objects that just happen to contain a reservoir of trapped air inside. This is analogous to foams such as the 'head' on a glass of beer or shaving foam, which are liquids that contain some air. Occasionally pupils will classify objects they are unsure about such as footballs into an imaginary intermediate set of solid/gas.

A second reason why materials might not be considered to be solids is that they are thought to be liquids instead. Soft solids such as plasticine go against some pupils' incorrect notions that all solids have to be hard and rigid, and because they can be moulded into new shapes are classified as liquids. Candle wax and butter are other soft solids that pupils can believe are liquids because they easily melt. Conversely, some pupils think treacle is a solid and not a liquid because it is more **viscous** (thicker) than water. Jelly is frequently considered not to be a solid because it is too soft and has been made by adding water, which is a liquid. Some learners believe that powders like sand or talcum powder are liquids because they can be poured, spilled and take the shape of their containers, even though each individual grain of sand/flour is in the solid phase (Figure 11.1a).

Reconstruction

Aside from using the arguments that have been presented in this section during teaching, a good way to start to deal with some of the misconceptions is by introducing the idea of state changes. Inform pupils that materials are not permanently solid, liquid or gas but can change depending on the temperature.[1] An experiment designed to discover the melting point of butter will help to elucidate this, and can be done, with care, using hot water incrementally added to a water bath (Figure 11.1b). Start with water straight from the cold tap in the water bath, then carefully add water from a hot kettle a little at a time, thus slowly increasing the temperature of the butter. When the butter liquefies around the thermometer bulb then this is the melting point temperature; note that butter melts at around 30°C and so a very hot day would not suit this activity. Conclude by stating that we give a material the label of being solid, liquid or gas by looking at its state *at room temperature*, and although the butter melts easily it is normally a solid. The same ideas can be reinforced during the activity of making jelly.

Younger children can begin to describe materials by using a feely box. Place objects in the box one at a time and ask children to use adjectives that best fit that object, and then finally they have to guess what the object is. Use a variety of materials including hard and soft solids, an open tub of salt, an open cup of fairy liquid, etc.

Solid	Liquid	Gas
Has its own shape	Takes the shape of the bottom of its container	Fills its container
Cannot change its volume	Cannot change its volume	Volume can be changed (can be compressed)
Particles very close together and fixed in position in a regular pattern	Can flow	Can flow
	Can be spilled	Particles far apart, free to move randomly at high speeds
	Particles very close together and not fixed in position	

Figure **11.1a** Characteristics of the three states of matter

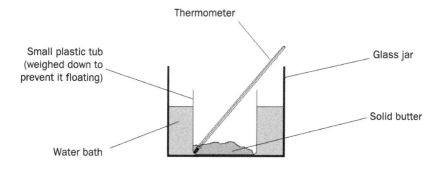

Figure 11.1b Determination of the melting point of butter

If pupils are ever in doubt about which state a material is in, cite mutual exclusivity by asking them which set they think it belongs in the most. Get them into the habit of judging a material to be solid, liquid or gas with no intermediate sets.

Sources: Jones and Lynch (1989); Russell *et al.* (1991); Stavy (1994); Stavy and Stachel (1984).

11.2 The comparative weight of a powder

Misconception

A solid is lighter when in powder form.

Scientific conception

Pupils may believe that if an object is ground down into tiny pieces to form a powder, it naturally becomes less heavy. This idea may derive from the correct observation that many familiar powders such as salt, sugar, flour, sand and coffee tend to feel fairly light if picked up as a handful.

This familiar sensation has some basis in truth. If you hold some powder in one hand (e.g. iron filings) and a similar sized whole piece of the same material in the other (e.g. a 100 g iron mass), the powder will indeed feel and weigh the lighter. This is because the powder is less dense than a whole continuous piece of material due to air spaces between the powder grains, and since the whole piece has no air spaces it is more dense, so an equal volume of it would be the heavier (Figure 11.2). However, it must be remembered that a single grain of powder is made from exactly the same substance as a larger piece of material, so has the same density as that larger piece. Therefore if a large bit is first weighed then completely filed down to powder and the grains are collected then weighed again they should weigh exactly the same as the original large bit because there has been no loss of mass. Just because the solid now exists as a powder, that does not mean that it has become any lighter.

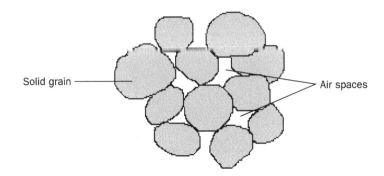

Solid grain ——————————○   ○—————————→ Air spaces

Figure 11.2 A microscopic depiction of how the grains of a powder might fit together

The more insubstantial nature of a powder may reinforce this misconception, e.g. the fact it can slip through the fingers easily. For this reason it is difficult to get hold of much of a powder in a single handful so you are unlikely to be able to hold enough material for it to feel oppressively heavy.

Reconstruction

Weigh a small piece of wood. Using a file, grind the piece down a little bit, carefully collecting all of the filings, then reweigh the filings together with the original piece to show that no loss of mass has occurred. There is a possibility of some loss as dust during the filing process so some practice might be needed to prevent a significant reduction in mass that would show up on the balance.

Passing a container of iron or copper filings around the class is a useful way to demonstrate that not all powders are light and insubstantial.

Source: Galili and Bar (1997).

11.3 Which is heavier – ice or water?

Misconception

If you melt a solid it becomes lighter.

Scientific conception

If a piece of ice is weighed, then left in a cup to melt completely and the resulting melted water weighed again some learners would predict a loss of mass. They may expect this because water when compared with ice appears to be more insubstantial, softer, and less of a tangible substance. Others may note that *volume* decreases when ice melts to become water, prompted by observations of the amount of space taken up

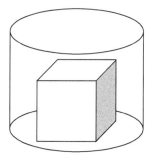 

Figure 11.3 The apparently large reduction in volume when ice melts

by an ice cube when compared with the seemingly small amount of melted water (Figure 11.3), or by the fact that water expands when it freezes to become ice, and so the mass of ice would probably reduce after melting. Similarly, pupils may believe that if candle wax is melted to form liquid wax its mass will also fall.

When any material melts its mass is always conserved because, although there has been a change in state, the number of particles in both the solid and liquid forms is the same, assuming no experimental losses due to evaporation, for example (see 13.6 for more on mass and particles). This conservation of mass occurs despite obvious changes in the volume of water during melting/freezing. For instance, many pupils will be aware that it is difficult to remove ice cubes from the freezer tray because the water has expanded during the freezing process (although they may believe that the mass of water has increased during its transformation into ice). Because ice expands during freezing it is less dense than cold water, and so when equal volumes are compared, ice is actually *lighter* than cold water.

The misconception might be linked to the incorrect idea that solid particles are closer together than liquid particles and so liquids must weigh less because there are fewer particles in a given space (10.1). Other contexts where pupils have failed to conserve mass include the belief that running water has more mass than still water, and when a liquid boils to become a gas there has been a decrease in mass.

Reconstruction

The misconception can be refuted experimentally in a fairly straightforward way by asking pupils to weigh a sealed jar containing an ice cube, waiting for it to melt at ambient temperature then reweighing the jar to show that the mass does not change. Be sure to wipe the outside of the jar just before each weighing to remove any external condensation.

As in 11.2, remind pupils that water is a substantial and heavy material by asking them to lift a 10-litre filled container – bearing in mind local health and safety regulations.

Sources: Galili and Bar (1997); Leite *et al.* (2007).

11.4 What happens to water once it has boiled?

> **Misconception**
>
> *Boiling and evaporation are irreversible changes.*

Scientific conception

In Year 5 pupils are introduced to the concept of reversible changes, which are situations where materials can be altered but are able to change back later to their original form. These are usually taught in the context of state changes, often using water as a particular exemplar (Figure 11.4).

In Year 6 pupils meet the concept of irreversible changes, where materials transform into something new and cannot easily be reverted back to their former condition, e.g. burning wood, cooking a fried egg. The misconception statement above reflects the belief that when liquid water becomes steam (liquid → gas) then the steam can never become water again. However, since state changes such as boiling are reversible then steam can be cooled and condensed to become liquid water again (Figure 11.4). The misconception would be reinforced by the observation that the clouds from a boiling kettle appear to dissipate into the air, seemingly lost for ever.

Reconstruction

Relate the issue to a familiar context by asking pupils *why do the insides of your kitchen windows sometimes become wet when someone is cooking?* Explain that when water is boiled in pans on the cooker it becomes steam and rises into the air; as the steam floats away from the hot cooker it cools and condenses back into liquid

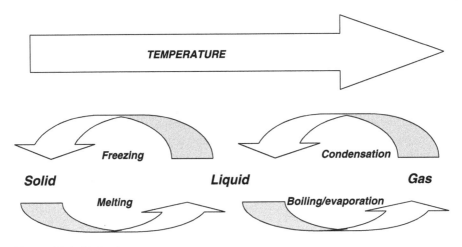

Figure 11.4 State changes

water, forming clouds of mist, some of which deposits itself on the cold window panes. One analogy is that when a person changes their clothing, e.g. school uniform, they look different, and may even behave differently, but are still the same person; that person is always able to change back into their original clothes. When liquid water boils and becomes steam it too changes its appearance and behaviour – it has 'changed its clothes', but is still essentially the same thing since condensing the steam allows it to become the liquid water that it was once before.

Pupils can hold a glass of ice water (carefully) above a cup of just boiled water and see how it becomes dripping wet on the outside. Asking pupils where the water came from can elicit some surprising responses, including the idea that the ice water from inside has seeped through the solid glass to the outside (also see 11.7). The discussion should eventually be steered towards the scientific idea of condensation in response to a drop in temperature, in order to show that the evaporation process is reversible. A further complication with this issue is that the white clouds that we see above boiling water are not technically in the *gaseous* state (as steam/water vapour), but instead in are the *liquid* state in the form of water droplets (see 11.5 and 11.6 for clarifications).

Source: Ahtee and Varjola (1998).

11.5 The disappearing puddle

Misconception

Liquids that evaporate or boil disappear for ever.

I think the water has dissapeard (sic). I think the air around us sucked the water up and the air made it into nothing because the air is stronger than the water. (Pupil, aged 9 years; Russell and Watt, 1990, p15)

Scientific conception

When asked to explain what happens when a puddle evaporates on a hot day some pupils will simply say that it has vanished in the heat. Similar responses can be elicited with a boiling kettle scenario, e.g. the belief that water becomes steam before disappearing off, never to be heard of again (11.4). Other pupils may suggest that the missing water has 'disappeared into the air', which is nearer to the truth.

Boiling is the state change that takes place when a liquid becomes a gas at its boiling point, which in the case of pure water is 100°C at normal atmospheric pressure; the gas produced by boiling is *steam*. On the other hand, evaporation is when a liquid becomes a gas below the boiling point; the gas produced in this case is *water vapour*, which is gaseous water below 100°C. A puddle disappears on a hot day not because the sun boils the water to 100°C; instead, the puddle is only heated to (say) 25°C and then slowly evaporates as water vapour. This water vapour then becomes part of the air around us, contributing to humidity; some will rise into the sky, cooling down in the process, and upon reaching a certain height condense back into liquid water to become part of a cloud.

The fact that evaporated water (vapour) from a puddle is invisible is likely to be the source of the misconception. A degree of imagination is required to envisage the unseen water vapour as still being present in the air all around us, or rising then becoming clouds in the sky which may eventually fall as rain again.

Reconstruction

Understanding the water cycle (Year 4) is a good way to dispel this misconception. Many pupils will remember the 'story of water' as it takes on different forms within the cycle (Figure 11.5), and the water cycle can be acted out by children as a classroom role play.

Stimulate a discussion about the unpleasant 'muggy' feeling associated with a hot, humid day being due to the air being 'very wet', i.e. lots of invisible water vapour is present in the air.

A container of water covered by clingfilm placed in the classroom in direct sunlight or on a radiator will catch evaporated water vapour on the inside, making it visible again in liquid form, showing that as water evaporates it does not simply disappear for ever. Using a control container without clingfilm for comparison, where the water appears to merely vanish, may help. Since this misconception is closely related to the misconception that boiling is irreversible (11.4), use of the pedagogies described there would facilitate the construction of acceptable scientific ideas.

Key Stage 1 children can create puddle prints. Make up batches of different-coloured water with food colouring. Get the children to use droppers to make small coloured puddles on an A4 plastic page protector, then leave this on the windowsill in direct sunlight, or close to a heat source such a radiator. When the water evaporates, coloured patches are left on the plastic. Take care with this exercise if your classroom has a carpet that will stain easily.

Sources: Bar (1986); Frankel-Hauser (1998); Russell and Watt (1990).

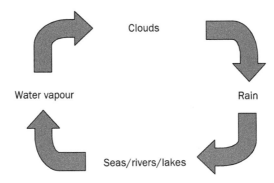

Figure 11.5 Simple representation of the water cycle

11.6 What are clouds made from?

Misconception

Clouds are made of gas.

Scientific conception

This misconception is relevant to all water clouds, including clouds in the sky, above a boiling kettle or those associated with weather conditions such as mist or fog. Water clouds look gaseous and behave macroscopically as a gas would – they float in the air, can flow, are able to fill a container, and possess an insubstantial quality, appearing to have no physical substance. However, these clouds are composed of water mainly in the *liquid* phase and not the gaseous phase. Examined micro-scopically, they would appear as water droplets suspended in the air. Because they are so tiny they have a very low weight and are able to be lifted by small rising air currents as you would find, for instance, above a boiling kettle, and so the droplets appear to behave like a gas – floating, flowing, etc. Within weather clouds in the sky you often have water droplets moving around in turbulent conditions, colliding with each other and joining together, becoming larger and larger until they are so big that their weight is too large to be supported any longer, and so fall as rain.

The misconception is reinforced by the everyday name we give to the clouds of water produced by a boiling kettle, pan of water or hot bath – *steam*. Scientifically, steam is water in the gas phase at or above its boiling point ($100°C$ with pure water at normal atmospheric pressure), and because water clouds exist below this temperature they are actually in the liquid phase as water droplets (Figure 11.6). Therefore in the classroom it is best to get into the habit of referring to these entities as 'clouds' or 'mist', instead of using the colloquial name 'steam'. If you watch a boiling kettle there is a small transparent area just above the spout, below where the clouds begin to form – this is true gaseous steam, which is invisible. The white clouds that are visible above this area are condensed water in the liquid phase (Figure 11.6).

A related misconception is the belief that powders are liquids when in fact they are tiny bits of solid (11.1). Powders behave macroscopically as a liquid, i.e. they flow, can be poured, spilled, and so on, but each individual bit is in the solid phase.

Reconstruction

As with 11.5, the state changes discussed here form part of the water cycle, so an understanding of the processes contained therein would help pupils appreciate that clouds are made from liquid water.

The teacher could demonstrate how holding a piece of tissue within the clouds above a boiling kettle (with care) makes the tissue damp as the water droplets are absorbed onto the tissue. Note that this is *not* an example of condensation (gas → liquid), since the drops in the cloud are not gaseous.

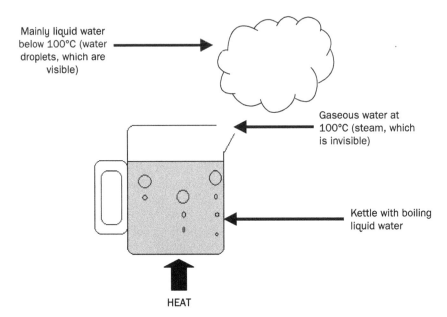

Figure 11.6 The different states of water associated with a boiling kettle

Relate familiar contexts to the idea that clouds are actually liquid water, for instance how a car windscreen quickly becomes wet when driving through fog, or cycling through fog can make your hair wet. Similarly, water can sometimes be seen collecting on the outside of aircraft windows when descending through cloud.

It should be noted as a final point that in reality the situation is slightly more complex since the white clouds produced by a kettle will actually contain *some* water in the gaseous state in the form of water vapour (see 11.4). Weather clouds also contain some water vapour and even some water in the solid phase, as ice or snow. Whether this information should be taught at the primary level is a matter for debate, since although it reflects correct science it might only serve to confuse pupils further.

Source: Dove (1998).

11.7 Why do some objects become moist when we take them out of the fridge?

Misconception

A cola can gets wet because liquid from the inside seeps through to the outside.

Scientific conception

Most children would be aware of this common experience which can especially be seen on a warm day when containers of cold drinks become invariably moist on the outside. However, children are usually at a loss if asked to explain why the water appears, and answers such as the misconception statement above represent attempts to make sense of the phenomenon. As with the other entries in this chapter, water vapour plays a vital part in the process. Invisible water vapour in the gas phase is present in the air surrounding the drinks can, and when it comes into contact with the cold can the water vapour cools and condenses into water in the liquid phase. We say that the cold temperature of the can is below the **dew point**, causing the water vapour to condense or 'become dew', therefore the can becomes moist as the liquid water become visible. In hot, arid environments where humidity is very low there is little water vapour in the air and so the phenomenon may not occur.

The mist that emanates from the family freezer when we open the door appears for the exactly the same reason – the freezer temperature is below the dew point and so water vapour in the air outside condenses into water droplets, visible as mist. At dawn, cold surfaces such as the ground or the metal body of a car can be wet with dew even if rain has not fallen during the night because temperatures have dropped to below the dew point.

Reconstruction

Pupils can be reminded that drinks cans made from aluminium are both waterproof and airtight so it is impossible for anything from the inside to seep through. A good demonstration of how water vapour is present in the air as humidity would be to wait for a rainy day when several children enter the classroom. The windows quickly mist up because liquid water from their wet clothes evaporates, becoming invisible water vapour in the air and giving the room a very humid atmosphere. This water vapour then condenses on the cold surface of windows to produce the misting. Pupils who habitually wear spectacles would be familiar with this experience.

Source: Osborne and Cosgrove (1983).

Note

1. Pressure also has an influence on state changes, although this concept is probably best left for the secondary years.

12

Earth science

12.1 Is there a difference between a rock and a stone?

> **Misconception**
> *Rocks are large, heavy and jagged. If smaller, they are stones. If smooth, they are pebbles.*

A rock is bigger than a stone. A stone is dead small . . . (Pupil, Year 2; Russell *et al.*, 1993, p33)

Scientific conception

During the teaching of a primary Earth science topic activities typically involve presenting to pupils a variety of authentic **rock** and mineral specimens. Some pupils may consider any pieces smaller than the palms of their hands too small to be called rocks; instead they are stones. The roots of this misapprehension probably lie in colloquial language, since to some children 'a stone' is any rock-like object that is small enough to be capable of being thrown a fair distance. This informal classification would include fragments of materials that are not technically rocks – for instance, pieces of brick or concrete would also be called stones (see 12.2). These beliefs are compatible with non-scientific definitions of the word 'stone'; however, there is a problem if pupils construct mutually exclusive sets – since a particular fragment of material is thought to be a stone because of its small size, then it cannot be a rock. This is likely to result in classification problems where pupils think small fragments of rocks such as granite or slate are non-rocks.

Similarly, a boulder may not be considered to be a rock because it is too big. Children may classify any smooth sample as being a pebble and not a rock. A rock can be defined scientifically as *any natural material that is a product of geological processes and consists of an aggregate of more than one mineral.* Therefore, whether an object is a rock or otherwise has nothing to do with its size, which means both a very small fragment and an entire cliff face are classified as rock.

Did you know?

Semantic differences in other cultures. Interestingly, in everyday American English use there appears to be less of a size distinction between a rock and a stone than exists in British English. In the USA a rock can be a smaller fragment, hence the American expression *people in glass houses shouldn't throw rocks.*

Reconstruction

A useful approach would be to alter pupils' semantic usage of the word *rock*. Instead of using the word to describe a particular object as 'a rock', insist that scientifically the object is 'made from rock' or simply 'rock'. When deciding whether to classify something as 'rock', its physical properties or qualities need to be looked at, irrespective of size or smoothness. For example, the teacher may wish pupils to differentiate between rocks and minerals, so an activity may involve inspecting samples and deciding on whether they consist of one pure substance (mineral) or several mixed together (rock); see 12.2 and 12.3 for further clarification of this distinction.

Source: Russell *et al.* (1993).

12.2 What exactly is a rock?

Misconception

Brick and concrete are examples of rocks.

Scientific conception

Upon cursory examination a brick is very rock-like. A small fragment from a damaged brick that has had its flat sides and corners broken away may look indistinguishable from any other fragment of rock such as sandstone. However, rock is a natural material (see 12.1) and a brick is not a natural material – it has been artificially manufactured by firing clay in a kiln, often along with additives such as lime to produce a hard and fairly brittle material ideal for use in building.

Likewise, concrete is not a natural material, being a mixture of cement, sand, gravel and water. Once liquid concrete has been poured into place, e.g. on a garden pathway, it sets due to a chemical reaction that binds the mixture together to form a dry, hardwearing solid. A piece of broken concrete can look very similar to rock such as conglomerate.

A related misconception is that a polished piece of marble or a granite paving stone is not a rock because it has been worked and so is no longer natural.

Reconstruction

Encourage pupils to overcome the inclination to call anything that looks rock-like a rock, reminding them that along with appearance and physical properties the source of a material also needs to be taken into consideration. As intimated above, sometimes the flat sides or corners of a brick or piece of concrete can reveal its artificial origin. A sorting exercise requiring pupils to separate a variety of objects into synthetic and natural would help. Younger children can inspect a rock collection and describe each specimen, commenting on its colour, texture, attractiveness, etc. They can also use a computer programme such as Microsoft PowerPoint to make collage of things that are made from rock such as dry-stone walls, driveways, roofs and statues.

Sources: Happs (1985a); Russell *et al.* (1993).

12.3 What exactly is a mineral?

Misconception

Minerals are precious small stones.

Scientific conception

Minerals are usually thought to be attractive, shiny, rare and used extensively in jewellery, e.g. rubies, sapphires, emeralds. Indeed, many minerals are jewels because of their beauty and rarity, and are gemstones; other minerals such as quartz are not rare and have low monetary value. So although the misconception statement is correct on one level it discounts other minerals that are less rare, attractive and expensive.

In contrast to minerals, pupils frequently consider rocks to be dull, commonly available and comparatively inexpensive. In fact some rocks such as the igneous horn-blendite are quite rare, and rocks that have high crystalline content such as schist can be naturally shiny and attractive. It is therefore sometimes difficult to generalize when trying to distinguish between rocks and minerals using appearance or rarity alone. Minerals are naturally occurring 'pure' chemicals that have been formed by geological processes; e.g. pyrite (fool's gold) is iron disulphide (FeS_2). Rocks, on the other hand, are natural mixtures of more than one mineral (Figure 12.3).

The distinction between rocks and minerals is confused by a colloquial use of the word 'rock' to describe mineral gems such as diamonds and sapphires when set in an expensive engagement ring. Some gemstones are not only natural and can also be produced synthetically in the laboratory, e.g. rubies, for use as a component in lasers.

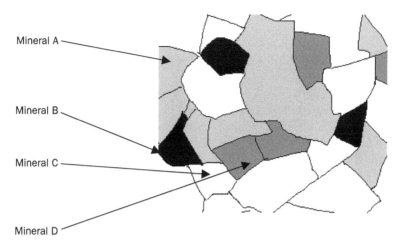

Mineral A

Mineral B

Mineral C

Mineral D

Figure 12.3 Microscopic view of a rock sample made up of four different minerals

Related misconceptions include that a rock is made up from a single substance only, and that rocks or minerals that are attractive are called crystals.

Reconstruction

With the traditional primary-level exercise where pupils examine rock/mineral samples in order to study their appearance and properties such as hardness, be sure to include quartz, calcite and other inexpensive minerals in order to show that not all minerals are gemstones.

To help pupils distinguish between rocks and minerals use a photograph (e.g. sourced from the internet) to show the microscopic rock structure of granite. Point out the individual minerals in the picture, which are usually interlocked like a jigsaw puzzle (as in Figure 12.3). Examination of an actual sample of granite using a magnifying glass would also reveal this pattern. Tell pupils that each piece of the jigsaw is a small bit of a pure chemical, called a mineral. To help underline this, using the classroom geology collection show pupils larger pieces of the same minerals that are found in granite (e.g. feldspar, quartz).

Source: Happs (1985a).

12.4 What causes earthquakes?

Misconception

All earthquakes are a result of volcanoes erupting.

Scientific conception

Associating earthquakes with volcanoes is a relatively common error. Both are dramatic and often violent phenomena that are unfamiliar to UK residents at first hand, and so represent exotic events whose causes are shrouded in mystery. Not living within an earthquake zone can lead to the construction of misconceptions about what exactly makes an earthquake happen.

Most earthquakes occur due to the friction generated when moving underground rocks rub against each other. This movement occurs where rock masses are divided by huge splits, or faults. Occasionally, enormous subterranean hunks of rock are snapped off during this rubbing and the immense amounts of released energy transmit vibrations outwards in all directions, eventually reaching the Earth's surface at the **epicentre** where they are felt as earthquakes (Figure 12.4a).

Figure 12.4b shows the location of earthquakes over a 35-year period, with the majority occurring along the boundaries of **tectonic plates** – the energy transferred from these vast, mobile sheets of rock can be pinpointed as the source of faults and consequently earthquakes. It can be noted when Figures 12.4b and 12.4c are compared that volcanic eruptions occur at the same locations as earthquakes; this is due to weaknesses in the Earth's crust at plate boundaries that are a common causal factor in both of these phenomena.

So typically, despite the two phenomena occurring in the same geographical regions, earthquakes are not triggered by volcanoes erupting; instead earthquakes are a result of the underground movement of huge sections of rock. That said, a minority of earthquakes *are* associated with volcanic activity when large amounts of magma are moving underground, and earthquakes have in the past acted as an early warning of some volcanic eruptions.

Other misconceptions that relate to the cause of earthquakes include the idea that earthquakes occur due to high winds or tornadoes. Also, converse to the current misconception, some people believe that all volcanic eruptions are caused by earthquakes.

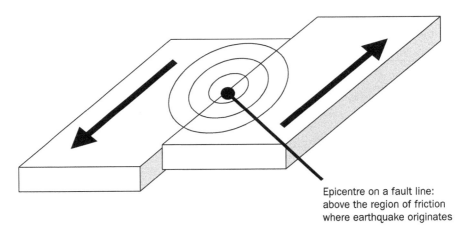

Epicentre on a fault line: above the region of friction where earthquake originates

Figure 12.4a Most earthquakes occur as a result of friction between moving masses of rock

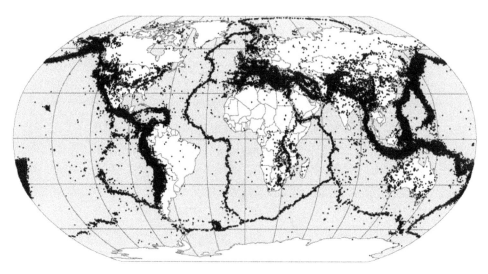

Figure 12.4b Earthquake epicentres 1963–1998 (NASA)

Did you know?

The world's most active volcano? One notable candidate for this title would be Kilauea in Hawaii, where activity in the form of lava flows has been a daily event since 1983.

Reconstruction

Showing pupils maps of earthquake and volcano zones similar to those in Figures 12.4b and 12.4c will help make the point that, although the two phenomena are often found in the same locations due to weaknesses in the Earth's crust, many earthquakes occur in the absence of volcanic eruptions.

Footage of the tragic Indian Ocean tsunami of 26 December 2004 could accompany explanations that tsunamis are caused by undersea earthquakes and not volcanic activity.

Source: Ross and Shuell (1993).

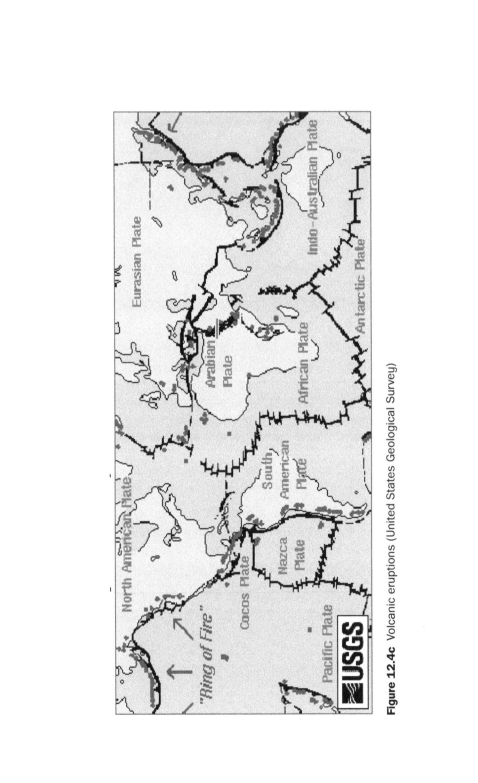

Figure 12.4c Volcanic eruptions (United States Geological Survey)

12.5 Which way is down?

> **Misconception**
>
> *The densest materials in the Earth are to be found at the South Pole.*

Scientific conception

Pupils may construct the idea that dense materials within the Earth such as iron have settled over time and filtered 'down', coming to rest at the 'bottom' of the Earth. This misconception is indicative of a naive, incorrect concept of up and down, as in space there is no ultimate frame of reference (Figure 12.5a). Since gravity acts towards the centre of the Earth and not the geographical South Pole, this is the true direction of 'down' if the Earth is the frame of reference (Figure 12.5b). Billions of years ago, when the Earth was forming, the denser materials that were in high abundance sank towards the centre under the influence of gravity, resulting in today's iron/ nickel core (Figure 12.5c).

Stories, sometimes exaggerated, of a wealth of natural resources such as metals and oil in Antarctica might further reinforce this misconception. A geographical misconception that is also a consequence of a naive concept of up/down is that on a map of Antarctica the direction *north* is always at the top of the map; however, north actually radiates in all directions away from the geographical South Pole (this can be shown using a globe).

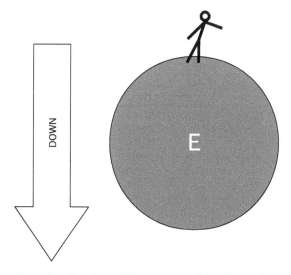

Figure 12.5a 'Down' is in the direction of the surface of the Earth where I am standing (misconception)

Reconstruction

A first step is to correct the naive concept of 'down' that acts as a source of the misconception, insisting that 'down' for anyone on Earth is towards the Earth's centre. Pupils'
beliefs regarding which way they consider to be 'down' can be elicited by using a
diagram similar to Figure 12.5d, asking pupils *how would the balls fall if the three
people were to release them at the same time?*

Although the internal structure of the Earth is beyond the primary science
National Curriculum, pupils could be introduced to the idea of the Earth consisting of
different layers and that the heaviest (densest) layers are found at the core, not the
South Pole.

Sources: Marques and Thompson (1997); Nussbaum (1985); Schoon and Boone (1998).

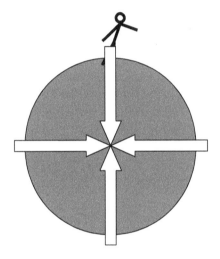

Figure 12.5b The true direction of 'down'

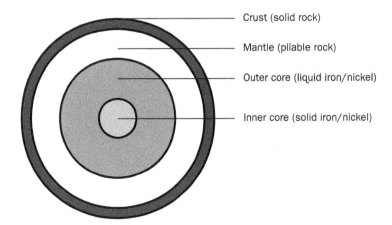

Figure 12.5c Internal structure of Earth (not to scale)

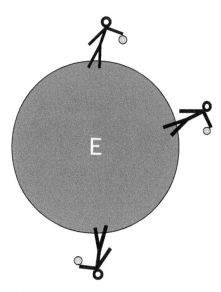

Figure 12.5d Eliciting pupils' ideas of 'down'

12.6 How do underground creatures breathe?

Misconception

Animals in soil breathe by coming to the surface.

Scientific conception

Informal observations carried out in the garden can yield sights of soil animals such as ants, ground beetles or centipedes crawling on the surface and then disappearing underground again, particularly when disturbed. Reasons given by pupils to account for this intermittent surfacing can include a need for air, analogous to how a whale, being a mammal, has no gills and so needs to periodically come to the surface of the sea in order to breathe.

While soil invertebrates similarly do not have gills so therefore need direct contact with air in order to absorb oxygen, there is in fact plenty of air underground. Soil is not a compact solid mass, and instead contains many air spaces within. Therefore these animals can breathe quite adequately whilst underground by utilizing these tiny pockets of air (Figure 12.6).

During rainy weather earthworms appear on the surface of soil, a phenomenon that can act as a source or reinforcer of the misconception. Worms absorb oxygen through the skin, and when soil becomes waterlogged they find it difficult to extract the oxygen and so surface in search of air, therefore in this particular case the animal does indeed surface in order to 'breathe'.[1]

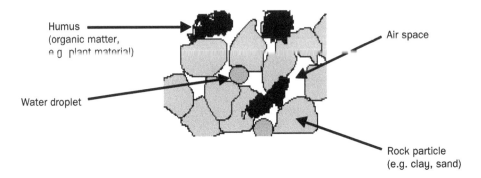

Figure 12.6 The basic structure of soil

Reconstruction

The incorrect idea that soil does not contain any air spaces lies at the root of this misconception. It can be demonstrated that soil is not a solid mass by asking pupils to spoon some soil into a small container such as an eggcup, and then to predict how much water they will be able to pour into the container before it overflows. It is surprising how much water can be added; this can be then accounted for by explaining that soil contains a myriad of air spaces that the water can squeeze into.

This activity can be extended by comparing different soils. Clayey soils placed in an eggcup will accept a smaller volume of water than sandy soils before overflowing because the clay particles are small, fit together more closely and exclude air. When soils are placed in a funnel[2] and water is poured over them, sand will hold scarcely any water, letting it run straight through; however, clay will let hardly any water pass through and instead slowly absorbs it, becoming sticky in the process. Farmers usually prefer an intermediate soil between the extremes of clay and sand for crops so that some air spaces are present, and also some water is held in the soil.

A spring or summer activity that is suitable for KS1 classes is to ask each child to study a 'circle of earth'. Cut pieces of string into 2 m lengths and ask children to make a circle with the string over an area of grass or dirt. The children then need to watch for any animal activity within their circle, for instance ants or ground beetles coming to the surface. If the ground is sprinkled with a very dilute detergent solution earthworms will be likely to appear.

Sources: Brass and Duke (1994); Frankel-Hauser (1998).

12.7 What can we do to help reduce global warming?

Misconception

I can help the problem of global warming by eating less red meat.

Scientific conception

The phenomenon of **global warming** and its causes are poorly understood by primary school children. To appreciate the underlying science we must look into how light energy from the sun affects the Earth. First, let us consider what happens with the **moon** (figure 12.7a), which unlike the Earth has no atmosphere. Light energy from the sun warms the moon's surface ❶. As the moon warms in this way it is constantly losing heat energy from the surface and nearly all of this heat escapes back into space ❷. This makes temperatures on the surface of moon very hot during the day and very cold at night (maximum 120°C; minimum –247°C), and these extremes of temperature are one of the reasons why the moon is unable to sustain life.

Figure 12.7b shows that, with the Earth, the fact that an atmosphere is present means comparatively less heat escapes into space. The atmosphere can be thought of as a 'blanket of gases' surrounding the Earth that keeps most of the heat in. As was the case with the moon, light energy warms the Earth ① and this heat is continually being lost from the surface. Most of the heat from the surface is transferred into the atmosphere ②, which becomes warm itself in the process. Some of this heat from the atmosphere escapes into space ③, although most is retained, and as a consequence the Earth's surface is kept warm ④. Therefore, the surface of the Earth is heated by two different processes, ① and ④. Life is able to exist on Earth partly due to the fact there are no extremes of daily temperature as there are on the moon. Like a blanket, the Earth's atmosphere keeps night temperatures relatively high by warming the surface. Temperatures during the day do not become excessively high because some of the sun's energy is absorbed by the upper atmosphere before it has a chance to warm the surface ⑤.

The Earth has been becoming progressively warmer over the past 100 years, and most scientists believe that this global warming is a result of human industrial pollution. Some gases in the atmosphere are very good at absorbing heat and then releasing that heat to the surface of the Earth. They are called **greenhouse gases,** the most important of which are carbon dioxide (CO_2) and water vapour. The amount of carbon dioxide in the atmosphere has increased since the late 1700s due to the consumption of **fossil fuels** such as coal, wood and petrol during industrial and other processes,

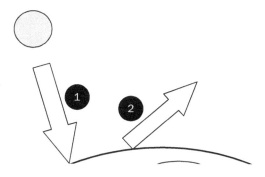

Figure 12.7a How the sun heats the moon (not to scale)

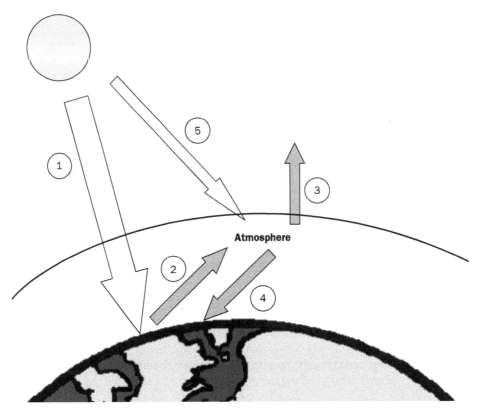

Figure 12.7b Explaining the greenhouse effect (not to scale)

which release carbon dioxide when they burn. Therefore the increasing levels of carbon dioxide means that more heat is retained by the Earth's atmosphere, which makes temperatures rise (Figure 12.7b, arrow ④). In effect, the atmosphere is becoming a more efficient 'blanket'. A minority of scientists however, believe that greenhouse gases are not the cause of global warming and that temperatures are increasing as part of the planet's natural cycle of warming and cooling.

Pupils can become confused about what might cause global warming and cite reasons such as radioactive waste, acid rain, the extinction of endangered species, not picking up litter, and, as the misconception statement above suggests, even eating red meat. Pupils are aware of a number of different contemporary environmental or health concerns that are frequently reported in the media, although sometimes they misunderstand or have forgotten the science underlying global warming and spuriously mix and match different causes and effects in this way. Scientifically acceptable methods to help the problem of global warming centre around the burning of fewer fossil fuels, thus stemming further excessive releases of carbon dioxide into the atmosphere. Some pupils mistakenly think that greenhouse gases 'trap' the sun's rays and heat the Earth like a greenhouse, which is a disadvantage of using the term *greenhouse* as a metaphor to help explain the process. The phenomenon of ozone depletion is frequently confused with global warming, and pupils may say that one is a cause of the other, although in reality there is some overlap. For instance ozone is a greenhouse gas, though depletion of the ozone layer does not directly contribute to global warming (see 12.8, next).

Reconstruction

The potential problems of global warming have been well documented and include the melting of the polar ice caps, sea level rises and climate change. Although an understanding of the greenhouse effect and its consequences is beyond the primary curriculum, upper KS2 teachers could consider discussing the ideas that underlie them as they are important for general scientific literacy. This is particularly relevant given the number of potential misconceptions about global warming. In Year 4 as part of the *Living Things* section teachers are required to explore the impact humans have had on the planet; lessons about global warming would fit in well here.

The idea that atmospheric gases can keep the heat in like a blanket can be demonstrated by asking children to compare how warm they feel when outside on cloudy and cloudless nights respectively. Clouds consist of water droplets, ice and water vapour (with the latter being a greenhouse gas), and during overcast nights clouds help keep in heat lost by the Earth's surface – therefore cloudy nights tend to be warmer and clear nights cooler. Some writers have suggested that the traditional approach of teaching environmental issues holistically as 'saving the planet' acts as a barrier to teasing apart the specific scientific ideas behind phenomena such as global warming. There are a number of animations available on internet sites such as YouTube that would help children understand the sequence of events that bring about global warming, but of course, these should be vetted by teachers beforehand for scientific accuracy.

Sources: Boyes and Stanisstreet (1993); Francis *et al.* (1993); Skamp *et al.* (2009).

12.8 What is ozone depletion?

Misconception

Holes in the ozone layer are caused by the greenhouse effect.

Scientific conception

Ozone gas (O_3) is a different form, or **allotrope**, of oxygen gas (O_2) consisting of three atoms instead of two. Together with all the other gases that make up the air we breathe, ozone is present naturally in Earth's lower atmosphere (**troposphere**) in very small concentrations. Most of the planet's ozone is, however, mainly located in the upper atmosphere (**stratosphere**) at an altitude of approximately 25 miles (40 km) above the surface as a discrete band of gas that envelops the Earth – the ozone layer.

Ozone in the atmosphere plays a vital role in sustaining life on our planet, and if it was absent all exposed life forms would quickly disappear. Most people are aware that ultra-violet (UV) **radiation** from the sun reaches the Earth's surface. This type of radiation can be beneficial as it stimulates vitamin D production in humans and is required for sun tanning, although at high intensities or with prolonged exposure harmful effects on exposed skin are possible, including premature aging and skin cancer. Ozone in the atmosphere allows some UV radiation to pass through to the surface, specifically types UV-A and UV-B, while it completely blocks type UV-C. This latter type is extremely dangerous to living things as it readily causes mutations in DNA resulting in genetic damage responsible for cancers, crop failures and other detrimental conditions.

Since the early 1970s scientists have noted that ozone levels are becoming progressively less. This is especially the case over the polar regions, where concentrations have been reduced to such an extent that large 'ozone holes' over the Arctic and Antarctic have been reported (Figure 12.8). However, the term 'hole' is a misnomer since some ozone is still present at the poles, although is very much reduced. In addition, it is important to note here that although colloquially one hears of 'holes in the ozone *layer*', ozone depletion mostly occurs in the lower troposphere close to the Earth's surface and less so in the discrete ozone layer high in the stratosphere, and so it is the presence of ozone in the atmosphere as a whole that is reduced. Clearly, depletion of ozone is concerning due to the possibility of increased transmission of deadly UV-C.

Scientists believe that synthetically manufactured chemicals are responsible for ozone depletion, particularly chlorofluorocarbons (CFCs) such as Freon, found in refrigerators and aerosol cans. These chemicals react with ozone, removing it from the atmosphere. Since the mid-1980s manufacture of CFCs has been largely phased out because of their connection to ozone depletion.

As stated in 12.7, pupils frequently confuse ozone depletion and the greenhouse effect and believe that greenhouse gases such as carbon dioxide are responsible for

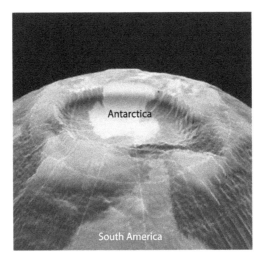

Figure 12.8 Computer-generated image of the South Pole showing ozone depletion in 2004 (NASA)

ozone depletion, or that holes in the ozone layer have caused global warming. As with global warming, pupils tend not to be familiar with the possible consequences of ozone depletion to the planet and may attribute general environmental or health effects such as more flooding, poisoned fish and more heart attacks. Some children optimistically believe that the holes in the ozone layer are plugged by greenhouse gases.

Reconstruction

As with global warming, ozone depletion is beyond the primary curriculum but is important for scientific literacy, so could also be introduced during the Year 4 *Living Things* topic, where the environmental impacts of human activity on the planet are discussed. In addition, similar pedagogies based on internet-sourced animations would help pupils' understandings and prevent confusions over different environmental phenomena. In recent years ozone depletion has been less prominent in the media compared with global warming and consequent climate change, which can only hinder pupils' familiarity and correct understanding of the process.

Sources: Boyes *et al.* (1999); Koulaides and Christidou (1999); Rye *et al.* (1997); Shepardson *et al.* (2011).

Notes

1. Although technically this is not breathing – see the Glossary definition.
2. Such as the cut-off neck of a 2-litre plastic drinks bottle.

PART FOUR

Physics

13
Forces

13.1 Does mass affect the speed of falling?

Misconception

Heavy objects fall at a greater speed than light objects.

Scientific conception

A pupil who has constructed this misconception would believe that if a man and a young child jumped at the same instant from a diving board into a swimming pool, the man would make the first splash because he is the heavier and so would have fallen more quickly. A reason commonly offered for why heavier objects fall with a greater speed is that as mass increases then gravity attracts objects with a greater force, i.e. 'gravity has got more to get hold of'.

If several objects of different mass are dropped simultaneously from the same height they will all hit the ground at exactly the same time, if **air resistance** effects can be negated. It is true that with several objects of different mass as in Figure 13.1 the heavier objects will be pulled by gravity with a greater force than the lighter ones, e.g. the 1 kg ball will experience a pulling force of 10 N and the 20 kg ball 200 N – these forces are each object's *weight*. However, the accelerations caused by these gravitational pulls will be exactly the same for each object and their speed of falling will be equal at a given height, so they will all hit the ground simultaneously. But the fact that all the spheres in Figure 13.1 **accelerate** equally seems intuitively wrong because if they all have different weights then why is the Earth not pulling the heavier ones faster?

To further understand this an additional concept needs to be introduced, that of **inertia**, which is the resistance of an object to its present state of motion. It is difficult for one person to get a stationary broken-down car in motion by pushing it, but once the car is moving the effort becomes less and the car can be kept moving by applying a smaller amount of force. Inertia prevents the person initially pushing the stationary car

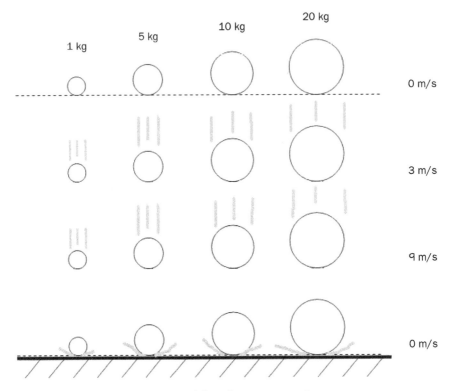

Figure 13.1 Objects of different mass fall at the same speed

with ease, and it also prevents the person stopping the car easily once it is moving – it is as if the car is purposely resisting any attempt to change its present state of motion. A similar situation applies to the falling spheres in Figure 13.1. The heavier spheres are indeed attracted to the Earth with a greater pull (weight), but because they have more mass the effort required to get them moving is also greater because of inertia, which inhibits any greater acceleration. Simply, with the heavier spheres the increased gravitational pull and increased inertia cancel each other out, with the result that each sphere is accelerated at the same rate and so falls with equal speed, regardless of mass.

Sometimes the opposite view to the original misconception is taken, with pupils predicting that lighter objects will fall faster because they encounter less air resistance. Indeed, the cross-sectional shape of the object can have a large effect on fall speed; for instance, a car falling whilst suspended from a parachute may have a mass of 1 tonne but will fall more slowly than a 100 g glass marble due to the parachute having a greater air resistance than the marble.

Reconstruction

Although in reality heavier objects will fall slightly faster than lighter objects of the same shape because of air resistance effects, the idealized scientific view can still be taught successfully because experiments can be arranged so that any differences are imperceptible to the human eye. Dropping different sized glass marbles or ball bearings simultaneously from the same height will give reliable outcomes that show them landing at the same time. Care must be taken to achieve a synchronized release as factors such as sticky fingers can be a source of error. Attempts to account for air resistance can be made by trying different experiments such as having a series of identically sized small plastic bottles or tubs, with each containing a different amount of mass.

Did you know?

A caveat. Despite the fact that we teach pupils the scientific view that all objects fall with equal speed regardless of their mass, an important caveat to the phenomena of falling objects is that within the Earth's atmosphere air resistance effects are extremely difficult to remove, which consequently makes lighter objects actually fall with a lesser speed. If the experiment depicted in Figure 13.1 were to be carried out in school there *would* be very slight differences in the falling speeds and the heavier objects would land first; whether these differences would be perceptible to observers depends largely on the height from which they are dropped. If they were released from a point several storeys high then the heavier balls would probably be seen to land first, but if dropped from 1 metre above the ground any perceived variation is unlikely, although electronic apparatus such as datalogger light gates would be able to detect significant differences. Thus the scientific view we teach is in fact idealized and bears little relation to the actual phenomena we reproduce in the classroom.

Teachers can make a video recording of two objects of different mass being dropped at the same time, which can then be played back in slow motion to show a simultaneous landing. There is a famous video available on the internet where the American astronaut David Scott drops a geological hammer and a falcon feather on the moon – where there is no atmosphere and so no air resistance – and both are seen to land at the same time. Trial and error will show that some objects are not suited for experiments designed to dispel this misconception; a golf ball and a ping pong ball have an equivalent diameter and different masses but the ping pong ball falls noticeably more slowly.

Key Stage 1 children can try marble painting. You will need a box lid with a piece of A3 paper in the bottom. Dip a marble in paint and roll the marble around the lid so that coloured tracks are produced. Add different coloured paints for more attractive patterns. Using different-sized marbles will show children how objects of differing mass move, with the larger marbles moving more slowly due to their greater inertia. To introduce KS1 children to the idea of forces read the story book *Oscar and the Cricket* by Geoff Waring. When talking to them about falling bodies specifically, *On the Way Home* by Gill Murphy is a good source.

Sources: Frankel-Hauser (1998); Gunstone and White (1981); Howe *et al.* (2012); Murphy (1982); Osborne (1984); Waring (2007).

13.2 What are the forces on projectiles?

Misconception

A ball in flight has a force that is propelling it forwards.

Scientific conception

The idea that anything moving forwards is being pushed by a constant force is extremely intuitive. It is very common for pupils to think that if someone throws a ball in their direction it only reaches them because it has been 'forced' throughout its flight (Figure 13.2a). They can feel this force if the ball is thrown hard towards them, and when they catch the ball the force runs out and is no longer acting.

In actuality there is no forward force on the ball during its flight. A force is a push or a pull, and the only time the ball is pushed is during the action of throwing. As soon as the ball leaves the thrower's hand it is no longer being pushed and during its flight it is actually decelerating due to air resistance – this is why when you are catching a ball, the further you are away from the thrower the slower the speed of the ball when it reaches you and so the 'softer' the catch.

Figure 13.2b shows the important forces that act when a ball is thrown. The thrower on the left of the diagram is applying a pushing force (**p**) to the ball during their throwing action. Also the ball's weight is pulling it downwards (**w**) and air resistance (friction, **f**) is pushing against the ball in the opposite direction to the pushing force. As soon as the ball leaves the thrower's hand it no longer is being pushed forward by anything, but continues on its path because the opposing force (**f**) is presently not large enough to stop it moving forwards; however, this air resistance force which is pushing the ball backwards makes it **decelerate**, slowing it down constantly. This reflects Newton's first law of motion, which states that an object must continue in motion (or remain at rest) unless acted upon by a force. In flight, weight still pulls the ball down which makes the ball describe an arc-shaped flight path instead of a perfectly straight line. Once the catcher on the right of the diagram has the stationary ball in their hands it is no longer moving so air resistance no longer applies, although weight is still pulling the ball downwards.

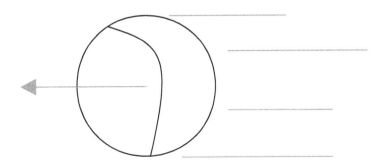

Figure 13.2a A projectile is acted on by a forward force during flight (misconception)

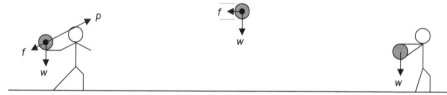

Figure 13.2b Forces acting on a thrown ball

Although the ball has no forward force in flight, our hands experience a pushing force when we catch it. This can be confusing as it represents an instance where something that has no pushing force generates a pushing force by itself. Considering Newton's first law of motion again, when we catch a moving ball we are actually applying a force with our hands to the ball in order to arrest its motion. The force that we feel is the equal and opposite **reaction force** of the ball pushing back on our hands, similar to when we push down with our hand on the edge of a table; the table feels like it is pushing back into our hand and leaves a visible impression on our skin (see 13.5).

If the ball were to be thrown in deep space, once it left the thrower's hand there would similarly be no forward force acting on the ball, and also because it is not near to the Earth or any other **heavenly body** it would not experience any weight force, nor any air resistance, which means it would be travelling forwards in space in a perfectly straight line with no forces at all acting on it. The ball would continue moving forward in this way for eternity with no reduction in speed until another force was applied to it, according to Newton's first law of motion. Other surprising examples of moving objects which have no forward force acting on them are a moving car with the engine turned off, a freewheeling bicycle, and a bullet in flight.

Famous scientists

Scientists can have misconceptions too. These misconceptions have historical precedents. Ancient Greek scientists thought that a projectile such as a thrown spear stays in flight because tiny air currents cause external forces to push and support it. In the fourteenth century AD the French thinker Jean Buridan challenged this view, insisting that a special force within the projectile was pushing it along and propelling it forwards during its flight; this force was *impetus*. Due to the influence of later scientists such as Isaac Newton, and contrary to our intuitions, we accept today that a projectile has no forward force acting upon it.

Related misconceptions include attributing animism to an object in flight, e.g. 'the ball fell down because it wanted to', and that **projectiles** are kept airborne because they are supported by forces in the air around them. Some learners think that a projectile flies because it contains a force greater than gravity, and when this force has been spent it begins to fall back down. (See also 13.4.)

Reconstruction

Since forces are invisible and we can only observe their effects it is often difficult to address any misconceptions that relate to them, a factor which contributes to their high incidence. A starting point would be to push a toy car across the floor and ask pupils to name the forces acting on the car once it has been released but is still in motion; this would elicit the misconception. Then remind pupils that a force has to be either a push or a pull and therefore, once released, no pushing force is being applied to the free-wheeling car. After the initial launching push has finished the car is constantly slowing down after release, and what they are seeing when the car appears to be moving along in a forward direction is the car actually being pushed backwards by friction.

When introducing the idea of forces to younger children get them familiar with the concepts of 'push' and 'pull'. Ask them to do a series of physical activities then ask them to decide whether they are applying a push or a pull, for instance kicking a sponge ball, lifting up a teddy, throwing a paper aeroplane, etc.

Sources: Driver *et al.* (1994); Piaget (1970); Watts (1982).

13.3 Does every force always have an opposing force?

Misconception
Forces always act in pairs that are equal and opposite.

Scientific conception

In Year 6 pupils learn in some detail about how different forces act on objects, and a common approach is to have pupils draw force arrows onto diagrams in order to show exactly where these forces are being applied, and their **magnitude**. Accepted conventions for drawing force arrows include that they must be drawn as straight lines with a ruler, touch the object where the force is being applied and show the direction of the force, with their length indicating the comparative size of the force.

Teachers typically introduce the idea that forces act in pairs alongside the concept of balanced and unbalanced forces, with pairs of forces usually acting in opposing directions for example as in a tug of war (see Figures 13.4b and 13.4c). In this context one of the two forces can be different from the other, which represents an unbalanced system. However, and although beyond the primary syllabus, teachers are generally aware that for every force there is an equal and opposite reaction, known formally as Newton's third law of motion. These two different ideas can be merged into an erroneous hybrid concept: *all forces act in pairs that are equal and opposite.* As a consequence, when pupils draw opposing force arrows onto a diagram they are routinely allocated equal magnitude (Figure 13.3a).

Leaving aside reaction forces for the moment, it is true that forces frequently act in opposing pairs on a system; however, these two opposing forces do not have to be equal in size. For instance, when a skydiver first jumps out of an aircraft, because they are falling comparatively slowly through the air, their weight force is greater than the air resistance force that acts in the opposite direction (Figure 13.3b). This is an unbalanced system so they accelerate downwards, gaining speed. The air resistance increases incrementally with the speed and eventually the two forces become equal (Figure 13.3a), the system now being balanced, and so no further acceleration occurs and the skydiver falls with constant speed (**terminal velocity**). For other situations where opposing pairs of forces can be unbalanced, see Figures 13.2b, 13.4c and 14.4c.

Reconstruction

The bald statement that forces always act in pairs is confusing to pupils as it can mean two different things: either an unbalanced situation where opposing forces can be different, or that every force has an equal and opposite reaction. It is easy to see how the misconception can arise from a merging of these two disparate concepts. Although it could be argued that presenting forces as pairs that act on a system retains a

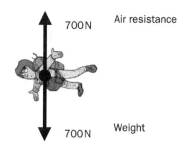

Figure 13.3a Equal and opposite forces on a skydiver

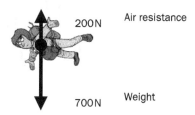

Figure 13.3b Opposing pairs of forces can be unbalanced

simplicity that is relevant to the study of mechanics at primary level, it is advised that teachers avoid making the statement that forces *always* act in pairs, and instead consider presenting examples where more than two forces apply, e.g. Figure 13.2b. The concepts surrounding Newton's third law and reaction forces are discussed later in 13.5 – however, these ideas are beyond the primary curriculum and, in the context of this present discussion about the difficulties pupils have correctly understanding the nature of opposing forces, it could be argued that the potential confusion created by their implementation at the primary phase might outweigh any advantages.

The frequent citing of instances from unbalanced systems will remind pupils that opposing forces need not always be equal in size. For example, when conducting the familiar experiment of running toy cars down a slope, ask pupils to draw a diagram of the system including force arrows on the car before and after release from the top of the slope.

Key Stage 1 children can see the effects of balanced forces by piling plastic bricks on top of each other. Run a competition to see who can make the tallest pile of bricks.

Source: Jones (1983).

13.4 A moving object has a large forward force and a small backward force acting on it

Misconception

If an object is moving, more force is being applied in the direction of movement.

Figure 13.4a Forces acting on a cyclist travelling at constant speed (misconception)

Scientific conception

Pupils in Year 6 are introduced to the concept of a system having its forces in either a balanced or unbalanced state. For example, in a tug of war each person pulls the rope the opposite way. If both people pull with the same force then no resultant movement occurs and the forces are balanced (Figure 13.4b); if one person pulls with more force than the other then there is movement in their direction because the forces are unbalanced (Figure 13.4c).

The simple tug-of-war system is a good way to illustrate the basic idea of forces being either balanced or unbalanced. However, pupils can generalize this to fresh

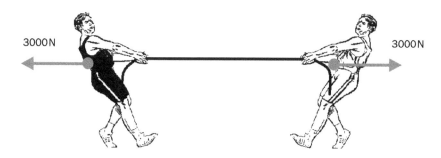

Figure 13.4b Balanced forces in a tug of war

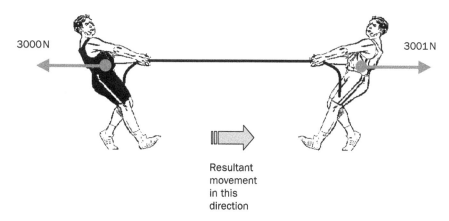

Resultant
movement
in this
direction

Figure 13.4c Unbalanced forces in a tug of war

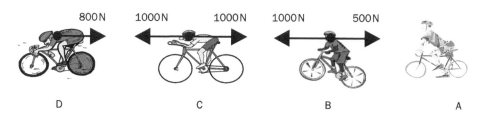

Figure 13.4d Balanced and unbalanced forces during motion

situations by making the assumption that if an object is moving then forces always need to be unbalanced, which is incorrect (Figure 13.4a). Using the context of cyclists experiencing different kinds of motion, Figure 13.4d shows how forces can be balanced or unbalanced depending on the relative magnitudes of forward and backward forces. Note that for clarity other forces such as weight and reaction forces have been ignored for these examples.

Cyclist A is not pedalling. There are no forward or backward forces acting. Forces are balanced (at zero) so no motion occurs.

Cyclist B has just started pedalling with a force of 1000 N and experiences air resistance/friction at 500 N. Forces are unbalanced so he accelerates and moves forwards.

Cyclist C pedals with a force of 1000 N and, because she is travelling at a greater speed than cyclist B, experiences a greater air resistance/friction of 1000 N. Forces are balanced so no further acceleration is possible and she travels at constant speed. She can try to accelerate again by pedalling with more force or reducing air resistance by adopting more of a racing tuck, so creating a new unbalanced system.

Cyclist D stops pedalling and applies the brakes. He is still moving forwards and experiences air resistance/friction of 800 N (including brake friction) with no forward force to compensate, so forces are unbalanced. He decelerates and eventually comes to a stop.

To summarize, referring to cyclist C, it can be seen that a state of balanced forces can indeed be associated with a moving body, which in this case is travelling at constant speed. Also, if forces are unbalanced then this always results in either acceleration or deceleration, in accordance with Newton's first law of motion (13.2). Note that the braking cyclist D is still moving forwards although no forward force is acting, a situation that is intuitively impossible; 13.2 explains this apparent anomaly.

A related misconception is that at a steady speed there are no forces acting on a body, when in fact forces do apply but cancel each other out so the body is at a state of equilibrium.

Reconstruction

This misconception represents a variant of 13.2 and so the corrective pedagogies described in that section are applicable.

Source: Driver (1983).

13.5 Reaction forces

Misconception

An object at rest has no forces acting upon it.

Scientific conception

In Year 3, pupils begin to associate pushes and pulls with moving objects and learn to call these actions *forces*. The forces acting within moving systems are easier for pupils to imagine because there are perceptible outcomes, e.g. an object moves faster, more slowly, or changes its shape. With static systems such as the book and table

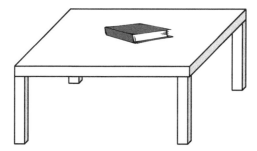

Figure 13.5a A stationary object on a table has no forces acting upon it (misconception)

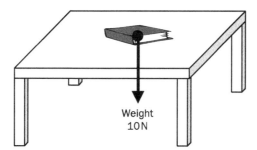

Figure 13.5b Weight pulls the book towards the centre of the Earth

in Figure 13.5a, nothing obvious appears to be happening and so it may be natural to assume that there are no forces present; in fact, there are a number of forces in play.

Weight[1] is a widely known force that with a little prompting many pupils would be able to name and correctly draw (Figure 13.5b). However, some may correctly understand that Figure 13.5a shows a balanced system, and so add another arrow that shows an equal and opposite reaction force (Figure 13.5c). They explain that the table is pushing up on the book in reaction to the book's weight, which balances everything out so there is no up/down movement.

This is a common misconception, the real situation being more complex. As the Earth pulls the book down (weight), the book also pulls the Earth up with an equal and opposite force – this is the true reaction force (Figure 13.5d). Although this reaction pull is real, the Earth is not lifted upwards by any noticeable or measurable amount because of its tremendous mass – it has so much inertia that it is just too heavy to be moved by a mere 10 N force (see 13.1). Besides, in the example given the table acts as a barrier between book and Earth inhibiting any further attractive movement between these two objects. Reaction forces were described by Isaac Newton in his third law of motion, explained simply as *to every action there is an equal and opposite reaction.*

In addition to these two forces there is another interaction to consider, taking place between the table and the book. The book is pressing down on the table and one

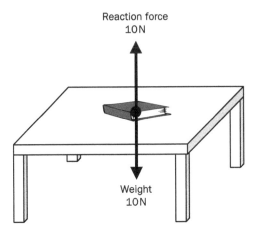

Figure 13.5c The reaction force misconception

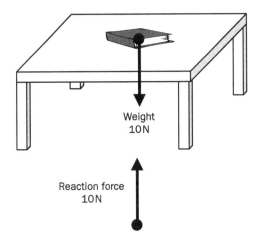

Figure 13.5d The book pulls the Earth upwards with an equal and opposite reaction force

can feel this force if one's fingers are slipped between book and table; this is the **contact force** (Figure 13.5e). As with the weight force previously discussed, the contact force generates its own reaction force as the table pushes back up on the book.

Note that weight acts from the centre of mass of the book (Figure 13.5d) and the contact force acts at the point of contact between book and table (Figure 13.5e). Also note that the contact force and the book's weight are equal, but this is not always the case, as when multiple contact forces are in play (e.g. Figure 13.5i). Figure 13.5f gives all forces that act on the system, and because all the upward forces are balanced out by all the downward forces, no net movement takes place so the book, table and the Earth all remain stationary.

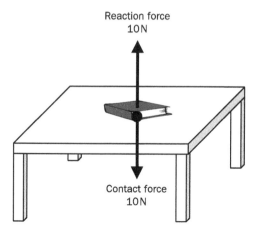

Figure 13.5e Contact force and reaction force

To further clarify, Figure 13.5g shows the forces acting on a person who has jumped into the air. Since he is clear of the ground there are no contact forces. The Earth is pulling him down and at the same time he is pulling the Earth up with an equal and opposite force.

If the person lands on the ground and then stands on one leg, all of his weight is transmitted through one foot and so his contact force with the ground will equal his

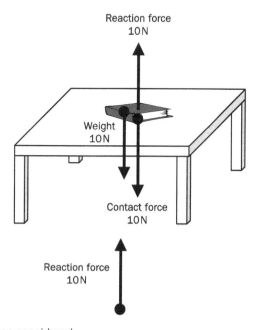

Figure 13.5f All forces considered

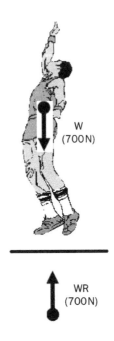

Figure 13.5g Forces acting when a person has no contact with the ground
W = Weight
WR = Reaction force of weight

weight (Figure 13.5h). The reaction forces remain equal and opposite to his weight and contact force.

If the person then stands on both legs and is perfectly balanced, since he has 'spread his weight', the contact force through each foot will equal half of his weight (Figure 13.5i).[2] The sum of both contact forces equals his weight.

Reconstruction

In Year 6, static situations as depicted in Figure 13.5a are introduced to the class in the context of balanced forces, and pupils are then required to name the particular forces acting on the system. This provides a good opportunity for misconception elicitation. Reaction forces are beyond the primary curriculum but opportunities to introduce them to the class might arise if Newton's third law ever crops up during discussions, as brighter upper KS2 pupils could be aware of the mantra *for every action there is an equal and opposite reaction*, and this idea has been known to cause confusion (13.4). How far the teacher wishes to go in explaining reaction forces is dependent upon the ability of the class. Introducing the additional idea of contact forces might merely act as a source of further confusion, testing the capabilities of even the brightest.

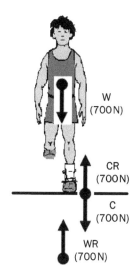

Figure 13.5h Forces acting when a person is standing on one leg

W = Weight
WR = Reaction force of weight
C = Contact force
CR = Reaction force of contact force

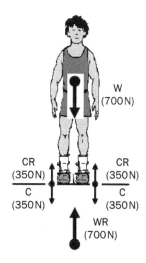

Figure 13.5i Forces acting when a person is standing on both legs

W = Weight
WR = Reaction force of weight
C = Contact force
CR = Reaction force of contact force

Ideally pupils need to have grasped the ideas behind balanced/unbalanced forces before reaction forces are introduced. As discussed elsewhere (13.4) reaction forces can be felt by pressing on the edge of a table with your hand – the table pushes you back with an equal and opposite force; in fact, it may leave a slight indentation on the skin. Inspecting the face of a well-used hammer will show dents where the nails have 'hit back' at the hammer due to the reaction force associated with each hammer blow.

The example of a tug of war where each side is pulling with exactly the same force helps learners to understand the idea that a stationary system can have forces constantly acting within it (13.4). Also, the familiar experiment where friction is studied by pulling masses across a horizontal surface covered with different materials such as sandpaper or glass can be used as a medium for teaching about the forces involved with stationary systems. With a rough material such as sandpaper as the surface, pull the masses horizontally using a Newton meter until they just begin to move, then back the force off slightly so you are still pulling but the masses are now stationary. Record this force as indicated on the Newton meter scale. Hold this position, and then ask the class *are there any forces acting on the masses?* Substitute the sandpaper for a smooth material such as glass, so that the masses now slide easily when a lesser pull from the Newton meter is applied. This should help learners appreciate that the constant friction force of the sandpaper was holding the stationary masses in place, opposing the constant pulling force as measured by the Newton meter.

Sources: Gunstone and White (1981); Jones (1983); Montanero *et al.* (2002); Viennot and Rozier (1994).

13.6 Is there gravity in space?

Misconception

There is no gravity on the moon.

[On Earth] you throw the can up it will come back down because you've got gravity in the air pushing down on top of the can. (Pupil, Year 6; Russell *et al.*, 1998)

Scientific conception

Usually prompted by images of weightless astronauts in science fiction films, pupils sometimes infer that there is zero gravity on the moon, planets, and in space generally. They can rationalize this by assuming that gravity only exists on Earth because of the presence of an atmosphere, and once a spacecraft crosses beyond the limit of the atmosphere, gravity disappears. Further reasoning can lead to pupils believing that the source of gravity is air pressing down on objects within the atmosphere. All of these ideas are at odds with conventional science.

To understand the basic nature of gravity requires an appreciation of the concept of *mass*. Every material object in the universe, including liquids and gases, is made from atoms, molecules or ions, called *particles* in primary science. Two identically sized small solid cubes made of aluminium and iron are placed on scales and their masses are found to be different (Figure 13.6a). The small iron cube has more mass for two reasons: first, an iron particle is heavier than an aluminium particle; and second, there are more iron particles present than aluminium particles.[3] The larger iron cube has a greater mass than the smaller iron cube because the former contains more particles. Therefore the mass of an object is a measure of how heavy each constituting particle is and also how many particles are present – considered simply, how much 'stuff' there is. Mass cannot be changed unless the object itself is changed, e.g. chipping a piece off an iron cube will reduce the mass of the cube because there will be fewer particles there.

If the two small aluminium and iron cubes were taken into deep space, held about a metre apart and then released, they would start to move slowly towards each other until they were touching. This is gravitational attraction, and is experienced by every object in the universe; note that it is nothing to do with magnetism. Pupils are surprised to learn that everything in the universe is attracted to everything else to a greater or lesser degree. The bigger the mass, the more intense the attraction, so on Earth if the two small metal cubes are placed on the floor, despite the same gravitational attraction still being present between them, they do not move towards each other because there is a far larger object that is attracting them instead – the Earth. Also, the further the distance between masses, the less the attraction, which is why in deep space the gravity from heavenly bodies is negligible. Gravity behaves according to a mathematical relationship known as an *inverse square law*, meaning that if the distance that separates two objects is halved, then the gravitational strength is quadrupled. Another aspect of this relationship is that as distance is increased, gravity drops off very fast, so over long distances its effects are extremely weak.

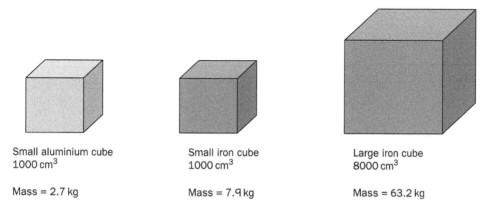

Small aluminium cube
1000 cm^3

Small iron cube
1000 cm^3

Large iron cube
8000 cm^3

Mass = 2.7 kg

Mass = 7.9 kg

Mass = 63.2 kg

Figure 13.6a Masses of iron and aluminium cubes. When the two smaller cubes are compared with each other, the aluminium cube has less mass because aluminium particles are lighter than iron particles, and are also fewer in number because they are less closely packed inside the cube

Objects in space such as the planets, moon and sun attract each other constantly with significant amounts of force. These heavenly bodies are huge so gravitational attraction is immense, especially from the sun, although the planets do not hurtle into the sun and burn up because they are skirting around the sun at high speed in **orbit**. A useful analogy is the motion of a roulette ball circling the wheel while bets are placed – it continues to circle smoothly and freely because it has enough speed to overcome being pulled towards the centre. After a while, because of friction the ball loses speed and falls into the wheel, eventually landing in a number pocket. Because space is a near-vacuum there is very little friction that is able to affect the planets, which like the roulette ball maintain enough orbital speed to avoid similarly being pulled into the sun.

Earth's gravitational attraction exerts a significant pull on all objects close to its surface; this force is their weight. As stated, this weight force is greater with objects that have a greater mass, and also when objects are closer to the Earth's centre (13.7), and the approximate weights of our two small metal cubes on Earth are given in Figure 13.6b. Weight is measured in newtons (N) and can be roughly calculated by multiplying the mass of an object by 10.

If the cubes were to be transported to the moon their weights would become less (Figure 13.6b). This is because the mass of the moon is only 17 per cent of that of the Earth and so will attract the cubes with only 17 per cent of the gravity force experienced on Earth. Note that the *mass* of the cubes does not change on the moon because the cubes have not changed and are still made of the same 'stuff'. Because the cubes weigh less on the moon, astronauts could throw them much further across the

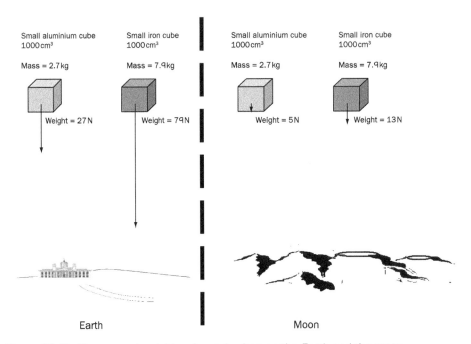

Figure 13.6b Masses and weights of metal cubes on the Earth and the moon

lunar surface than they could on Earth. Conversely, at the gaseous surface of the giant planet Jupiter, gravity is 2.5 times that of Earth so if a person weighs 700 N (70 kg) on Earth, they would weigh 1750 N on Jupiter (equivalent to 175 kg on Earth).

To summarize, gravitational attraction exists between all objects because they have mass. Particularly large objects such as planets, moons and stars exert huge gravitational forces and so all objects close to their surfaces will experience a significant and noticeable gravitational pull. Only in deep space far away from these heavenly bodies will gravity be negligible. Since the weight of an object is the force it experiences due to gravity, weight can change depending on where the object is; on the other hand, its mass can never change without changing the object itself in some way.

Related misconceptions include the idea that gravity occurs due to the Earth's magnetic field exerting a force. Alternatively, some learners think that the fact the Earth is spinning causes gravity to occur, and with **KS4** secondary physics students when the idea of **centripetal force** is introduced this misconception may be reinforced.

Reconstruction

Video clips that are freely available on internet sites such as YouTube show American Apollo astronauts walking on the moon and experiencing gravitational forces, although these forces are clearly less when compared to Earth's. The idea that the presence of air is required in order for gravity to work can be difficult to correct. A video clip of the same astronauts inside their spacecraft journeying to and from the moon will serve to show that even though air is present inside the craft, the astronauts can still experience weightlessness.

Pupils can become confused if they see videos of astronauts who are weightless orbiting the Earth within space shuttles or space stations. This can reinforce the misconception that gravity disappears just beyond the atmosphere. In fact gravity is still powerful at the altitudes navigated by these craft but the act of orbiting will create the sensation of weightlessness in spite of one's body still experiencing a significant weight force (see 13.7 and 14.4).

Sources: Bar *et al.* (1997); Driver (1983); Russell *et al.* (1998); Stead and Osborne (1980); Vicentini-Missoni (1981).

13.7 Can gravity change?

> **Misconception**
> *Gravity becomes stronger the further you are from the ground.*

Scientific conception

Pupils understand that if an object falls from 20 metres above ground level it will land with more force than if dropped from a height of 1 metre. This can lead to the belief that at the 20 metre point the force of gravity must be greater in order to cause the extra landing force. The idea is encapsulated in the well-known adage that a dime dropped from the top of the Empire State Building in New York City would land with so much force as to have the potential to kill a passer-by on the pavement below. Other manifestations of the misconception include that if a car was pushed up a gradient it would be more difficult to push nearer the top of the hill than nearer the bottom because gravity increases with height.

These beliefs are contrary to how gravity actually behaves. Gravity causes an attractive force to be exerted on objects towards the centre of the Earth; scientifically this is known as the object's weight. As an object's distance from the centre of the Earth increases then the gravity becomes less, making it weigh less. For instance, if a woman who weighs 800 N at sea level boards an airliner which then climbs to 30 000 feet, she would weigh 1 N less (equivalent to 100 g). If the same woman were then to be launched into deep space her weight would be approximately 0 N because she would be distant from the centre of the Earth, as well as from other heavenly bodies, and so she would be weightless and able to float freely. Therefore an object has to be raised to great heights above the Earth's centre before there is any noticeable change in gravity, and in everyday contexts close to the Earth's surface the weight of an object remains constant regardless of height.

The reason why an object dropped from a tall building lands with such force is not because there has been an increase in gravity. Throughout an object's fall it is constantly being pulled by an unchanging force (its weight), which makes its speed become continually faster while it falls, or accelerate. This acceleration is approximately 10 metres per second for every second it is falling; i.e. 1 second after release its speed is 10 m/s, after 2 seconds the speed is 20 m/s, and so on. So the higher that an object is dropped from, the more time is spent falling so the greater its final speed when it lands (but see 13.3).

A variant of the misconception is the belief that gravity increases the further away you are from the Earth's surface until you leave the atmosphere when gravity immediately becomes zero. This implies that gravity has something to do with air pressure (see 13.6). Incidentally, it is very common, though incorrect, to think that astronauts in Earth's orbit are weightless because there is no gravity – in fact gravity is strong at altitudes where spacecraft orbit the Earth, and so the astronauts' weights would actually approximate their weights on the Earth's surface. Apparent weightlessness is experienced because being in orbit means that the astronauts are constantly falling; it is similar to being in a runaway lift that has had its cables cut. The lift's occupants would be able to float around freely and experience apparent weightlessness because both lift and occupants are in a state of freefall. The situation of a spacecraft in orbit is different than the aforementioned weightlessness encountered in deep space where gravity would be truly absent or negligible due to the immense distance from the Earth and other bodies. In all of these instances of apparent weightlessness, all objects will still have a significant weight force acting upon them.

Secondary pupils can confuse an object's weight with its potential energy, which does increase with height. Some learners think that gravity becomes zero at the Earth's surface because an object is no longer falling, again an idea that is analogous to potential energy (related to 13.5). Others argue conversely that gravity is exclusively present only at the surface of the Earth and objects not in contact with the surface are free of its influence, which is why birds are able to fly, although in aeroplanes gravity is trapped inside.

Reconstruction

The misconception can be elicited by asking the class *at which point on a slope would gravity be at its most powerful?* A simple way to refute the error is to have pupils time a toy car running down a slope with a fixed angle first at table-top level and then at floor level. Use the reasoning that if gravity were more at greater heights then the car would run faster down the slope when it was at the table top, and slower when at floor level. This could be extended by repeating the experiment on different floors of a multi-level building. Reinforcement could involve suspending an object by a Newton meter at different heights above the ground to show there is no change in the measured weight of the object, so gravity must be constant. Of course, if the difference in heights were large enough then it *would* be possible to measure weight differences due to weaker gravity, e.g. by using an accurate pair of bathroom scales to weigh a person at sea level then in an airliner at cruising altitude.

Sources: Driver (1983); Ruggerio *et al.* (1985); Watts (1982).

Notes

1. Pupils sometimes call this gravity, which is acceptable.
2. Note that each contact/contact reaction force should be touching the foot, but for clarity they have been drawn slightly to the side.
3. A men's rugby union team of 15 players plays a game against a boys' rugby league team of 13 players. This might be thought of as an uneven match – the combined mass of the men's team is greater than that of the boys' team because the men are heavier and there are more of them.

14

Floating and sinking

14.1 Why do some objects float and others sink?

> **Misconception**
>
> *All light objects float; all heavy objects sink.*

Scientific conception

When predicting whether a material will float or sink, pupils will often use the perceived weight of the material as the main or only criterion. But it is impossible to decide categorically if a material is 'heavy' or 'light' when there is no further point of reference. That is to say, one cannot baldly claim that gold is heavier than feathers because the amount of each is a vital factor – a barrel of feathers would be heavier than a single gold ring. To make fair comparisons of heavier/lighter we also need to consider how much of a material is there; in science this is done by assessing the amount of space each object takes up, i.e. its volume. The scientific concept of density gets around the problem by taking into account how much an object weighs (its mass to be precise) as well as its volume (Figure 14.1a). For example, a 1 cm³ cube of steel has a mass of 8 g, so its density would equal 8 ÷ 1 = 8,[1] while a 1 cm³ cube of expanded polystyrene has a mass of 0.1 g, so its density would equal 0.1.

A simple yet correct way to think about the question of whether something will float or not is to consider how its density compares with that of water. Pure water has a density of approximately 1 at room temperature, and materials with densities greater than 1 (such as steel) will sink in water; those with densities less than or equal to 1 (such as expanded polystyrene) will float (Figure 14.1b). In 14.3 the idea that

$$\text{density (g/cm}^3) = \frac{\text{mass (g)}}{\text{volume (cm}^3)}$$

Figure 14.1a The equation for determining the density of an object

objects of different densities float or sink is taken further and applied to different contexts.

If the steel cube from Figure 14.1b were hammered very flat then shaped into a sealed, hollow sphere it could be made to float on the surface of the water (Figure 14.1c). This is because although its mass is still 8 g, its volume has been greatly increased and so its density has been reduced to a point that is below the density of water (1). This is the reason why ships that weigh thousands of tonnes are able to float – they have lots of empty space inside so their overall densities are less than 1. An alternative and more sophisticated way of looking at why objects float is considered in 14.4, embracing the concept of **displacement**.

Pupils can attribute other qualities of an object aside from weight when deciding whether or not it will be able to float. Objects that are flat or wide are thought more likely to float, as are smaller items – a good way to elicit this latter misconception is to show a short and long length of candle and ask the class which they expect to float and which they expect to sink. Some pupils believe that hard or sharp objects are more likely to sink.

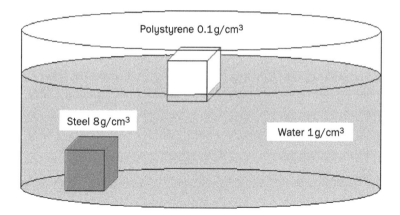

Figure 14.1b Comparative densities and floating

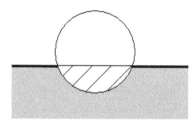

Figure 14.1c Floating sealed steel hollow sphere (shaded area shows displacement)

To summarize, whether an object floats or sinks in water depends on its density. A solid object with no air spaces inside such as a 1 cm^3 cube can only float if the density of its material is less than or equal to that of water (1). However, a material whose density is greater than water's (e.g. steel) can be made to float if it can be shaped in a way that increases its volume so that its density becomes less than 1.

Reconstruction

The misconception can be addressed by having pupils experiment with a collection of 'heavy' things, some of which sink (e.g. 100 g mass), and some of which float (e.g. filled Thermos flask), as well as 'light' objects that sink (e.g. small iron nail) and float (e.g. inflated balloon). In addition, ask pupils to make a single piece of plasticine first sink and then float by remoulding its shape. The concept of comparative densities, although beyond the primary curriculum, should be within the grasp of brighter upper KS2 pupils.

Younger children can explore whether a variety of objects float or sink as part of a messy play session. Collect together about 10 objects and ask children to predict which will float and which will sink, then ask them to test their predictions by trying the objects in washing-up bowls partly filled with water.

Sources: Biddulph and Osborne (1984); Carr *et al.* (1994); Hewson (1986).

14.2 Can something be floating and sinking at the same time?

Misconception

*An iceberg is **floating** and sinking at the same time.*

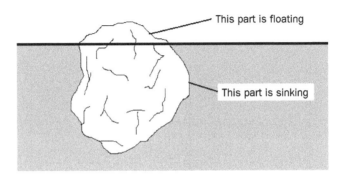

Figure 14.2a The submerged part of a floating iceberg is sinking (misconception)

Scientific conception

As discussed in other parts of this book, some words have different conversational and scientific meanings which learners tend to find confusing. In an everyday context it would be acceptable to say that the submerged part of a floating object such as an iceberg has sunk because it has 'gone underwater'. However, during primary science lessons teachers need to make a clear dichotomous distinction when deciding whether an object is either floating or sinking – it can never do both at the same time. In the case of the iceberg it is floating, because it is suspended in a **fluid**.

Suppose, for instance, that the iceberg was quite small and a large, heavy heli-copter lands on top. The extra weight causes the iceberg to become totally submerged and continue to move downwards because it can no longer be supported by the water it floats in, until it rests on the sea bed (see 14.4). During its descent through the water the iceberg is no longer technically floating because its downward motion indicates that it is no longer being suspended in a fluid, and instead is sinking.

Consider a submarine that is submerged 50 metres below the surface of the sea and maintaining a constant depth, neither rising nor descending in the water. Is it floating? The answer is yes, because even though it is below the surface it is still suspended in a fluid. Learners who think that the submarine is not floating would be using the everyday definition of floating that limits the distinction to objects that are on the surface of a liquid. If the same submarine starts to rise towards the surface it can still be regarded as floating; if it begins to dive towards the sea bed it is sinking, and no longer floating; when it comes to rest on the sea bed it is no longer sinking because it is being supported by a solid surface (Figure 14.2b).

In terms of densities, a sinking object can be defined as something that is denser than water, and a floating object is less dense or has equal density. Beyond scientific

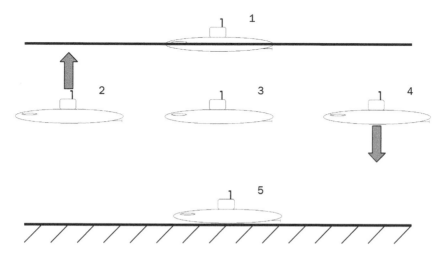

Figure 14.2b Floating or sinking? Arrows show direction of movement; see Figure 14.2c for further description

Submarine	Circumstance	Floating	Sinking
1	Stationary on the surface of the sea	Y	N
2	Ascending	Y	N
3	Stationary at constant depth	Y	N
4	Diving	N	Y
5	Stationary on the bottom of the sea	N	N

Figure 14.2c Floating or sinking table

definitions of floating and sinking, 14.1 and 14.3 discuss the reasons why certain objects float and others sink.

Since air is a fluid, all of the above instances also apply to contexts such as a rising hot air balloon (floating) and a skydiver (sinking). Similarly, confusion can arise when everyday meanings clash with scientific ideas. For instance, it would be acceptable for a pupil to write in a story during a literacy lesson that a leaf falls from a tree and floats down to the ground, but scientifically the leaf is sinking, and not floating.

Related misconceptions include that a person in the sea wearing an inflated life jacket is sinking but the life jacket itself is floating, and if people on the water's surface are swimming they are floating but if they are panicking they are sinking. With submerged objects learners may think that something that is keeping a constant depth just below the surface of the water is floating, but if an object is holding its depth near to the sea bed it is sinking.

Did you know?

Icebergs. The iceberg in Figure 14.2a is approximately 90% submerged because ice has a density of just over 0.9 g/cm^3. This is a perennial problem for shipping as it is difficult to know how close one can sail to an iceberg since its large submerged portion tends to be invisible from the surface. The RMS *Titanic* infamously sank after colliding with an iceberg below her waterline.

Reconstruction

It is important that pupils consider what the whole object is doing when making judgements about whether it is floating or sinking. In Figure 14.2a considering the entire iceberg instead of the parts above and below the water's surface simplifies any decision, as it is clearly not sinking. Also, encourage pupils to think about the vertical motion of an object, i.e. whether it is moving upwards (floating), downwards (sinking) or keeping a steady depth/height (floating). Using sets of closed questions to challenge the thinking of pupils could help them to incrementally construct meanings that are more scientific. Teachers might apply a series of questions to a misconceiving pupil thus:

T. *Is an iceberg sinking or floating?*
P. The top bit floats and the bottom bit sinks.

T. *If a coin is dropped into the water will it be sinking or floating?*
P. It will be sinking because it will be moving down.

T. *Is a ship that is taking in water and slowly disappearing under the surface floating or sinking?*
P. Although a bit is showing above the surface it's moving down which means it is sinking.

T. *How about an iceberg then?*
P. Well, it isn't moving down so it has to be floating.

Teachers can reinforce the scientific meanings of floating and sinking during traditional practical activities such as investigating if differently weighted objects float or sink in tap water and salt water. If pupils are allowed to make and use physical props such as a **Cartesian diver** this should help them understand more clearly the phenomena of floating and sinking. Note that a model iceberg can be made by freezing a carton of milk.

Sources: Biddulph and Osborne (1984); Carr *et al.* (1994); Joung (2009).

14.3 More about floating

Misconception

Wood is denser than water.

Scientific conception

The concept of density that pupils construct may differ from that embodied within the scientific definition. As discussed in 14.1, the density of an object is its mass divided by its volume. Imagine a variety of materials were available to you as equally sized solid cubes exactly 1 cm^3 in volume. Some of these cubes such as gold (density 19.3), tungsten (19.3) and lead (11.3) would feel heavier than the rest because they are high-density materials. The cubes of low-density materials would feel comparatively lighter, for example soap (0.8), rubber (0.4) and expanded polystyrene (0.03). Medium-density materials include glass (2.6), concrete (2.4), aluminium (2.7) and titanium (4.5).

Pupils may correctly relate density to being how heavy something is for its size, but if asked to imagine whether a piece of wood is denser than a sample of water they commonly cite the wood as being the more dense. The reasoning behind this decision might include the fact that wood is solid and hard while water is less substantial and soft. Experience with lifting a heavy wooden piece of furniture would strengthen this association. However, if the density values are examined, water (1.0) is significantly denser than common woods such as pine (0.4) and elm (0.6). Even comparatively heavy woods like teak (0.7) and mahogany (0.8) are less dense than water, and very light woods such as balsa (0.1) have a low density.

A simple way to discover whether a material is more or less dense than water is to see if it floats. If immiscible liquids of different densities are mixed together in one container they will separate out into different layers with the denser liquids on the bottom and the less dense on top (Figure 14.3a).[2] Similarly, all of the aforementioned woods will float on water, showing that water must be the denser material because it has formed a 'layer' underneath the wood, pushing the wood upwards. That said, a minority of woods are denser than water and will sink, such as ebony (1.1) and lead-wood (1.4). Also, if some porous woods are given time to become saturated with water they can eventually sink; bogwood found in peat layers is very waterlogged and so is ideal for aquaria because it sinks to the bottom of a tank without the need to be weighted down.

Reconstruction

Pupils can carry out an activity where they predict what would happen if a variety of woods were to be placed in water and then test their predictions practically. During discussion of conclusions explain how the woods that float must have a lower or equal density to water, and any that sink have a higher density. Samples of

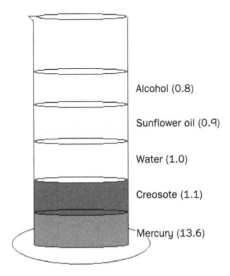

Figure 14.3a Liquids of different densities form layers (if immiscible with adjacent layers)[2]

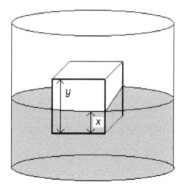

Figure 14.3b Density and floating ability

ebony can be secured from commercial collections of different cuboid materials that are commonly found in primary schools, or in a cupboard containing apparatus used in static **electricity** experiments, since it has been traditionally used as an insulator that is capable of holding a charge. Old black piano keys would be another source.

This activity can be extended by asking pupils to measure with each sample the proportion of floating wood that lies below the waterline (x) and the overall height of the wood (y). After dividing x by y the samples can then be placed in rank order of 'floating ability' and compared to the actual density values, since the less dense woods will be more buoyant and have a greater proportion of their bulk above the water line and vice versa (Figure 14.3b).

A more pupil-friendly version of the cylinder depicted in Figure 14.3a can be made by using safer liquids such as cooking oil, treacle, syrup and water.

To help dispel the misconception that water is a low-density material ask upper KS2 pupils to attempt to lift a substantial amount, for instance a filled 15-litre water cooler bottle. Of course, local health and safety regulations concerned with the lifting of heavy objects must be considered in carrying out this activity.

Source: Galili and Bar (1997).

14.4 Can an object lose its weight?

Misconception

An object floating in water is weightless.

Scientific conception

Experiences such as swimming can lead pupils to believe that a floating body possesses zero or negligible weight in water. If asked to name the forces acting on a stationary floating ship they might deny that any force is present at all. As explained in 13.6, every object is constantly being pulled towards the Earth by a pulling force called weight (or gravity), so even a swimming or floating body will have a weight force acting on it. The apparent sensation of weightlessness felt during swimming is due to water supporting a swimmer's body to a certain degree; in fact water will push upwards onto any partly or wholly immersed object with a force called **upthrust** (sometimes called buoyancy). With a stationary floating object, because there is no resultant up or down motion, the forces are balanced, so weight must be equal to upthrust (Figure 14.4a).[3]

The misconception can manifest itself during experiments that use Newton meters to investigate the forces at play when objects are immersed in water. When a 3 N metal object is weighed in air there are two forces acting (reaction forces excluded): the weight of the object pulls downwards and the tension of the spring pulls upwards an equal amount (Figure 14.4b). The scale on the Newton meter indicates the tension and reads 3 N.

When the same metal object is immersed wholly in water there is an apparent loss in weight as the Newton meter now reads only 2 N, and the whole apparatus actually feels less heavy; pupils may conclude that the water has made the object become lighter (Figure 14.4c). However, because the object has not changed in any way it is still attracted towards the Earth by the same amount of force, so its weight remains the same at 3 N. Water supports the object by providing an upthrust of 1 N; thus there are two forces acting upwards and one downwards that cancel each other out (2 N + 1 N = 3 N), resulting in no movement and a balanced system.

So the reason why an object feels lighter when partly or wholly submerged is that the water's upthrust pushes up against its weight. It is easier to pick up a heavy stone from the sea bed than from the beach – a submerged stone does not weigh any less than it would on the beach because it is the same object whether in or out of the water – the only way to make it weigh less would be to break it into smaller pieces. Note that in the case given in Figure 14.4c weight is greater than upthrust and this is why the metal object would sink if released from the Newton meter (i.e. the upward

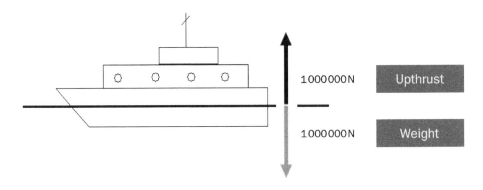

Figure 14.4a The forces acting on a stationary floating object are balanced

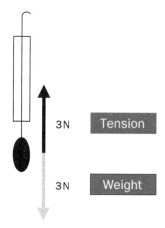

Figure 14.4b Forces acting on a metal object weighed in air using a Newton meter

tension force of the spring is removed). If the upthrust were equal to the weight as in Figure 14.4a then the object would be able to float on the surface due to balanced forces.

In 14.1 it was stated that an object floats or sinks depending on whether its density is greater or lesser than the density of water. A more sophisticated way of looking at the same phenomenon is by thinking about upthrust within the context of something called displacement. As a floating steel sphere settles into water it pushes aside a volume of water equal to the shaded area in Figure 14.1c. This displacement can be easily measured by lowering the sphere into a dish that is filled to the very brim with water, having arranged for any overflow to be caught by a washing up bowl/bucket and then weighed. If this displaced volume of water weighs (say) 80 N then we could predict with absolute accuracy that the metal sphere on its own would also weigh 80 N. That such an exact prediction can be made is due to the work of the Greek scientist Archimedes, who discovered in the third century BC that any floating object displaces exactly its own weight in water, hence the 80 N steel sphere would displace 80 N of water. Furthermore, the upthrust provided by the water is exactly equal to the weight of displaced water, i.e. 80 N, and considering the points made earlier in this

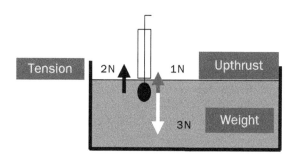

Figure 14.4c Forces acting on an immersed object

section this is why a balanced system exists with floating objects. If the hollow sphere were made of lead then it would sink lower into the water. If the lead sphere became completely submerged and began to sink this would be because, for instance, the displacement of water is 200 N and the metal itself weighs 300 N. To summarize, if the displaced water weighs *less* than the weight of an object then the water cannot support it and it will sink; if the displaced water weighs *the same* as the object, then it floats.

There are other misconceptions that involve erroneous ideas related to upthrust. Some pupils may believe that a ship floats due to being supported by constant upward water currents, or by the force of its oars/engine. Others think that the depth of water beneath a floating object is a deciding factor as to whether an object floats or sinks, e.g. something that floats in shallow water will sink in deeper water. Some learners confuse the concept with water pressure and think that the upthrust force will increase the deeper an object sinks. Other misconceptions include the idea that the upthrust increases as either the area of the base of an object increases, or its weight increases.

Famous scientists

Archimedes and the King's golden crown. The King of Syracuse asked Archimedes to ascertain whether or not the royal crown was indeed pure gold. Gold has an unusually high density, so a simple way was to first weigh the crown, then melt it, and finally reshape it into a cube so its volume could be calculated, and hence its density. Of course the King forbade this, though after prolonged thought an alternative solution eventually came to Archimedes while taking a bath. He realized that the submerged crown would displace its exact volume when placed in water, famously crying 'Eureka!' (I've found it). To this day, in science we still call the special vessel used to measure an object's displaced volume a 'Eureka can'.

Reconstruction

If pupils have been taught and understand the idea of balanced forces, a useful way to elicit the misconception is to ask the class which forces they think act on a stationary floating ship – they may reply instinctively that either no forces or just weight are present. Remind them that since the ship is stationary there have to be balanced forces acting, i.e. something pushing up with a force equal to the weight, otherwise the ship would sink, and that this force is called upthrust. It would also be good practice to mention that the upthrust is *not* a reaction force to the ship's weight (13.5).

Although using Newton meters to quantitatively demonstrate the presence of upthrust is useful, such an activity lies outside the primary curriculum. That said, pupils do have to be familiar with the meaning of the word 'upthrust' and so teachers may feel that such an experiment is warranted.

Having pupils pushing down an inflated party balloon (or an empty 2-litre plastic bottle with its lid on) into a bowl of water is a tried and tested method of showing the powerful nature of some upthrust forces; because you are pushing down against the weight of water equal to the balloon's considerable volume it is difficult to completely submerge the balloon. This can be extended by repeating with a similar sized ice balloon, where less pushing effort is required by the pupil because the weight of the balloon is greater and so assists their downward push. The ice balloon can also be used to show that 'heavy' objects can float (14.1).

Sources: Bar *et al.* (1994); Parker and Heywood (2000).

Notes

1. Density values given in the book are assumed to be in grams per cubic centimetre (g/cm^3) unless otherwise stated. Thus, these values are equivalent to the **relative density** of an object/material.
2. Note that this diagram is for information only. Creosote and mercury are hazardous and should not be used in the classroom in this way.
3. Note that, in the figures in this section, force arrows are not touching the object that is experiencing the force. This goes against convention, but has been done so that the diagrams are easier to interpret.

15

Electricity and magnetism

15.1 What are the different ways that a bulb can be connected to a cell?

Misconception

Electricity works by simply coming out of one end of a cell.

Scientific conception

Preschool children understand through experience with electrical toys that cells ('batteries') do something vitally important in making devices work. Exactly how cells achieve this is not widely known, although pupils construct ideas similar to the adult notion of energy, where a cell gives up some of its 'stuff' to an appliance; when the stuff has run out, then the appliance no longer works and the battery is dead. Colloquial expressions such as *it's run out of juice* illustrate this useful analogy. Some pupils may relate the stuff to a kind of fluid inside the cell, which when connected pours into the appliance as water flows through a hosepipe. For these particular learners the misconception statement above would be a rational conclusion – it is called the unipolar model of electrical flow (Figures 15.1a and 15.1b).

The unipolar model is incorrect. Electricity can indeed be analogized in simple terms as a flow of water, although the flow must take the form of a continuous loop. Figure 15.2b shows how electricity exits the **positive terminal** of a cell, travels through wires around the circuit, passes through a bulb, goes through more wires then

Figure 15.1a The unipolar model of electrical flow (misconception)

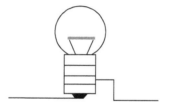

Figure 15.1b How wires connect to a bulb

finally re-enters the **negative terminal** of a cell. If the positive and negative terminals are not connected in an uninterrupted loop then the electricity cannot flow around, the bulb does not light, and the circuit is said to be broken.

As electricity travels around a circuit and passes through wires, bulbs or other components it loses energy. Thus after a period of time a connected cell runs down because it is constantly losing energy, usually as heat, light, kinetic or sound, and eventually will need replacing with a fresh cell.

Be safe!

Working with electrical circuits. The circuits used by primary children are usually quite safe and there is little danger of electrocution. This is because the source is normally low **voltage** cells (batteries) or in some cases **DC** power units that convert mains electricity to a safe level with low voltage and current. A real risk is the danger of overheating due to the pupil inadvertently building a short circuit. This is quite common, particular with novices, as they accidentally connect the terminals of the cell directly together with no intervening components such as bulbs or buzzers. This creates very low resistance within the circuit (see later) as the current only has electrical wires to push its way through, and the all the wires and connections quickly become very hot. This is usually accompanied by a smell of burning and in some cases the plastic covering the leads begins to melt, potentially creating a fire hazard. It is good practice before the lesson to ask the class to let you know immediately whenever they smell burning, at which point you must try to find where the short circuit is and disconnect it. A different risk is the danger of cutting fingers on broken glass bulbs. Ask children not to screw them down into their holders too firmly, which is the usual cause. Finally, it is worth mentioning to the children that they are not permitted to use the mains supply. During a science lesson I once spotted a child trying to connect two leads directly into the mains plug socket, a situation which had potentially fatal consequences.

Reconstruction

Year 4 pupils can carry out a practical activity where they are given a bulb, two wires and a cell and set the challenge of making the bulb light up with a minimum of teacher input. This activity is suitable for eliciting the unipolar misconception, as some children will first attempt to make the bulb light using only a single wire attached to one cell terminal. Trial and error will help them realize that both ends of the cell need to connect to the bulb for it to work, and so facilitate the construction of a correct scientific model of an electrical circuit. Note that although this activity is excellent for correcting the unipolar misconception, it will not discriminate between clashing current and current consumption misconceptions (15.2 and 15.3).

Pupils may need some direct guidance in order to make the bulb come alight, as the wires need to touch the bulb in two distinct places: the outer metal screw casing and the metal 'blob' on the underside (Figure 15.1b). Some pupils may attempt to touch the wires to the glass surface of the bulb, and this can be linked to later discussions about materials being conductors and insulators. Use a webcam linked to an inter-active whiteboard when carrying out a close-up demonstration of exactly where the wires need to go.

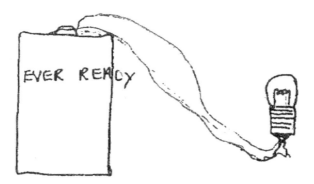

Figure 15.1c Child's drawing (aged 10 years) possibly depicting the unipolar model (misconception) (Osborne *et al.*, 1991, p32)

Although the Programme of Study states that electricity should first be introduced in Year 4, even KS1 children are capable of building their own circuits. Providing a cell, bulbs, motors, buzzers, light-emitting diodes (**LEDs**), etc. and allowing some teacher-directed exploration will allow younger children to see what happens when different components are introduced into a simple circuit. A good way to introduce the idea of electricity to KS1 children is by reading the story books *The Lighthouse Keeper's Lunch* by Ronda Armitage, and *Oscar and the Bird* by Geoff Waring.

Sources: Armitage (2007); Driver (1983); Tiberghien and Delacote (1976); Waring (2009).

15.2 How does electricity move around a circuit?

Misconception

Electricity comes out of both ends of a cell.

Scientific conception

As discussed in 15.1, pupils commonly understand that cells give up some of their 'stuff' to devices, and may construct the analogy of a kind of fluid that leaves the cell, flows through the wires and then finally enters a component such as a bulb, making it work. This 'hosepipe' representation as embodied in the unipolar model (Figure 15.1a) can be extended to the idea that electricity is pushed out from both ends of a cell to feed a device. Construction of this more advanced double hosepipe variant can be due to a pupil correctly understanding that both terminals of a cell need to be connected for a component to be able to work. Because the electricity is depicted as meeting in the middle of the circuit with nowhere else to go this is termed the clashing currents model of electrical flow, and is not a correct scientific representation (Figure 15.2a).

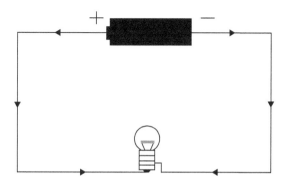

Figure 15.2a The clashing currents model of electrical flow (misconception)

Although the water flow analogy can be useful in helping to understand how electricity moves around a circuit, it is better to think of the water/electricity as travelling in a continuous loop in a similar manner to cars driving around a one-way circular racetrack. The electricity leaves the cell from the positive terminal only, travels around the wires, through components, then back into the cell at the negative terminal (Figure 15.2b). As explained in the context of the unipolar model misconception, the cell eventually runs down as energy is lost to the surroundings.

Reconstruction

Although an understanding of the direction of electrical flow is beyond the primary curriculum, it is valuable if teachers are able to recognize and correct misconceptions such as the clashing currents model, should they appear. A practical way to illustrate which path electricity is taking through a circuit is to connect a household **multimeter** in series to different parts of a circuit, as this piece of apparatus will show positive or negative readings depending on the direction of electrical flow.

Asking pupils to connect LEDs to different parts of a circuit will result in the LEDs lighting up in some places and not in others. This is because LEDs will only turn

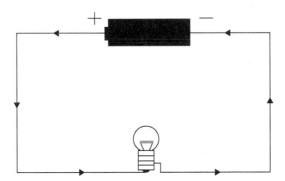

Figure 15.2b Scientific model of conventional electrical flow

on when electricity flows through them in one direction – they are a kind of one-way street. Using these observations, pupils can draw a diagram of the circuit that shows which way they think the electricity is flowing.

Sources: Chiu and Lin (2005); Driver (1983).

15.3 What is current?

Misconception

A circuit uses up electric current.

Scientific conception

Figure 15.3a[1] shows how some pupils might depict the behaviour of electric current in a simple DC circuit consisting of one cell, two bulbs and three wires. They understand (correctly) that 'electricity' or current comes out of one cell terminal, travels around the circuit passing through bulbs and wires, then re-enters the cell at the opposite end. They believe that bulbs use up current so its value diminishes during the journey around the circuit, represented by the size of the arrows on the diagram. Also, because there is less current available in the right-hand side of the circuit, bulb B is the dimmer of the two bulbs. These conclusions are a consequence of the incorrect idea that current is constantly being depleted by a live circuit, or the current consumption model of electrical flow.

This misconception has been previously identified in a variety of age groups with high frequencies of occurrence and is difficult to correct. Within a simple DC circuit as depicted in Figure 15.3a the current remains constant throughout, but to understand why this is the case it is important to think about what current actually is. Within the atoms of a metal conductor such as the copper wire in a circuit there are tiny subatomic particles called *electrons*. These electrons are not tied to any one atom,

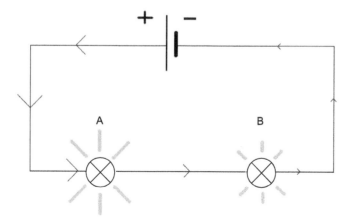

Figure 15.3a Current consumption model (misconception)

instead being able to randomly wander up and down the wire; they are known as *free electrons*, and collectively as a *sea of electrons*. When the two terminals of a cell are connected to the wires to make a circuit, the sea of electrons is attracted to the positive cell terminal and so they move *en masse* through the wire towards that terminal, causing electrical flow (Figure 15.3b). During their journey the moving electrons pass through the very thin tungsten filament of a bulb and cause it to glow because of friction from the collisions with the tungsten atoms, then come out the other side of the bulb and enter the wire on their way to the cell. When the electrons reach the cell terminal they enter the cell; at the same time more electrons leave the cell at the opposite terminal and enter the wire, with this replenishment keeping the number of electrons in the circuit constant.

Thus, the electrons that make up current are in a kind of self-contained system and so their overall number is never reduced in the circuit.[2] Because of this, bulbs A and B in Figure 15.3c will have equal levels of current, and if you were to use a multimeter to measure the current at any point in the circuit you would always get the same reading. Since bulb brightness is an indicator of current size, the two bulbs would be equally bright.

When a circuit is switched on, its bulbs will light instantaneously. It makes sense to assume that the electrons are therefore travelling very quickly around the wires within the circuit, and a commonly held idea is that current travels at the speed of light. However, the electrons would only pass through the type of circuit shown by Figure 15.3c at a rate of around 5 cm each minute because they are constantly colliding with and being slowed by metal atoms within the wires and bulb filaments in the circuit.[3] The reason why the bulbs come on instantly is that electrons do not have to be sent all the way from the cell to the bulb, they are already present in the bulb and the wires as free electrons (Figure 15.3b). The cell in Figure 15.3b can be considered as a kind of pump that is pushing electrons along as they pass through it. As soon as the cell starts 'pushing' then all the electrons in the chain will start moving immediately, and as they pass through the bulb they cause it to light up without any delay.

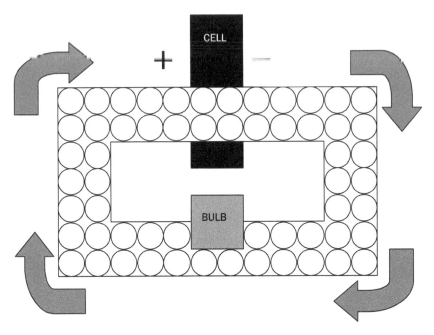

Figure 15.3b A simple model of electron flow in a series circuit (electrons not to scale)

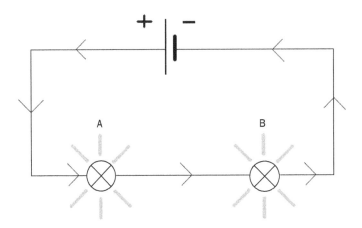

Figure 15.3c Scientifically correct model of electrical flow

Within a domestic household electric circuit the situation is different as the electricity is **alternating current (AC)**, where the current flow is not constantly in the same direction but instead changes direction very rapidly, 50 times a second. The electrons in an AC circuit are pushed along a wire first one way then the opposite way, which ends up with them only moving a few millimetres each way through the wire.

Nevertheless, although individual electrons do not travel very far through the wires, a bulb can be made to light up because the sea of electrons as a whole is pushed in the circuit in alternate directions.

Another misconception that is a consequence of the current consumption model is that a **resistor** placed into a circuit near to the positive terminal of a cell would reduce the brightness of a bulb, but if placed near the negative terminal would have no effect on bulb brightness (Figure 15.3d). This is because it is believed that current flow through a bulb can only be affected if something is placed 'before' or upstream of the bulb, as with a river. In fact, because you are working within a closed system, a resistor placed anywhere in a simple DC circuit will have the same diminishing effect on the current and reduce the brightness of the bulbs.

The reader might have noted that the directions of flow in Figures 15.3b and 15.3c oppose each other – this is not an error. In diagrams of electrical circuits current is conventionally drawn as arrows travelling from the positive terminal of the cell, through the circuit towards the negative cell terminal, i.e. anticlockwise in Figure 15.3e. This is termed conventional current, and although recognized and accepted worldwide

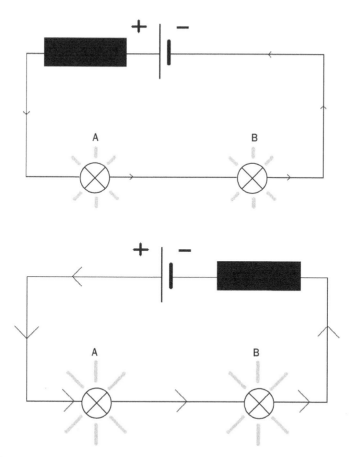

Figure 15.3d Upstream/downstream resistor misconception

by electricians, its direction of flow is actually scientifically incorrect. In fact, electrons are negatively charged so travel in the reverse direction away from the negative terminal and towards the positive, i.e. clockwise in Figure 15.3f (opposites attract, likes repel). Therefore within conductors such as metal wires, current can be considered to be a flow of negative charge. There are historical reasons why the direction of conventional current is incorrect and is a source of perennial confusion for students at all levels of education, who may generate the corollary misconception that because conventional current travels towards the negative terminal it is a flow of *positive* charge. Also, serving to confuse the situation further, electric flow can in other contexts be due to particles other than electrons; for instance, during electroplating, positively charged particles in solution such as copper ions are responsible in part for electrical flow. In the primary classroom to avoid unnecessary confusion the conflicting directions of flow tend not to be shared with pupils, who are usually presented with the conventional direction, i.e. from the positive cell terminal to the negative.

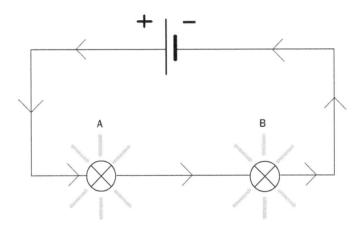

Figure 15.3e The direction of conventional current flow

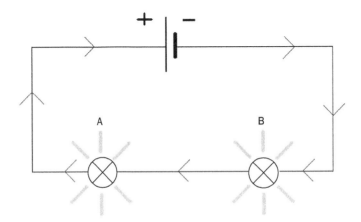

Figure 15.3f The direction of electron flow

Did you know?

A circuit loses energy, not current. A cell does not last for ever, eventually running down because it 'gives' something to the circuit that it cannot take back . . . so what exactly is it losing? It has already been stated that electrons exit the negative terminal of the cell, travel around the circuit and enter the positive terminal. A cell is a kind of pump that recycles electrons in the circuit by using energy, and gradually this pump loses its capacity to do this because it loses energy, which cannot be recovered. Chemical energy within the cell drives this process, which during the life of a cell such as in Figure 15.3c is converted to electrical energy in the wires, then heat and light energy in the bulbs which is finally lost from the circuit. So this circuit does not lose current in the form of electrons (they cannot leave the self-contained system – see Figure 15.3b), but loses energy as heat and light which makes the cell gradually run down, and the electrons circulate more slowly. When the chemical energy within a cell is exhausted it can no longer drive electrons around a circuit and becomes flat. With rechargeable cells the chemical energy can be restored by using the mains electricity to reverse the chemical processes within the cell (see chapter 19 for more on energy changes and transfers).

Reconstruction

Although the word 'current' is not used in the primary curriculum, the concept that a cell supplies some kind of 'stuff' to the circuit in order to make things work is implicit within activities. Teachers may extend brighter pupils by introducing the idea of a travelling entity called current that is present within the wires and components of a circuit. A good way to elicit the current consumption misconception is to ask the class to predict the comparable brightnesses of a string of several bulbs in a series circuit arranged as in Figure 15.3b. Pupils then build circuits to test their predictions and note that bulb brightness is actually the same, so refuting the misconception. The teacher can reinforce this by using a household multimeter to demonstrate that the measured current at any point in the circuit has the same value.

There are technical aspects of this experiment which can confound misconception correction, or even reinforce some misconceptions. The bulbs should be all of the same rating (e.g. 1.5 V) and need to be tested by the teacher prior to the lesson so that they indeed all have the same brightness because there are sometimes variations; especially watch out for the odd rogue bulb of a higher rating that is much brighter. If pupils find there are minor variations in brightness then ask them to swap bulbs around in the circuit in order to show that the variation is due to the bulb itself, and not its position/order within the circuit.

A popular KS3 role-play activity is to have pupils pretending to be electrons travelling around the room, which represents different parts of a DC circuit, and if the concept of current is introduced to primary children then this pedagogy could be similarly utilized.

This is known to be a very resistant misconception. Misconceiving pupils may persuade themselves that there is indeed a difference in subjective bulb brightness when there is none in order to preserve their theory. Others may reason that their string of bulbs does have equal brightness but the current re-entering the cell is reduced at some point after leaving the last bulb. The concept of energy is not introduced in primary science and is perhaps best avoided in this particular context. When energy is introduced at KS3 it represents a regular source of further confusion for pupils who find it difficult to remember the difference between electrical current and electrical energy.

Sources: Glauert (2009); Shipstone (1984); Tiberghien and Delacote (1976).

15.4 What is voltage?

Misconception

Voltage makes a circuit work by travelling around the wires.

Scientific conception

Although the volt as a unit of measure is used frequently in primary electricity topics when describing cells, during lessons teachers rarely tend to offer any further meaning or context. Pupils may consequently construct their own ideas as to what volts and voltage actually are. They appreciate that different cells have different voltages and that the higher the voltage the more 'stuff' a circuit is given, making bulbs brighter and buzzers noisier. If this train of thought is taken further pupils can imagine that the voltage runs around the wires and components making everything work. However, as discussed in 15.3, although there are indeed tiny subatomic particles called electrons that travel around the circuit, a measure of the number of these electrons passing a given point within a circuit at any one time is current, not voltage.

Voltage is renowned in science education as being a poorly understood and difficult concept and is best thought of at a simple level as a kind of pushing force generated by a cell that causes current (electrons) to flow around a circuit. The more volts a cell can provide the greater the pushing force so making the bulbs in a circuit brighter. As a cell runs down over time its voltage will decrease accordingly. The cell in Figure 15.4a is using 6 V to drive the circuit containing two bulbs; in addition to the cell's voltage, the diagram, which is typical, shows that there are also volts present within the circuit itself, across each bulb. Note that the sum of the volts associated with each bulb approximately equals the total number of volts delivered by the cell, as if the bulbs have shared the cell's voltage between them, i.e. 2.9 V + 2.9 V = 5.8 V; the missing 0.2 V represent the 'share' taken by the wires in the circuit.[4] However, the fact that the bulbs' voltage is shown on the diagram can act as a source of confusion that encourages learners to believe that volts appear to have been sent around the circuit when actually *the circuit does not contain any volts.*

To make this clearer, we need to think about voltage not as something physical and moving like current, but as a measure of difference. The voltage differences

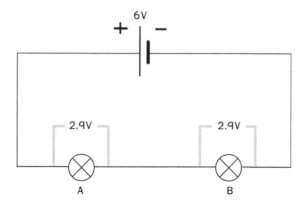

Figure 15.4a Voltage measurements within a simple DC circuit

within the circuit in Figure 15.4a are shown in Figure 15.4b as a slope, with the volts in the column on the left of the diagram representing the height of the slope. Voltage starts high when current leaves the cell at the positive terminal (6 V) and gradually falls to 0 when current enters the cell at the negative terminal. Each bulb has made the voltage drop by 2.9 V, and each long wire by 0.1 V, explaining why by the time the current enters the cell on the far right of the diagram the voltage has become 0. As current passes through each bulb the voltage drops significantly so voltage is not something present within each bulb; instead, it is a measure of the drop in 'height' on either side of a bulb. Current can be imagined as like a ball, only being able to move if there is a downhill slope for it to roll down – from left to right in Figure 15.4b. As current passes through each bulb there is a large drop in height (voltage), and as it runs through each long wire there is a smaller drop. As the current enters the cell at the negative terminal it is at the lowest point on this imaginary slope, and the job of the cell is to boost it back up to the highest point, ready to leave the positive terminal for another trip around the circuit. If a bigger 12 V cell were to be substituted into the same circuit then the drop across the bulbs would be greater, approaching 6 V for each bulb, and they would glow much more brightly.

If a circuit contained one small bulb and one buzzer, the measured voltage across the buzzer would be greatly in excess of that across the bulb. It is as if the buzzer is greedy and takes nearly all the cell's voltage for itself, leaving little for the bulb, which as a consequence glows very dimly, if at all. This can be conceptualized more correctly as the voltage drop across the buzzer being massive compared with the drop across the bulb.

In summary, volts are not something that travel around a circuit. Instead they are a measure of the driving force that causes current to move, just as a slope causes a ball to roll downhill; the scientific name for this driving force is **potential difference**. If there were no difference in volts within the circuit, current would not be able to flow.

This misconception can be reinforced if pupils notice that the small bulbs used in school experiments each have a voltage rating stamped on them, which may suggest

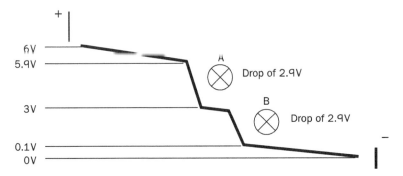

Figure 15.4b Voltage drops across a simple DC circuit

to them that volts are physically entities that travel through bulbs. This value merely lets the user know what cell voltage is required to light the bulb, and if a much higher voltage is supplied to the bulb in error, for instance by connecting several cells in series, the filament may melt and the bulb blow.

Related misconceptions include the idea that voltage is the amount of electricity stored in a cell. As discussed in the box on p. 187, cells do not contain electricity but instead act as a source of chemical energy that can be transformed into electrical energy. Therefore a 'charged' cell actually contains no charge until it is connected to a circuit. Another common though erroneous idea is that voltage is an inherent and subordinate part of the current within a circuit. Although current within a circuit needs a voltage in order to flow, the current and voltage are separate things, and the voltage is a causative agent for current flow. In this section voltage has repeatedly been analogized as a 'driving force', but it must not be thought that any macroscopic mechanical push or pull exists within circuits during current flow. The 'forces' take the form of attractions between positive and negative charges that have been created by chemical processes occurring within cells.

Reconstruction

At the primary level the concept of voltage is usually kept simple, for instance being related to how bulb brightness increases with the number of cells of a certain voltage connected into a circuit. As with the concept of current (15.3), if misconceptions of voltage do appear it is preferable if teachers attempt to correct them, so laying better foundations for future study at secondary school. One way to explain voltage without using the more complex idea of potential difference is to say that when current leaves a cell it is given a kick and sent on its way around the circuit. To illustrate this, draw a cartoon foot that kicks circular objects (current) out of one terminal of a cell and gives them a reason to move around the circuit. The bigger the cell's voltage the larger the foot, and so the bigger the driving force.

With very bright upper KS2 children teachers may wish to introduce the idea of voltage dropping at different points of the circuit. A household multimeter can be used to show how volts drop across components, with these voltage losses then being drawn by pupils as a slope (as in Figure 15.4b).

Sources: Osborne (1983); Shipstone (1985).

15.5 Are all metals magnetic?

Misconception

All metals are magnetic.

Scientific conception

When school children play or experiment with magnets they can quickly realize that only metallic objects can be attracted. Sometimes they over-generalize and assume that magnets are capable of attracting all metals; in fact only three metals are magnetic: iron, nickel and cobalt. This includes any **alloy** that contains any of these metals, e.g. a steel paper clip is magnetic because steel contains iron. If a magnet is able to attract a metal this also means that the metal itself can be turned into a magnet given the right circumstances. Surprisingly there are some non-metallic materials that are magnetic, for instance iron oxide, which does not contain **elemental** iron. These materials can be turned into *ceramic magnets*.

Other magnet misconceptions include the ideas that a barrier such as a piece of paper will stop the influence of a magnet, and a magnet would cease to work in the absence of gravity.

Reconstruction

An activity where pupils can experiment by attempting to attract a variety of different metals using a magnet can serve as a useful refutation exercise for this misconception. Be sure to include common non-magnetic metals such as aluminium (drinks cans), brass (some keys) and tin metal. Lead metal should be used only with care and with classes where there is no probability of hand to mouth contact, and hands should be washed after use.

One unexpected outcome is that tin metal is not magnetic but a tin can is. What we colloquially call 'tin' cans are actually made mostly of steel, which is magnetic, and only have a thin tin coating to prevent rusting. An interesting activity is to have a collection of 2p coins of different ages – pupils will find that only some are magnetic – those dated after 1992. This is because after 1992 such coins began to be made with a steel core, whereas before they were made from solid bronze, which is a nonmagnetic metal.

There is scope with this topic to set pupils practical homework where they have to solve problems using fridge magnets, for instance write a list of ten objects that a fridge magnet will stick to.

One way to remember the three magnetic metals is the acronym 'FeNiCo', which represents the chemical symbols for iron, nickel and cobalt, respectively.

Sources: Finley (1986); Meyer (1991).

Notes

1. For brevity, conventional circuit symbols are used to depict components in 15.3 and 15.4.
2. Over time the cell will run down, making the electrons in the circuit slow down. Note that current is not a measure of the total amount of electrons within a circuit, but the number of electrons passing a certain point in the circuit in a given time.
3. It is like trying to push your way through a very crowded room; scientifically this is termed resistance, and the more difficult it is for electrons to pass through a material the higher that material's resistance. The thinner the material the greater the resistance, as is the case with tiny tungsten bulb filaments, which can be analogized as a crowd of people all trying to get through a narrow tunnel at the same time (see Figure 15.3b). With higher resistance the electrons travel through the wires more slowly, and so current is less.
4. Also note that in reality a 6 V cell would probably be providing a little less than its stated voltage when measured with a meter due to the fact that a small amount of voltage is needed to overcome the cell's internal resistance.

16
Light

16.1 Where is light present?

> **Misconception**
>
> *Light is only found in bright areas.*

Scientific conception

In an everyday sense 'light' can be defined as any area that is illuminated, e.g. *we need some more light in here*, or *is it light outside yet?* As a consequence, pupils understand light as being a general quality of a particular location, which conflicts with the scientific idea of light as a form of energy that travels from one place to another. Figure 16.1a shows a source illuminating a flat surface in a dark room where pupils believe that light is present at only the source and the surface because these are the only areas that are visibly lit up. In fact, because light is travelling from the torch bulb towards the flat surface, light can also be said to exist in the area in between, in the form of a beam (Figure 16.1b). This beam can be made visible by various means (see *Reconstruction*). We are not able to see the travelling beam making its way across the room because light travels at an extremely high speed, approximately 300 000 km per second.

The conventional scientific way to depict light in diagrams is by using arrows that show the path taken by the travelling light and also its direction – these are light rays, and are shown in Figure 16.1b.

Even if pupils understand that light is a travelling entity the misconception that it only exists in bright areas can still persist. For instance, in a room lit by a single candle they may say that light only travels as far as the objects that are illuminated, and does not penetrate into the dark corners of the room (Figure 16.1c). They believe that the light merely fills a limited space and then stays still. However, the fact that a person is still able to see the candle even if they stand in unlit areas of the room means that light rays must have permeated the entire room, travelling from the candle to the observer's

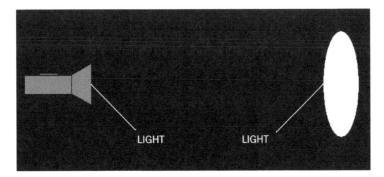

Figure 16.1a Light exists in bright areas (misconception)

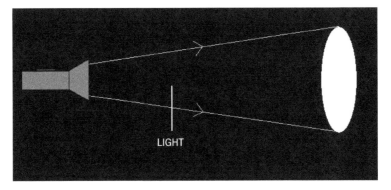

Figure 16.1b Light within a beam

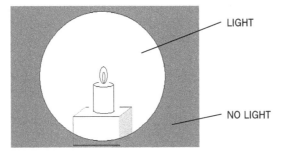

Figure 16.1c Candle illuminating a dark room (misconception)

eyes. Returning to the torch example above, light therefore not only exists at the source, within the beam and on the illuminated surface, but also fills the whole room.

Other erroneous ideas related to travelling light include the view that light does not travel at night-time, which is why darkness occurs. Conversely, some pupils believe that light travels further at night, which explains how during the daytime artificial sources such as car headlights and torches are more difficult to see.

Although beyond the primary curriculum – so it is not necessary to share this with pupils – make a mental note that light is a form of **electromagnetic radiation** that is visible to the human eye. Other forms of electromagnetic radiation are invisible, such as infra-red, ultra-violet, microwaves, radio waves and cosmic waves.

Be Safe!

Using a laser pointer in the classroom. These devices (also called laser pens) transmit laser radiation, which is high-intensity coherent light in a narrow beam. They can potentially cause permanent eye damage if the beam is shone directly into the eye. That said, laser pointers have been used by teachers and presenters in the UK for many years with no reported incidents of injury. Many laser pointers are classified as low risk, and the likely result of the laser beam accidentally entering the eye is a dazzling flash with temporary blindness (spots before the eyes) and disorientation. Other pointers are more powerful, for example lasers producing a green beam, and so must be used with greater care. In the primary classroom let common sense prevail. They are useful tools, but use them when demonstrating light phenomena only if you are sure the beam will not be shone directly into the eyes of the audience.

Reconstruction

Experiments that deal with the concept of travelling light ideally require a room with an effective blackout capability, preferably having thick black curtains or blinds. Pupils can make a torch beam visible by sprinkling a little flour into the area of the beam. Teachers can show this more effectively by substituting the torch with a whiteboard laser pointer, using appropriate safety precautions. These activities can start to convey the idea that light is not merely a quality at a location but is actually moving from one place to another. Relate this to a projector beam in a dusty cinema, and for a dramatic demonstration of the principle ask pupils to shine a bright torch at home outside in a dark garden on a foggy or misty night. Torch beams are often overtly depicted in cartoons or animations and these can serve as a reminder that light travels from source to illuminated object.

Light a candle in a dark classroom and ask the class to draw how far they think the light has travelled. Send some pupils into the dark areas of the room, then ask them if they can still see the candle. Explain that if they can, then the light must still be reaching these dark areas to some degree because seeing light means some of it has entered your eyes. If they draw a ray diagram of the candlelight and its penetration into dark corners this would help reinforce the scientific concept.

Introduce KS1 children to light by reading the story book *Oscar and the Moth* by Geoff Waring.

Sources: Driver *et al.* (1994); Galili and Hazan (2000); Guesne (1984, 1985); Waring (2006).

16.2 How do we see things?

Misconception

We see things because light travels from our eyes towards an object.

...when the light is on our eyes we can read the words. (Pupil aged 10 years; Osborne *et al.*, 1990).

Scientific conception

Pupils commonly draw ray diagrams in a way that suggests they believe that in order for something to be seen light has to travel from the eye and connect with the object (Figure 16.2a). In fact, the reverse is true. We see an object because the eye is able to absorb light rays travelling from the object, so stimulating electrical and chemical signals, which are sent to the brain. Thus the correct way to draw light rays is moving *towards* the eye and *away* from an object (Figure 16.2b).

However, this is only part of the story. We can only see an object when it is illuminated by a luminous light source such as an electric bulb or the sun, as the object cannot generate light rays of its own accord (unless the object itself is a source). Light travels from the source to the object, reflecting off the object and into the eye (Figure 16.2c).

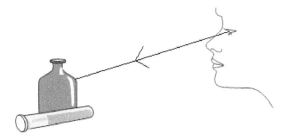

Figure 16.2a Light travels from eye to object (misconception)

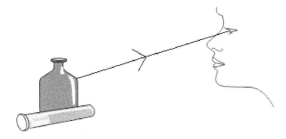

Figure 16.2b Light travels from object to eye

Figure 16.2c A luminous source illuminating an object in order to make it visible

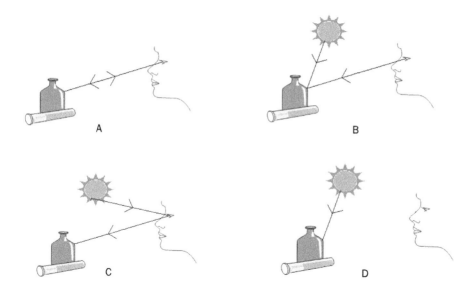

Figure 16.2d Some variant misconceptions

There are several variations to the original misconception and each is discussed next, illustrated by the ray diagrams in Figure 16.2d:

1   *Misconception A.* Although the pupil understands that light travels from object to eye, there are remnants of the original misconception resulting in a model comprising of an oscillating light ray that goes back and forth.
2   *Misconception B.* The way in which the sun has illuminated the object has been correctly drawn. However, the original misconception still persists; the everyday phrase *looking at things* may act as a trigger, possibly indicating the belief that we can only see things if we consciously look for them (see 17.1).

3   *Misconception C.* The depiction might suggest that the pupil believes it is the eye that requires illumination in order to 'send' light rays towards the object.

4   *Misconception D.* Since the object is illuminated but no light then leaves the object towards the eye, this variant could be a manifestation of the misconception that light is only present in bright areas (16.1).

Some pupils have problems with the idea that light is able to reflect off surfaces that are non-shiny, and think reflection is limited to mirrors, **plane glass**, water, etc. There are also several misconceptions related to sources of light (16.3), for instance that no external source is required in order to see an object, with the consequence that humans can just about see things in total darkness.[1] When drawing light rays from a source such as a candle directly to the eye, pupils may tend to correctly draw the ray as in Figure 16.2b, but when drawing rays from a non-source, they may revert back to the original misconception (Figures 16.2a and 16.2e).

Reconstruction

Early on in the topic get pupils into the habit of including the light source in their ray diagrams, where appropriate. This will underline the idea that the reason why we can see something is that light *from* a source reflects *from* the object's surface and *into* our eyes. Pupils need to think of this journey being taken by one continuous ray of light from source to eye (via object), as shown in Figure 16.2c.

Research has shown that pupils can understand the scientific model more if the object is replaced by a mirror and they are asked to draw the journey of the light rays; use a torch or candle as the source, not the sun (Figure 16.2f). The teacher can demonstrate with more clarity if a whiteboard laser pen is used as the source and the beam

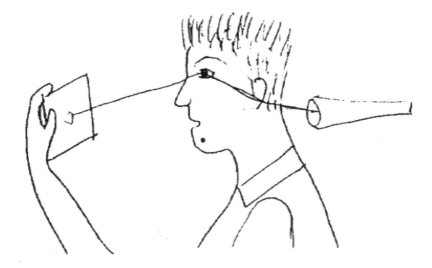

Figure 16.2e Child's drawing (aged 11 years) showing light entering the eye from a torch, and light travelling from the eye to an object (misconception variant C, Figure 16.2d) (Osborne *et al.*, 1990, p25)

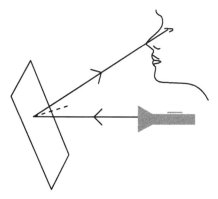

Figure 16.2f Using a torch and a mirror to help correct the misconception

sprinkled with flour, but it is obviously important for safety reasons *not* to view the beam's reflection as shown in Figure 16.2f and instead to direct the beam towards an unoccupied area of the room (see 16.1 for more on this technique).[2]

Younger pupils are capable of learning the differences between sources and non-sources of light. Ask children to draw and colour examples of things that can make their own light, and things that cannot.

Sources: Fetherstonhaugh and Treagust (1990); Osborne *et al.* (1990); Watts (1985).

16.3 Why does the moon shine?

Misconception

The moon is a source of light.

Scientific conception

In Year 1, pupils learn that objects such as a torch, fire or the sun create their own light and are called *sources*. However, some pupils over-generalize and can end up thinking a light source is anything that is bright or shines, for instance a mirror, a bicycle reflector or the moon. These objects are merely good *reflectors* of light and do not generate their own light, and if no source were available then they would not be visible. The moon is a very bright object when viewed in the night sky because it is reflecting light from the sun and directing some of it down towards the Earth. The moon is therefore not a light source, and if the sun were to suddenly stop shining then the moon would likewise fall into darkness.

There are other misconceptions that are related to light sources. Some pupils have difficulties understanding that dim illumination such as from glowing embers counts as a light source. When asked to list sources of light, electrical appliances are more commonly cited than natural sources such as the sun.

Reconstruction

Ask the class to investigate whether objects are light sources or not by observing them while the room is darkened; sources will appear brighter than they do in a normally lit room, and non-sources will be darker. A good way to elicit the misconception is to hold up a piece of reflective clothing that is illuminated by a bright torch in a dark room – the reflective areas can be made to glow very brightly – and ask pupils whether or not the clothing is a source of light. Switching the torch off will show that since the clothing becomes dark it is not making its own light so cannot be a source, and is merely an excellent reflector. Revising the idea of reflecting light using ray diagrams will remind pupils that light is able to bounce off objects and that materials that are shiny will reflect more light into our eyes than others that are dull.

Showing pupils pictures of the **phases of the moon** can help dispel the misconception since if the moon were a light source like the sun then parts of it could not be in shadow (18.7). Photographs of the Earth and other planets from space will demonstrate that all objects in the **solar system** shine to a certain degree due to their reflecting light from the sun. On the other hand, stars like the sun are sources of light.

Source: Şahin *et al.* (2008).

16.4 Where do shadows originate from?

Misconception

My shadow is always there inside me and bright light can push it out.

Scientific conception

Primary children tend to hold non-scientific ideas about what shadows actually are and how they behave. In line with the misconception statement above they can sometimes believe that a shadow is an integral part of every object that is constantly present but not always visible. They think a shadow is another facet of the object, as well as being an accurate representation; for instance the shape of a shadow is always a perfect replica of the shape of the object. This 'Peter Pan' model of a shadow is at odds with scientific concepts that explain the passage (**transmission**) of light through objects.

An object can be broadly categorized as falling into one of three categories depending on the amount of light that is able to be transmitted through it. A transparent object such as a clear pane of glass allows the passage of more or less all light which is why we are able to see things on the other side with a good degree of clarity. A translucent object allows only the passage of some light, so when looking through an object such as frosted glass things appear undefined and lack detail. An opaque object does not allow any light to be transmitted. Because opaque objects block light completely there is an area behind the object where no light is present – this area is devoid of any light so appears black to us – a shadow (Figure 16.4). Translucent

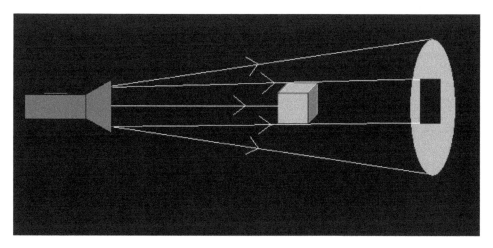

Figure 16.4 Shadows occur when opaque objects block light

objects can also cast shadows but because they allow some light to be transmitted these shadows are hazy with no sharp defined edges, and never completely black. Note that although Figure 16.4 shows an opaque cube absorbing the central light ray, this is merely for illustrative purposes and is not a comprehensive depiction as some light will be absorbed and some will be reflected from the cube (see 16.5).

Linked to the idea that a shadow is simply another facet of an object is the confusion some children have over the concepts of 'reflection' and 'shadow'. They will sometimes say 'shadows are reflections', meaning that an object's shadow is an accurate representation of that object, similar to an image that can be seen in a mirror. Children frequently draw shadows as mirror images complete with details included within the shadow itself; for instance when drawing a person's shadow they will include facial features, intricate aspects of clothing, etc.

> *I think a shadow is a reflection from the sun. Sometimes when you look in a pond you see a reflection. When you go somewhere where it can reflect you see your shadow.* (Pupil statement, Guest, 2003, p15).

Other misconceptions about shadows include the understanding that the brighter the light source the taller a shadow would become, or shadows only appear in the presence of bright light. Although children can usually predict where their own shadow would fall in relation to a light source such as the sun, they are less successful when attempting similar predictions with the shadows of objects other than themselves.

Reconstruction

Shadows are covered in Year 6 within the Light topic. Children are required to understand that shadows are caused when a light source is blocked, and carry out experiments that investigate the conditions that influence the size, shape, sharpness, etc. of shadows. As discussed, if pupils are asked to draw their own shadows some might include details within the shadows such as faces, and these ideas can be easily refuted by afterwards examining real shadows, ideally outside in the playground on a sunny day.

Misconceptions relating to shadows' size, shape, etc. can be tested using traditional investigations that will be familiar to primary teachers where the distances between the light source, object and screen are systematically changed to see how the shadow changes. Making shadow puppets is an engaging exercise for younger children and subsequent discussions centred on the nature of shadows can help them construct simple though scientifically acceptable ideas at a young age, such as which kinds of objects block light to cast a shadow, and which do not. Also, on a sunny day in the playground children can draw around their partner's shadow using chalk and then compare the shape and size of their shadow with those of others in the class.

Sources: Feher and Rice (1985); Galili and Hazan (2000); Guest (2003); Tiberghien *et al.* (1980); Watts and Gilbert (1985).

16.5 Why do we see rainbow colours when light passes through a prism?

Misconception

White light is pure; coloured light is white light with impurities in it.

Scientific conception

We depend on sunlight or indoor electric lighting to provide illumination so that we can see and interact with our surroundings. These sources produce **white light**, and what might not be immediately obvious is that white light consists of several types of different coloured light mixed together. These differently coloured constituents can be observed by using a prism to split white light; this is called **dispersion** (Figure 16.5a). These colours are the visible **spectrum**, and this method of splitting light was first described by Sir Isaac Newton in 1671. Newton decided that there were seven distinct colours in the spectrum (which can be remembered by the acronym ROYGBIV), although it is debatable whether indigo and violet can be distinguished separately. Rainbows are spectra produced when there is rain in the air and tiny water droplets act like individual prisms to reflect and disperse white light, creating an apparent bow-shaped image in the sky.

The human eye contains light-sensitive cells within the **retina** which are capable of detecting colour. These cells are called *cones* and there are three different types: red, green and blue. Red cones detect only red light, green cones only green light, and blue cones only blue light. There are no cones that detect other colours such as pink or brown, and for this reason red, green and blue are termed the three **primary colours**. Objects that we see around us have a particular colour for two reasons. First, it depends on which colour light they absorb, and, second, it depends on the colour of

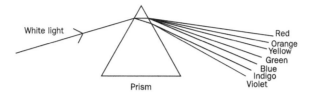

Figure 16.5a Dispersing white light into its constituent colours

light that the object is illuminated with. Looking at the examples below that have been illuminated with white light, if we see a white cube, then the object must have reflected all the white light back towards our eye, and absorbed no light (Figure 16.5b (i)). If a different cube is seen as red, then it has reflected red light towards our eye, but where has the green and blue light gone that was within the original white sunlight? The cube must have absorbed the green and blue light and reflected only red (Figure 16.5b (ii)). When objects appear black, no light is reflected towards the eye so the cube must have absorbed all the white sunlight (i.e. red, green and blue) and reflected no light at all – when we perceive black this means absence of any reflected light (Figure 16.5b (iv)). These phenomena can be linked to everyday experience. In summer white clothing feels cooler because it has reflected all visible sunlight, while conversely black clothing feels warmer because it has absorbed all sunlight.

Clearly, we also capable of perceiving a wide range of colours other than red, green and blue. As can be seen from figure 16.5c when light of the primary colours is mixed, **secondary colours** can be made; these are yellow, magenta (purple) and cyan (turquoise). For example, red and green light mix to produce yellow light, so a daffodil flower appears yellow because it is reflecting both red and green light together (see Figure 16.5b (v)). We see other hues apart from the primary and secondary colours because different coloured light mixes in different proportions. If mixed light is 90% red and 10% green then this would appear more orange than yellow. Note that in the art world the primary colours are traditionally red, blue and yellow. These are different to the scientific primary colours because they are concerned with the mixing of paints on a palette, which produce different colours to when beams of light are mixed.

Other colour misconceptions include the belief that when light of different colours are mixed they always produce darker light, and that when an object is illuminated with coloured light, the light adds its own colour to the object, or the light stops certain colours within the object from escaping (instead of the object reflecting and absorbing different colours).

Reconstruction

Any detailed treatment of colour theory is beyond the primary curriculum and pupils in Year 6 are required only to experience simple phenomena such as rainbows and the colours of soap bubbles, and practise using prisms to disperse white light. This would usually include teaching the concept of white light being a mixture of many colours,

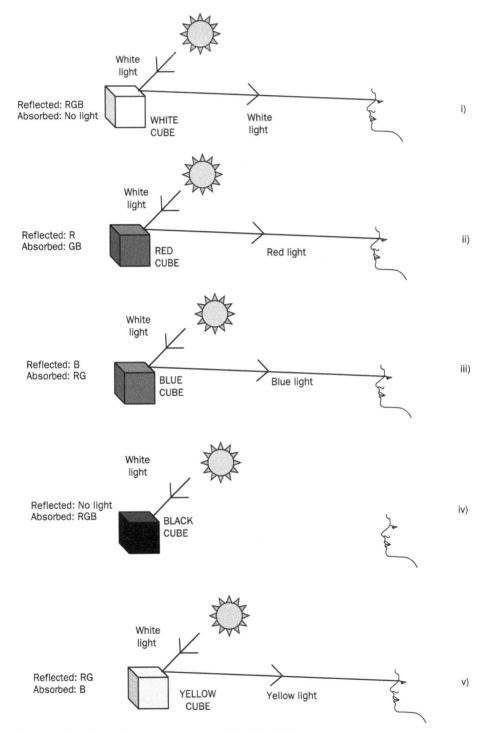

Figure 16.5b Why objects appear as a particular colour

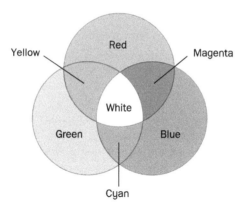

Figure 16.5c Mixing the primary colours of light

and pupils can be stretched by mixing light beams of different colours themselves using coloured cellophane stretched over torches. To be effective these activities require reasonably powerful torches and a darkened room.

When dispersing light using a prism it is tricky to achieve the correct angle for a spectrum to appear and readers are recommended to refer to Figure 16.5a as a rough guide. The incoming beam should just clip the prism apex. Place an A4 white card screen where you expect the spectrum to appear. Once a spectrum is produced, a second prism can be introduced close to the spectrum beam which will recombine it back into white light again, so reinforcing the idea that white light is a mixture. Similarly, children will enjoy constructing a coloured card spinner with a small pencil pushed through the centre; when it is spun the colours merge and the whole spinner appears white – this is Newton's disc (Figure 16.5d).[3]

Simple spectra can be produced by using an old CD and holding a torch just above its shiny surface at a slight angle, then placing a white card screen also above the surface to catch the spectrum. Even simpler, if children peer through a prism directly at a light source such as an overhead light or table lamp (never the sun); with the prism held close to the eye an attractive spectrum can be viewed. Finally, a laser pen is a powerful source of light that teachers can use with care to demonstrate reflection and absorption of light due to colour. When shone onto white card the laser light looks very bright as close to 100% of the light is reflected, while on black card there is practically no reflected beam due to the near total absorption of light.

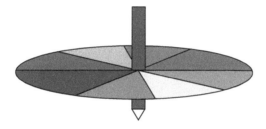

Figure 16.5d Newton's disc spinner

Sources: Anderson and Smith (1983); Feher and Meyer (1992); Galili and Hazan (2000); Guesne (1985); Martinez-Borreguero *et al.* (2013).

Famous scientists

Sir Isaac Newton. It could be argued that Newton (1642–1727) was the most versatile, prolific and talented scientist in history. He is renowned for formulating many different laws and theories about the physical world that explain the phenomena of light, sound, gravity, planetary motion and mechanics. Many of his ideas are still valid today. He is however, less well known for his achievements in the field of mathematics, which include the development of modern calculus.

Notes

1. One study found that this misconception was more common with city children who, because of environmental light pollution, may have had little experience of total darkness; with a sample of rural children this misconception was less prevalent.
2. Note that the **angle of incidence** is equal to the **angle of reflection**.
3. Carry out an Internet search to determine the colours of the disc using the search terms 'Newton's disc' or 'Newton's spinner'.

17
Sound

17.1 How does sound travel?

> **Misconception**
>
> *For a sound to be heard the listener has to actively concentrate on it first.*

The noise goes through the air to people who are listening. If they're not listening they'll only hear a bit of it . . .' (Pupil, aged 7 years; Watt and Russell, 1990, p16)

Scientific conception

Primary aged pupils sometimes have a concept of sound that is quite different from the scientific model. Some correctly understand that a sound such as a ringing telephone has a source but believe that the sound itself is only present inside their ears, with no appreciation that sound is a wave that travels from one place to another. Others may depict sound as travelling between source and listener but think that the person doing the listening needs to be consciously focusing on the sound before it can be heard. If no listener is present then the sound cannot be heard, and some pupils even believe that if a sound is being made by a person playing a musical instrument then the player cannot hear it unless they actively concentrate on the sound they are producing. This misconception has parallels with a philosophical conundrum: if a lonely tree falls in the forest with no one around does it make a sound? The scientific answer to the riddle is yes, it would still generate a sound wave that travels outwards from the source and is capable of being heard.

The misconception is also analogous to the idea that we have to actively look at something with our eyes in order to see it, as evidenced by ray diagrams that show light travelling *away* from the eye and towards an object being viewed (16.2). This can manifest itself with representations of sound waves being drawn *from* listener to source, and the everyday phrase *listening to* implies that active and conscious human involvement is necessary. Another indication is drawing sound as travelling only from

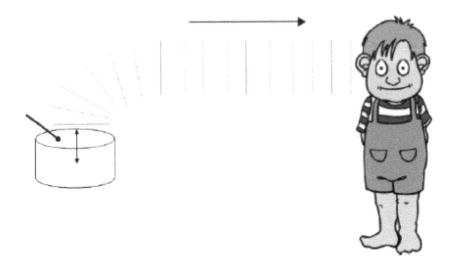

Figure 17.1a Sound travels only to the listener (misconception)

the source directly to the listener and nowhere else (Figure 17.1a); drawn correctly, the wave should be shown as being transmitted in all directions from the source like circular ripples in a pond. Some young children are, however, capable of constructing scientific models of how sound travels (17.1b).

Reconstruction

Elicit the misconception by asking the class to draw a diagram that shows the journey of a sound. Pose the question that if everybody leaves the room will a ticking clock still be making a sound (or a ringing mobile telephone, or any other continuous sound that can be generated)? Test the idea by tape-recording the sound with the room vacated.

The misconception that conscious listening is required for a sound to be heard can be challenged by surprising the class with an unheralded noise such as a tinkling bell while they are working quietly. As the bell gets their attention explain that even though no one was 'ready' for the sound they were still able to hear it anyway. Therefore sound will reach them regardless of whether or not they firstly concentrate on the source. Extend their thinking by introducing the concept of sound as a travelling wave by demonstrating echoes in a suitable location on the school premises – flat, tall walls bordered by a large open area are good, and a loud whistle makes a suitably brief, sharp note.

Key Stage 1 children can be led around the school on a 'listening walk'. Back in the classroom they list as many sounds as they can remember, and try to name the source of each sound, then describe the sound itself: whether it was loud, pleasant, high pitched, etc. The story book *Oscar and the Bat* by Geoff Waring provides a good introduction to basic concepts inherent within the topic of sound.

Sources: Linder (1993); Waring (2007); Watt and Russell (1990).

Figure 17.1b Picture drawn by a 7-year-old child explaining how we hear a sound (Watt and Russell, 1990, p29). 'In the playground it gets to you because you listen. Yes it would get to you if you didn't listen because your ears don't stop listening. They're listening all the time even at night. You hear them with your ears.'

17.2 Can sound waves be stopped?

Misconception

Sound cannot pass through obstacles.

Scientific conception

This belief seems to fly in the face of common experiences such as sitting inside a classroom and being able to clearly hear noises from outside in the playground. Pupils can rationalize this by arguing that even if windows and doors are closed, sound is able to seep into the room via tiny unseen gaps. They believe that if they sat in an airtight box then they would be totally insulated from outside sounds.

When a sound wave hits a barrier such as a single glazed window, some of the energy does not penetrate because it is either reflected off its surface or absorbed into the material. However, a significant amount of the wave's energy is able to enter the glass and come out of the other side, entering the room. In fact sound travels quite effectively through solids such as glass and wood, and this is the reason why we are able to hear sounds from outside while in a room with all the windows and doors sealed. Therefore a person placed in a sealed box would still be able to hear sounds from the outside providing the walls of the box were not too thick, e.g. 1 metre of concrete (although tapping directly on thick concrete from the outside would transmit sound through to the interior). 'Soundproofing' a house involves steps that remove energy from sound waves by building barriers that increase their absorption, for instance by placing lead metal or foam into wall cavities, and using double or triple glazing.

A related misconception is that muffling a sound such as a ringing mobile telephone tightly with a pillow makes the sound wave slow down as it travels from the pillow through the air to our ears, which quietens the sound. In this case the speed of transmission through air would actually be the same as its speed without muffling, although the energy of the transmitted wave would be reduced, which is why the sound is quieter. Because sound needs a medium (solid, liquid or gas) to travel in, a sound wave can never pass through a vacuum. Thus, science fiction films that depict loud explosions in space are scientifically erroneous.

Reconstruction

The misconception can be refuted experimentally in a number of different ways. An easy method is to find a box such as a Tupperware container, proving to the class that it is airtight by holding it submerged in a bowl of water. Put aside the bowl and water and place a mobile telephone inside the Tupperware container, seal it, then make it ring. This can be developed into an investigation where layers are added to the outside in order to discover the muffling properties of different materials. Sound intensity is preferably measured using dataloggers or similar electronic devices that give quantitative values.

Other ways to demonstrate that sound is able to travel quite readily through solid materials include the use of tin can and string telephones, or scratching on a desk while holding your ear flat against its surface. If your school has metal railings, tapping them with a hammer will produce sound waves inside the railings that travel surprising distances which can be measured by having pupils placed at different points away from the source of the tapping. Link this to anecdotes of people who have been lost in the desert sending out Morse code messages by banging on a metal pipeline. A similar experiment can be carried out inside the school using heating pipes (take care when hot), mimicking a method of communication supposedly used by occupants of prison cells. Further anecdotal examples include North American Indians listening for approaching horses by putting their ears to the ground, and the Western outlaw Jesse James using metal rail tracks to listen for an approaching train, both of which show that sound tends to travel further through solid material than through the air.

Sources: Asoko *et al.* (1991); Eshach and Schwartz (2006).

17.3 What is a sound wave?

Misconception

High sounds are loud, while low sounds are quiet.

Scientific conception

When a sound is described in a scientific context as being high or low then this usually refers to its **pitch**. For instance, a high-pitched sound is made by a tinkling glass and a low-pitched sound by a bass drum. Pupils can confuse pitch with loudness, and when a teacher refers to a high sound they may imagine a loud explosion, and think that a low sound is like a quiet whisper. These errors can be compounded by everyday terms such as *speaking in a low voice*. Pitch and loudness are in fact two distinct qualities of sound and are explained later in more detail, but first it must be clarified exactly what is meant by the term 'sound wave'.

Imagine dropping a small pebble into a pond. The water is disturbed as ripples travel outwards creating a series of concentric water waves, and the distance between each ripple is the same. With a sound wave, a different pattern develops and the concentric circles have varying distances between them (Figure 17.3a). Places where the circles have been squeezed together are called *compressions* (C) and places where the circles have been pushed apart are *rarefactions* (R). A series of compressions and rarefactions make a **longitudinal wave**.

Figure 17.3b shows how individual air particles behave in a sound wave after a tambourine skin (T) is struck. Before striking, the air particles are at rest and let us assume they are equidistant (i). When the tambourine is given a single tap, the skin bends slightly outwards causing air particles close to it to be compressed together (ii).

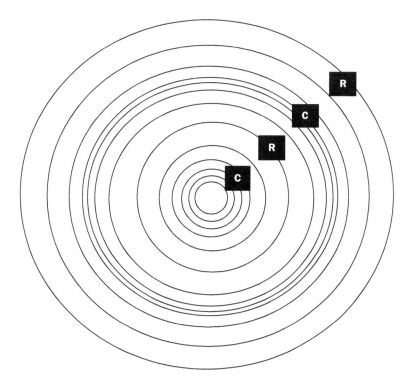

Figure 17.3a Sound waves travelling away from a central source

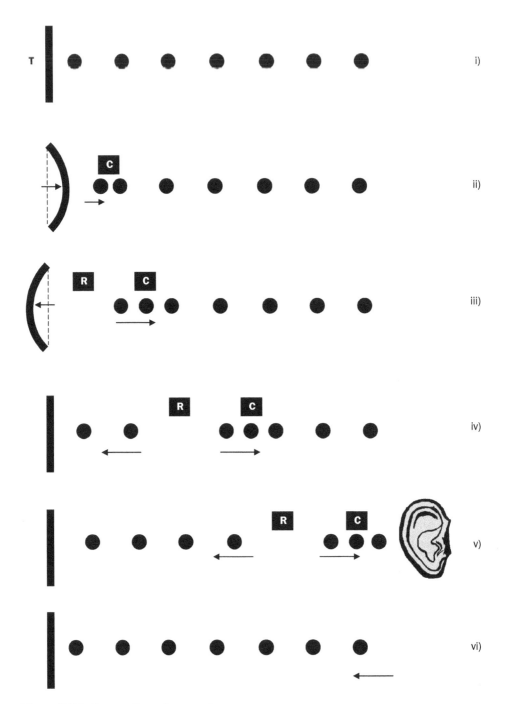

Figure 17.3b Propagation of a sound wave

As in a line of falling dominoes, these compressed particles cause the next particles in line to also be compressed (iii). As the particles close to the tambourine return to their original position, a gap appears causing an area of rarefaction (iii) and (iv). The compression and rarefaction continue to be passed down the line of air particles as a 'wave of sound' until they come into contact with a human ear (v). Within the ear is a thin flap of skin, the eardrum, which reacts to the compression and rarefaction by expanding inwards and outwards. This vibration is passed on via tiny bones and fluid-filled tubes, eventually being converted to electrical signals that are sent to the brain, and the listener becomes conscious that a sound has been made. After the wave has been passed along, or **propagated**, the air particles return to their original position (vi). For simplicity, this model shows a single vibration being propagated while in reality a sound wave consists of several vibrations travelling simultaneously with hundreds, thousands or millions of compressions and rarefactions being present at any one time, dependent on the distance travelled by the sound wave and its **frequency** (see later).

With water ripples it is easy to think the water moves horizontally outwards across the surface away from the source. However, if you watch a floating object, as the ripples pass the object will merely bob up and down and it does not move horizontally in the direction of the water wave. This is because individual water particles do not travel outwards – instead they vibrate around a central position. As can be seen from the previous series of diagrams (Figure 17.3b) a similar situation exists with air particles when a sound wave is propagated. The particles do not travel very far away from their original position and return back to this position as soon as the sound wave has passed. Some learners on the other hand incorrectly believe that a sound wave is like a rush of wind, with air moving *en masse* away from the source. The maximum distance that a particle moves away from its original position represents the **amplitude** of the wave, while the distance between successive compressions (or rarefactions) is the **wavelength** (Figure 17.3c).

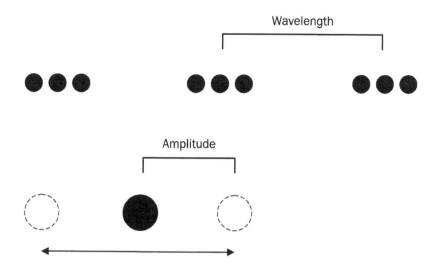

Figure 17.3c Wavelength and amplitude

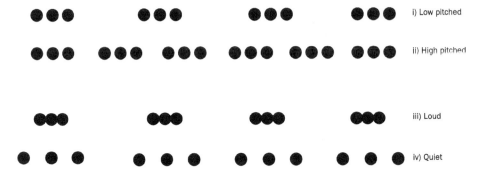

Figure 17.3d Pitch and loudness

Figure 17.3d attempts to show in a simple way how particles behave to produce sounds of differing pitch and loudness. If the compressions and rarefactions are spread wide, the wavelength is large (i) and the sound will be low pitched (e.g. a clap of thunder). With a high-pitched sound (e.g. a soprano voice) compressions and rarefactions are closer, and wavelength is less (ii). With a loud sound (e.g. pneumatic drill) individual particles move relatively long distances away from their rest positions so have large amplitudes (iii), and with a quiet sound (e.g. falling leaf) they hardly move at all, having small amplitudes (iv). Note that with 17.3d (iii) and (iv), the wavelength is not altered so the sound will be of the same pitch; only the loudness is different. As a sound wave moves away from its source it becomes gradually quieter so the amplitude of the wave is constantly decreasing as it travels. To summarize, sounds have different pitches because they have different wavelengths, and sounds have differing loudness because they have different amplitudes.

Finally, for completeness sake it is important to mention one other quality of a wave. If an observer were to count the number of compressions (or rarefactions) passing a given point in one second, then this is the wave's *frequency* (measured in hertz, or Hz). High-pitched sounds have high frequencies, while low-pitched have low frequencies. Frequency can also be described as the number of vibrations made by a source in one second. So with the tambourine in Figure 17.3a if the skin vibrates 100 times per second then its frequency would be 100 Hz. The frequency of a source would equate to the frequency of any sound wave it produces, therefore the frequency of the sound wave in Figure 17.3a would also be 100 Hz. Sounds are nearly always described in relation to their frequencies and not their wavelengths.

Related misconceptions include the belief that a sound wave is made from its own material and travels between air particles, and a sound wave exerts a force on the air that it travels through, pushing air apart to make a pathway.

Reconstruction

The idea that high sounds are loud and low sounds are quiet can be addressed by encouraging pupils to use correct scientific terminology – exclusively refer to high or low when discussing pitch, not loudness. Teaching the difficult idea of longitudinal waves is beyond the primary curriculum, although bright upper KS2 classes would be capable of understanding a simplified model. Traditionally, teachers demonstrate the longitudinal waves made by a slinky spring when the coil is outstretched across a long desk or the floor, and a quick flick of the hand sends waves through the coil that travel slowly enough to be easily observed. If necessary, the waves can be filmed using a video camera and played back in slow motion. Animations of longitudinal waves can be sourced from the internet.

An interesting everyday example of the phenomenon can be experienced when driving along a busy motorway, and has been called the phantom traffic jam. One can be travelling at normal cruising speed then suddenly have to slow down or stop because there is a queue of slow-moving traffic ahead. Shortly afterwards, the queue mysteriously dissipates and traffic moves freely again. When viewed from an aerial camera, a longitudinal wave is seen to pass along the line of traffic as one car at the front brakes excessively, which causes the person behind to also brake, and so on down the chain of cars. There are videos available on internet websites such as YouTube that show the phenomenon in action.

Other aspects of sound waves can be demonstrated, for instance testing the range of frequencies that children are able to hear. Humans typically only hear sounds within the range of 20 Hz to 20 000 Hz, and the ability to hear the higher frequencies diminishes with age. There are free, easy-to-locate online programmes available for download for this fun experiment.

Key Stage 1 children can make sounds of different pitch by having a series of plastic bottles each having a different level of water inside. Blowing across the mouth of the bottles produces a whistling noise, and the class could co-operate by becoming an orchestra and play simple tunes such as *Frère Jacques*.

Sources: Linder (1993); Linder and Erickson (1989); Watt and Russell (1990); Whittaker (2012).

Notes

1. This model is a simplification since in reality air particles would not be stationary. Particles would be darting around at great speed in random directions – the diagrams instead depict the 'average position' of particles. Note, however, that this random kinetic motion of air particles is not a sound wave. For clarity the model only illustrates the behaviour of a single line of air particles instead of a more realistic state of masses of particles propagating sound waves in all directions, as in Figure 17.3a.

2. Although water waves are a useful analogy, they are transverse waves and not longitudinal waves and the particles behave differently, e.g. they move up and down at right angles to the direction of the wave, instead of side to side.

18

Earth and space

18.1 Flat Earth

Misconception

The Earth is flat.

Scientific conception

There are several variants of the flat Earth misconception. A selection of five is presented here in a hierarchy that starts with the simplest conception of a flat Earth and ends with the most 'scientific' (although still a flat Earth misconception).

1   *We live on a flat body whose sides and bottom spread infinitely.* This simple model of the Earth is based on everyday perceptions that tell us that the surface of the Earth is flat, that is to say it exists only along a single horizontal plane (Figure 18.1a). With this construction there is no end to the Earth below our feet, **laterally** (sideways), or above our heads vertically until it meets the sky. A corresponding misconception is that space starts at the Earth's surface and extends infinitely above our heads, upwards and outwards.

2   *We live on a flat body whose bottom spreads infinitely.* Pupils who have heard that the Earth is round may think of it as a cylinder, so creating a hybrid between a flat Earth and a more scientific construction (Figure 18.1b). The surface of the Earth is flat although the sides do not extend infinitely as in model 1; instead

Figure 18.1a Infinite Earth (misconception)

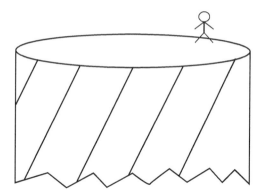

Figure 18.1b Earth as an infinite cylinder (misconception)

there are boundaries. The bottom of the Earth is either infinite or connected like a pedestal to a fixed point a great distance below the surface. The Earth is not a discrete object that exists in a disconnected state. It would be possible to walk/ sail off the edge of the Earth.

3   *We live on a flat disc.* Figure 18.1c shows the Earth as a flat, round, discrete object that is separate from the rest of space (its bottom has limits). This is a variant of the idea that heavenly bodies such as the Earth, sun and moon exist only as flat, two-dimensional objects. Depictions of planets and stars in textbooks are two dimensional, and some pupils may not automatically make the imaginative leap to thinking about them as being three-dimensional spheres. In popular fiction Terry Pratchett's *Discworld* is a mixture of models 2 and 3, although it is not known to what extent reading Pratchett's books contributes to the construction or reinforcement of children's flat Earth misconceptions.

4   *Earth is a sphere and we live inside it.* Learners accept that the Earth is three dimensional and spherical, although all life and space exists within the sphere itself, and we live on an internal flat area (Figure 18.1d). This essentially preserves the flat Earth concept and is consistent with the idea that where the Earth ends at the horizon, the heavens (i.e. space) begin (as with model 1); the idea that the heavens were transposed onto the inside of a rounded surface reflects how the sky actually appears to an observer, as a huge dome, and was accepted as fact in some ancient cultures.

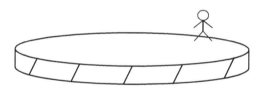

Figure 18.1c Earth as a flat disc (misconception)

Figure 18.1d Spherical Earth housing all of space (misconception)

5 *Earth is a sphere although there is a flat part where we live.* This is a compromise where learners accept that the Earth is spherical but remain essentially flat-Earthers (Figure 18.1e). In the minds of these learners this construction fully explains how photographs and video clips from space can show a spherical Earth, because we either live on the flat opposite side to that which is being photographed, or the flat bits are too small to be picked up

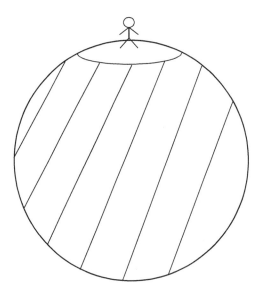

Figure 18.1e Spherical Earth with flattened localizations (misconception)

on the picture. Another variant where the scientific concept has been accepted although warped to a degree is the view that the planet Earth is spherical and exists out there in space, while where we live is a flat plane, unrelated to that planet.

These misconceptions are examples of how some ideas in science are counterintuitive in the sense that our immediate, everyday perceptions clearly tell us that the Earth's surface consists of terrain that extends flatly on a horizontal plane. Because of scale and perspective, we cannot easily appreciate the Earth's actual spherical shape by standing on its surface. That said, the Ancient Greeks were able to conclude that the Earth is a sphere and even made a reasonably accurate estimation as to its circumference. Despite this early work, the idea that the Earth was flat persisted through the centuries in several cultures and even as recently as the seventeenth century Chinese sailors 'knew' that they had to be careful when in certain waters otherwise they would fall off the edge into oblivion (model 3).

Contemporary views of educated people are aligned with the scientific, spherical Earth model, although a tiny minority, such as the members of Flat Earth Society, still argue for the opposite case.

Reconstruction

Ask the members of the class to show you where we live on a three-dimensional **globe map** of the Earth, as younger pupils may be aware of a globe map but have not yet

Figure 18.1f The Blue Marble (photographed by the crew of *Apollo 17*, December 1972)

Figure 18.1g A ship travelling towards the observer crosses the horizon

made the connection that it represents the planet we inhabit. The use of video images that show the Earth as three dimensional and spherical can reinforce the scientific view. For instance, clips from modern science fiction films or TV series offer outstanding **CGI** effects that render planets and other heavenly bodies as three-dimensional objects. Following a journey that involves the characters landing on a planet from space may show that the journey ends on the planet's surface and not its interior (as with model 4).

It might be difficult to challenge pupils who accept that the Earth is a sphere but the little localized area immediate to them is the exception, being flat. Classic stories of sailors who spotted approaching ships by first observing their masts over the horizon before the hull appeared, would help pupils appreciate that the whole Earth's surface is curved, including 'our bit' (Figure 18.1g).

Sources: Arnold *et al.* (1995); Jones *et al.* (1987); Nussbaum (1985); Nussbaum and Novak (1976); Vosniadou and Brewer (1990).

18.2 What is at the centre of the solar system?

Misconception

The Earth lies at the centre of the solar system, with the sun and the planets orbiting around it.

Scientific conception

Pupils at the primary stage can sometimes believe that the Earth is at the centre of space/the universe and every other heavenly body orbits around it (Figure 18.2a).[1] Sources of this misconception include the apparent motion of the sun across the sky, which gives the impression that the sun is circling the Earth once a day (18.3).

Supported by these observations of the sun's daily motion and by religious dogma, the **geocentric** (Earth-centred) model (Figure 18.2a) was widely acknowledged until the sixteenth century when the Polish astronomer Nicolaus Copernicus proposed a **heliocentric** (sun-centred) alternative with the sun at the centre of the solar system, which is accepted today as the correct scientific view. Figure 18.2b shows an eighteenth-century Icelandic manuscript of a geocentric model, with the Earth at the centre being orbited by (listed outwards from the middle): the moon, Mercury, Venus, the sun, Mars, Jupiter and Saturn.

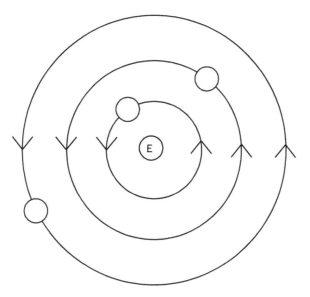

Figure 18.2a Classic geocentric model of the solar system, showing three orbiting bodies (misconception)

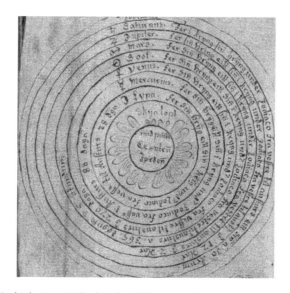

Figure 18.2b Historical geocentric drawing (misconception)

The modern heliocentric view has the sun at the centre of the solar system being orbited by the eight planets, their moons, and other smaller bodies such as comets, asteroids and **dwarf planets** (Figure 18.2c).

There are other non-scientific models of the solar system based on both geocentric and heliocentric beliefs. The heliocentric model shown in Figure 18.2d assumes

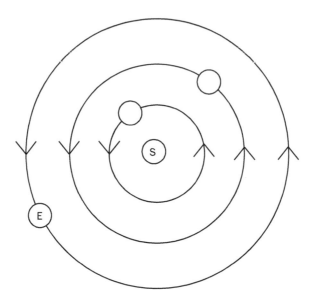

Figure 18.2c Modern heliocentric model of the solar system (only three orbiting bodies shown, including Earth)

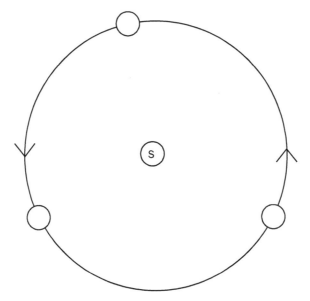

Figure 18.2d Planets have a shared orbit (misconception)

that all the planets are found at around the same distance from the sun and share the same orbit path. In fact, the outermost planet, Neptune, is 75 times further away from the sun than the closest planet, Mercury.

Figure 18.2e shows a variant of the previous misconception, only the Earth and moon are seen as special entities that deserve their own shared orbit, independent of

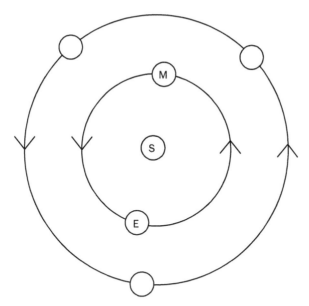

Figure 18.2e Heliocentric model with Earth and moon having dedicated orbit (misconception)

the other planets. This variant may appear in conjunction with the misconception shown in Figure 18.3e.

The converse of the previous misconception has also been identified, instead being based on a geocentric model (Figure 18.2f).

Famous scientists

A dangerous idea. In the time of Copernicus the belief that the Earth was not at the centre of the universe was contrary to religious dogma that was ruthlessly enforced by the Catholic Church and her agents. His heliocentric theory was published shortly before he was to die, supposedly so he could avoid the attentions of the Inquisition. Galileo was an outspoken advocate of heliocentrism and helped Copernicus's ideas survive his death. As a result, Galileo was vigorously pursued by the Church and eventually charged with heresy. Contemporary accounts report that he was lucky to escape execution, being sentenced instead to house arrest lasting a life term.

Reconstruction

An effective way to teach that the sun and not the Earth is at the centre of the solar system is through familiarization using diagrams and/or video images of space sourced from internet websites such as YouTube. With this particular misconception a good strategy would be to elicit from pupils any non-scientific ideas at the beginning

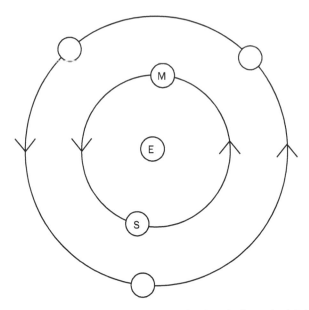

Figure 18.2f Geocentric model with sun and moon having dedicated orbit (misconception)

or midway through a space topic and then challenge them directly using engaging video imagery such as used in the context of a journey across the solar system that will help pupils construct a scientific heliocentric model. Typically, role play is used as an adjunct with pupils pretending to be planets, the sun, earth, the moon, comets, etc., and moving around in a manner in accordance with heliocentrism.

Sources: Parker and Heywood (1998); Sharp (1996); Taylor, *et al.* (2003).

18.3 Why does day become night?

Misconception

The sun moves around the Earth; this is why day and night occur.

[At night the sun] changes into a moon. (Pupil, aged 9 years; Osborne *et al.*, 1993, p37)

Scientific conception

Commonly as part of an Earth and Space topic, the class will fix an upright stick into the ground then record the position and length of the stick's shadow over the course of a day. Using these data it can be concluded that the sun appears to move slowly

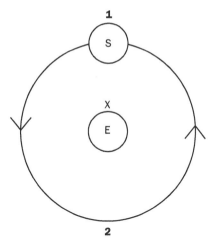

Figure 18.3a The geocentric model (misconception)

across the sky from east to west (in the northern hemisphere). In order to explain this apparent motion some pupils will deduce that the sun completes one circuit (orbit) of the Earth once every 24 hours (Figure 18.3a). If a person stood at X on Earth and the sun was at location 1 then it would be daytime for that person; 12 hours later when the sun reaches location 2 it would be night-time for that person because the Earth is directly blocking any incoming sunlight. During this time the Earth is stationary, remaining fixed in position, and does not spin.

Although this geocentric model might make perfect sense to pupils, it is scientifically incorrect. The sun lies at the centre of the solar system, and the planets, Earth included, orbit around this central point (18.2). However, the phenomena of day and night cannot be explained by the heliocentric model alone; instead they occur due to the fact that the Earth is spinning on its axis.

Figures 18.3b and 18.3c represent a correct heliocentric model where the Earth follows a roughly circular orbit around the sun, making one complete circuit every 12 months (365¼ days); at the same time, the Earth spins on its axis once every 24 hours. The sun is only able to illuminate half of the Earth at any one time, with the other half being in darkness, shown shaded on the diagrams. In Figure 18.3b it would be daytime for someone at position X because they are standing on the illuminated half of the Earth. Twelve hours later the Earth has spun half way around and for the person at X it would be night (Figure 18.3c). Note that although 12 hours have passed the Earth has not moved along its orbit path any noticeable amount – the Earth is indeed orbiting the sun, but day and night occur only due to the fact the Earth is spinning on its axis. Pupils are often confused by the fact the Earth both orbits and spins simultaneously, being two completely separate motions that occur independently of each other, and will incorrectly say things like *day and night are caused by the Earth orbiting the sun*. They may also confuse the times taken for each motion, and will declare that *the Earth orbits the sun every 24 hours*.

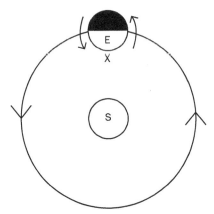

Figure 18.3b Daytime at X

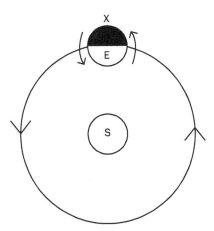

Figure 18.3c Night-time at X

There have been a number of related misconceptions that have been noted concerning the causes of day and night.

1   *Night comes because the moon blocks sunlight.* Although this is based on a correct heliocentric model, the moon does not have an orbit path around the sun that is separate from the Earth's orbit (18.6). This misconception is related to the belief that the moon only appears in the sky at night (18.8).

2   *Clouds are responsible for day and night.* Some pupils believe that when the sun disappears at night it is hiding behind clouds. During the day the moon cannot be seen because it too is now hiding behind clouds.

3   *The sun and moon swap places to cause day and night.* This geocentric model represents another attempt to explain why the sun comes out during the day and the moon during the night (but see 18.8). One source of this confusion might be

the analogue wristwatches that show a tiny sun rising at daytime and a tiny moon rising at night. A variant of this misconception is the idea that although the sun and moon are in positions as depicted by Figure 18.3e, they do not orbit the Earth and instead remain fixed in place, with day and night occurring instead due to the Earth's rotation. This is an interesting blend of correct (Earth spins) and incorrect (geocentric) science (see also Figure 18.2d).

Reconstruction

In the primary classroom the scientific view of the cause of day and night can be taught by demonstration using a globe of the Earth and a light source in a darkened room. Quite a strong source (e.g. an overhead projector or a slide projector) is required in order to obtain a clear distinction between light and shade on the globe. An interactive whiteboard projector that is fixed in position would not be suitable because of reflections from the whiteboard itself. If the light source is kept static and the globe placed a couple of metres away fully within its beam, then the globe should be half illuminated and half in shadow. If a small sticker or some Blu-Tack is then placed where the UK is located and the globe then spun on its axis, this will correctly show why we experience alternating daytime and night-time, and also how the sun appears to move across the sky from east to west from the perspective of an observer on Earth. Remember to spin the globe in an anticlockwise direction as you look down onto the North Pole.

There are variations of this approach that use role play, with pupils taking the part of the sun and the spinning Earth. Several of the misconceptions discussed in this

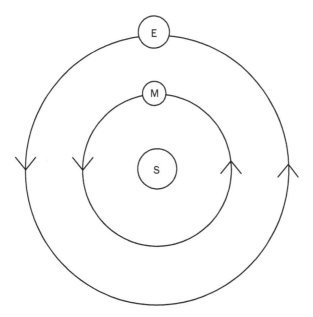

Figure 18.3d The moon blocks the sun (misconception)

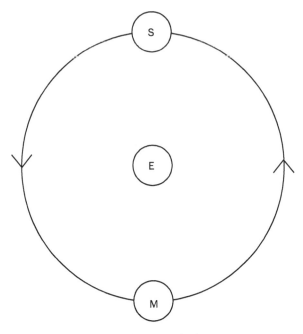

Figure 18.3e Alternate sun and moon (misconception)

section are associated with the idea that the moon only comes out at night, so correction of this represents a good starting point (18.8).

Sources: Baxter (1989); Osborne *et al.* (1993); Parker and Heywood (1998); Sharp (1996).

18.4 How does the sun rise and set?

Misconception

The sun simply rises upwards in the morning then sets downwards at night.

Scientific conception

Some pupils believe that the sun rises vertically above the horizon in the morning, stays in exactly the same position in the sky during the day, and then sets in a vertical direction below the horizon at night at the same spot from which it rose that morning. This simplified notion of sunrise and sunset fails to take into account how the sun is seen to move across the sky. During the course of a sunny day if one were to record the position of the sun in the sky every couple of hours then an arc-like motion would be observed (Figure 18.4d).

The sun rises from the east then sets towards the west. In the northern hemisphere the sun is seen to move from left to right across the sky while in the southern

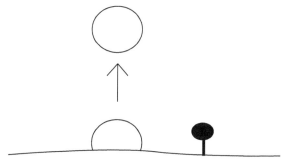

Figure 18.4a Sunrise (misconception)

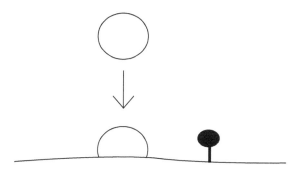

Figure 18.4b Sunset (misconception)

hemisphere the reverse is true. At midday the sun will be at the highest point in its arc, and it is commonly believed that at this time the sun is directly overhead. However, this is only the case if the observer is situated at more equatorial regions between the Tropics of Cancer and Capricorn on the day of the **summer solstice**. In the UK the sun is never seen directly overhead – even in high summer it reaches an angle of only around 60°. Note that diagrams such as Figure 18.4c may reinforce the misconception that the sun is directly overhead at midday.

The sun only *appears* to describe an arc across the sky; the Earth's rotation is responsible for giving this false impression and the sun is actually stationary with respect to the Earth (18.3). This misconception can exist merged with the idea that when the sun sets, the moon is seen to rise in the same place in the sky in a similar vertical fashion, replacing it, so is a variant of the misconception shown by Figure 18.3e.

Be safe!

Staring directly at the sun. Warn children that if they stare directly at the sun, even for very short periods or when wearing dark sunglasses, there is a high probability of permanent retinal damage. The possibility of eye injury increases greatly if the sun is observed directly through a telescope, binoculars or any other optical instrument.

Figure 18.4c Child's drawing showing the position of the sun at morning (a), midday (b) and afternoon (c) (misconception) (Osborne et al., 1993, p43)

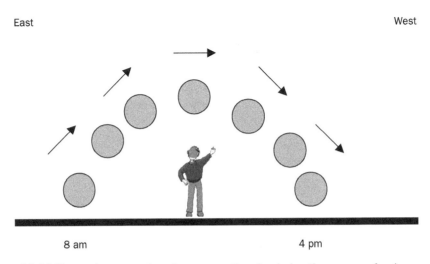

East   West

8 am   4 pm

Figure 18.4d The sun's apparent motion across the sky during the course of a day

Reconstruction

Daily records of a stick's shadow as described in 18.3 will make it plain to pupils that the sun does not remain static in the sky during the course of the day; instead it describes an arc. A quicker way to show this is to ask pupils on a sunny day to go outside and draw chalk marks around the shadows made by the edges of buildings, fence posts, and other fixed features. Returning to the chalk marks 20 minutes later will reveal that the shadows have moved, and these observations can be linked to the sun's apparent motion. Inside the classroom the teacher can demonstrate using a torch as the sun and a vertical rod that when the sun moves in an arc from left to right, the rod's shadow moves in accordance, and also becomes shorter at midday and longer in the mornings and evenings when the sun has just risen or is about to set.

Another idea is to sit a pupil in a swivel chair (the spinning Earth) and have a volunteer stand stationary a couple of metres away shining a torch beam (the sun) in the chair's general direction. As the chair is slowly spun anticlockwise, the stationary torch will appear to move across the pupil's field of vision from left to right, which is similar in one way to how an observer on Earth sees the sun appearing to move across the sky during daylight hours. The traditional mantra *the sun rises in the east and sets in the west* is useful to encourage the understanding that the sun does not simply rise and set in the same place.

Sources: Schoon and Boone (1998); Sharp (1996).

18.5 How big are the Earth, sun and moon?

Misconception

The Earth, sun and moon are of a similar size.

Scientific conception

As part of an Earth and Space topic pupils need to know the relative sizes of these three heavenly bodies. Textbooks commonly portray the solar system as the eight planets, the sun, and occasionally other objects such as comets, asteroids and dwarf planets. Because of the vast distances between these objects in real space, diagrammatic representations of the solar system in books (including this one) are never drawn to scale and for ease of presentation are compressed onto either one page or a double-page spread. Similarly, in reality there are huge differences between the comparative sizes of heavenly bodies, so also for convenience textbooks sometimes depict them as all being of a similar size. For many pupils this could be one origin of the misconception.

That said, many textbooks use a more realistic scale and show the sun as being much larger than other bodies in the solar system (as in Figure 18.5a), although the planets and moons may remain incorrectly portrayed as being of similar sizes. Pupils

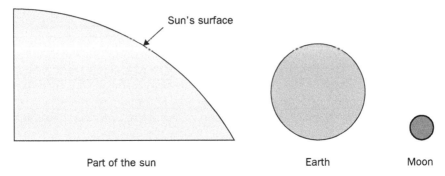

Part of the sun   Earth   Moon

Figure 18.5a Comparative sizes of the Earth and moon, drawn approximately to scale, with segment of the sun at 5% of scale

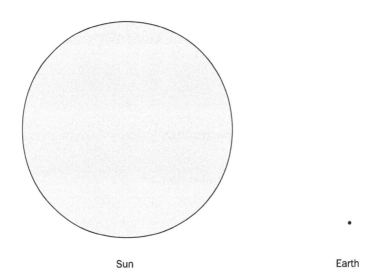

Sun   Earth

Figure 18.5b Comparative sizes of the Earth and sun, drawn approximately to scale

therefore may correctly conclude that the sun is very large, though incorrectly think that the Earth and moon have comparable diameters.

The moon's diameter is just over a quarter of that of the Earth's (Figure 18.5a); the sun's diameter is about 109 times that of the Earth's (Figure 18.5b). So on a comparative scale, misconceiving pupils tend to believe that the moon is bigger than it actually is, and/or that the sun is smaller than it actually is.

Reconstruction

Use three-dimensional models to show comparative sizes. The difference between the sizes of the Earth and the moon can be shown approximately to scale by using a full-size soccer ball and a tennis ball, respectively. On a much larger scale the difference between the sun, the Earth and the moon can be approximated by using a basketball, a peppercorn and a handwritten full stop on a piece of paper, respectively.

Sources: Bryce and Blown (2012); Sadler (1987).

18.6 The moon's orbit

> **Misconception**
>
> *The moon orbits around the Earth.*

Scientific conception

Although the statement by itself could be interpreted as being correct, Figure 18.6a shows that the pupil has constructed a different meaning from that implied by the scientific view. In this case an error in semantics regarding the word *around* has led to the construction of a non-scientific model, with the moon circling the sun around the outside of the Earth's orbit.

Figure 18.6b shows the correct arrangement, with the Earth orbiting the sun while the moon simultaneously orbits the Earth. The moon orbits the Earth approximately once every 28 days – the Ancient Romans observed and recorded the moon's phases in order to measure the passage of time and divided the year into 12 parts, or *months* (both *moon* and *month* have the same etymology). Note that it is correct to state

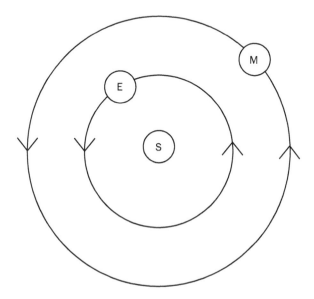

Figure 18.6a The moon has its own dedicated orbit around the sun (misconception)

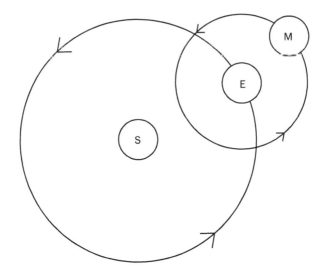

Figure 18.6b The scientific view

that the moon is going around the sun, but incorrect if you say that it is *orbiting* the sun (at primary school level, at least).

Reconstruction

Since this misconception represents a non-scientific model of the solar system it could be corrected in similar ways to those discussed in 18.2, e.g. role play with one pupil being the Earth and circling the sun, while another plays the moon and circles the Earth. While teaching it is best to avoid expressions along the lines of *the moon orbits/ goes around the sun*; it is preferable to say *the moon orbits the Earth and the Earth orbits the sun.*

Source: Sharp (1996).

18.7 What causes the moon's phases?

> **Misconception**
> *The Earth's shadow is responsible for the different phases of the moon.*

Scientific conception

Over the course of consecutive days and nights the illuminated part of the moon changes shape (Figure 18.7a); these shapes are the phases of the moon. It is commonly believed that part of the moon lies in darkness because the Earth casts its own shadow

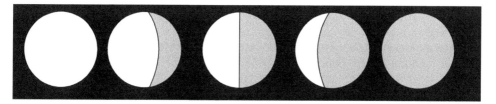

Figure 18.7a Phases of the moon: full, gibbous, half, crescent, new

Figure 18.7b Illuminated sphere

onto the surface of the moon. This makes perfect sense if one considers the relative positions of the Earth, sun and moon in space – the sun acts as a light source, and the Earth and moon lie on approximately the same horizontal plane so one would expect them to regularly cast shadows on each other (Figure 18.11a).

However, for reasons discussed later in 18.11, it is a relatively rare occurrence for the moon to be in the Earth's shadow (and vice versa), these events being called lunar **eclipses**. The dark portion on the moon that is visible with the different phases is not due to another heavenly body such as the Earth casting its shadow; it is merely a consequence of the particular way that any sphere is illuminated.

Figure 18.7b shows how a strong light source directed towards a white sphere in a darkened room illuminates the nearest hemisphere. Because light travels in straight lines the torch beam is unable to 'go around the corner' and reach the far hemisphere, which is in darkness. This is precisely what happens when the moon is lit by the sun in space. The shadows associated with the phases of the moon are therefore not a consequence of being in the shade of the Earth; in fact, the moon is in its own shadow.

The moon makes one complete orbit of the Earth approximately every 28 days, as shown on the inner circle of Figure 18.7c. The representations of the moon within this inner circle depict how the moon would be lit up in space by the sun at different stages throughout its journey, presuming the position of the sun is as indicated at the top of the diagram. The outer images on Figure 18.7c show how the moon would look as viewed from Earth at each stage. Thus, since a full moon is observed on day 14, it will have gradually become completely enveloped in shadow to form a new moon by day 28. The intermediate stages are gibbous moon (days 17–18), half moon (days 19–23), and crescent moon (days 24–27). At day 28 the process starts again with the new moon becoming gradually more illuminated as the days pass, going through the crescent, half and gibbous stages and finally becoming a full moon again by day 14. Although diagrams of this type are frequently used when teaching the moon's phases, pupils

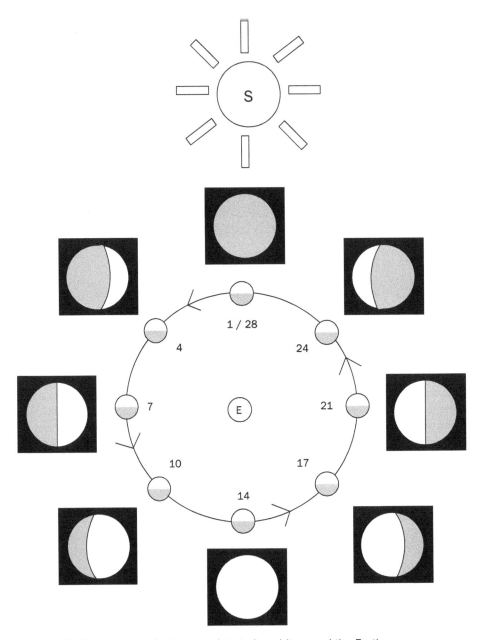

Figure 18.7c How the moon's phases relate to its orbit around the Earth

often have difficulties in interpreting them. This is particularly because they have to locate themselves on the diagram on Earth looking across at a specific moon from the inner circle, then imagine how that moon would appear to them in reality, and draw the appropriate phase (outer images).

Note that the new moon is sometimes depicted in textbooks as a very thin sliver of a crescent and not totally in shadow, since the origin of the phrase lies in the naming the first bit of light that appears after being totally in darkness as 'new', or reborn. The half moon is sometimes called either last or first quarter, phrases which should be avoided in the primary classroom because of the potential confusion with the gibbous or crescent phases.

The misconception can be linked to the incorrect assumption that there will be a lunar/solar eclipse every 28 days, so the Earth cannot avoid casting a shadow on the moon (18.11). Other reasons given by pupils to account for the moon's phases include passing clouds, the Earth turning on its axis during the night so we look at the moon from a slightly different angle (associated with the misconception that the moon passes through all of its phases during the course of a single night), and as the moon gets further away from the sun, less light reaches it so there is more shadow.

Reconstruction

It is a good idea to start by demonstrating how a sphere is illuminated in a darkened room. A white hockey ball makes a good moon, and a strong light source must be used such as a powerful torch, overhead projector or slide projector. It helps if the beam is made as narrow as possible so as to cut down on reflected light, which helps to make a clear boundary between illumination and darkness on the sphere. This can be extended to demonstrating how different phases can be seen according to the angle at which the viewer looks at the ball (as depicted in Figure 18.7c), and then related to the moon's orbit around the Earth.

Diagrams such as Figure 18.7c can be confusing if used alone and so are commonly utilized in combination with a class practical activity. A ping pong ball that has been painted half black makes a fair representation of an illuminated moon. Confusion can be minimized if you ask the pupil to imagine that their head represents the Earth with the 'moon' held at eye level, and a fixed point in the room such as the teacher's desk is chosen to be the sun. Pupils then move the moon around their heads in a circle, noting the different proportions of light and darkness at different stages of the journey; these can then be directly correlated with the moon's phases. Pupils can have difficulties keeping the moon at its correct orientation as it moves around their heads, i.e. with the white half constantly pointing towards the part of the room nominated as the sun.

To support the learning associated with this practical task a traditional activity is to ask pupils to record at home how the phases of the moon change over the course of several nights. This is one reason why space topics have traditionally been taught during the winter months, when the sun sets before children have to go to bed. As an alternative the moon can be observed during daylight hours but the phases are more difficult to see as clearly.

Sources: Baxter (1989); Sharp (1996).

18.8 Can the moon be seen during both daytime and night-time?

Misconception

The moon only appears at night.

Scientific conception

This misconception can have a variety of origins as discussed in 18.3 and 18.4, including favouring an incorrect geocentric model of the solar system. The root of the misconception may be less sophisticated, lying in childhood experiences of picture books that naturally associate the moon with night-time. For instance, 'the man in the moon' is commonly depicted as a character who is ready to go to sleep (wearing a nightcap, carrying a candle), and the nursery rhyme *Hey diddle diddle* is illustrated as a night scene.

> Hey diddle diddle,
> The cat and the fiddle,
> The cow jumped over the moon . . .

The moon rises and sets in the same way as the sun and for the same reason – the Earth rotates on its axis once every 24 hours (18.3). Since the moon orbits the Earth approximately every 28 days, its relative direction from Earth changes significantly every day. This means that on a particular date if the moon is seen to rise during the night-time, 14 days later it will be rising during the daytime. Thus, in Figure 18.8, with the positions shown in the top diagram the moon will be visible only during the daytime, and in the bottom diagram it will be seen exclusively during night-time.[2] Note that there will be times in between when the moon appears both during day and night

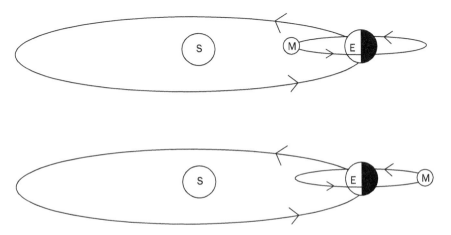

Figure 18.8 Relative positions of the Earth, sun and moon over a 14-day period

over a 24-hour period. Also note that over the 14 days as represented by the two diagrams at the scale depicted, the Earth will have only moved comparatively slightly in its orbit around the sun.

Reconstruction

Show a child's picture book that includes a typical cartoon 'man in the moon' character who has come out at night and then ask pupils *would he ever make an appearance during the day?* If the weather outside is clear and it is the correct time in the month, take the class outside and show that the moon can indeed be visible during daylight hours. A bright class might be capable of grasping the underlying principle as depicted in Figure 18.8.

Source: Sharp (1996).

18.9 What causes the seasons?

> **Misconception**
>
> *It is hotter in summer because the Earth is closer to the sun.*

Scientific conception

The idea that the distance between the Earth and the sun is responsible for seasonal change is common. Figure 18.9a shows that at different times of year the Earth–sun

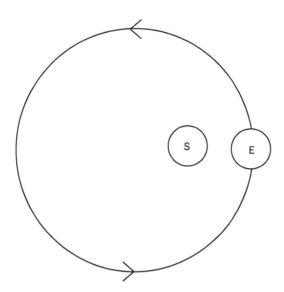

Figure 18.9a When the Earth is close to the sun it is summer (misconception)

distance indeed does differ because the sun is not exactly at the centre of the approximate circle described by the Earth's orbit path (greatly exaggerated in the figure). It makes sense that during the period that the Earth is closest to the sun it receives more heat and therefore this time must be summer, and conversely when the Earth is furthest away it must be winter. However, the actual reasons for the changing seasons are more complex.

The Earth's axis is an imaginary line running through the geographical North and South Poles. It is widely known that the Earth, like all planets, spins on this axis in the same manner that one is able to spin a globe map of the Earth. However, the Earth does not spin 'straight' in space with its axis at right angles to the plane of its orbit around the sun; instead, the Earth is tilted over on its axis at an angle of 23.5°, as can be commonly seen with globe maps. This tilt is evident in Figure 18.9b but has been exaggerated for clarity.

Referring to Figure 18.9b, in December the Earth's northern hemisphere is facing more away from the sun when compared with the southern hemisphere – we say that *the northern hemisphere is tilted away from the sun.* For this reason it is winter for northern hemisphere countries in December, including the UK. Six months later in June the opposite situation applies, with the northern hemisphere tilted towards the sun, making it summer in the UK. Australia on the other hand, being a southern hemisphere country, experiences summer in December and winter in June, because

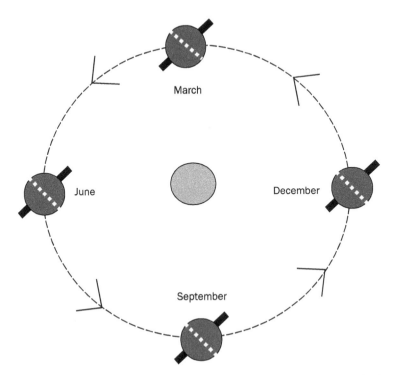

Figure 18.9b Seasonal change and the Earth's tilted axis. (The central circle is the sun and the outer circles represent the Earth at different times of the year.)

the southern hemisphere is tilted towards and away from the sun respectively at these times of the year.

In March the northern hemisphere is half way between being tilted towards and away from the sun, and correspondingly the weather features associated with spring in the UK are intermediate between those of summer and winter. The same can be said for September (autumn).

But why should having the hemisphere where you live tilted towards the sun create hotter weather? Perhaps surprisingly, this is nothing to do with the fact that because of the tilt the northern hemisphere is slightly closer to the sun. The real reason is due to differences of sunlight intensity. Figure 18.9c shows how parallel light from the sun travels through space and hits the Earth. Looking more closely at the surface of the Earth at points A and B (Figures 18.9d and 18.9e), the angle of the Earth's

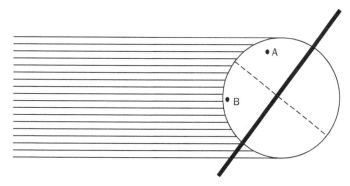

Figure 18.9c Sunlight intensity at two different points on the Earth's surface

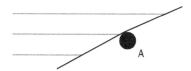

Figure 18.9d Sunlight intensity at point A

Figure 18.9e Sunlight intensity at point B

surface affects the concentration of sunlight hitting each point. The length of the drawn lines representing the Earth's surface at A and B is the same, as is the denseness of the light travelling from the sun (distance between 'beams'), but more beams of sunlight are able to hit at B when compared to A. Since sunlight carries heat energy, the length of Earth's surface at B will be warmer than at A because the sunlight is more concentrated at B, and more spread out at A.

In Figure 18.9c the Earth's northern hemisphere is tilted away from the sun, so as previously discussed it will be winter at point A (December). Conversely, since the southern hemisphere is tilted towards the sun, it will be summer at point B (also December). Nearer the equator there are typically two seasons, wet and dry, because the sunlight intensity does not change enough over the year to cause the temperature variations required for there to be four distinct seasons.

Other misconceptions have been recorded where pupils have attempted to account for the reason why summer temperatures are hotter. These include the sun spending less time behind the clouds, the sun burning hotter during the summer months, changes in plant life triggering seasonal change (instead of vice versa), the cold outer planets having stopped taking heat from the sun, and the angle of the Earth's tilted axis having changed.

To summarize, temperatures are hotter in summer mainly due to differences in the intensity of sunlight hitting the Earth's surface (Figures 18.9c–e). These differences cause seasonal change because the Earth lies on a tilted axis, which makes the northern and southern hemispheres take turns at being tilted towards and away from the sun over the period of a year (Figure 18.9b).

Reconstruction

Understanding the ideas behind seasonal variation is beyond the primary curriculum. However, pupils may still be likely to express ideas reflecting this misconception during an Earth and Space topic and ask questions about the causes of seasons, and attempting to correct it during the primary years would be time well spent. Using the same set-up as described in 18.3, an illuminated globe in a darkened room can be a useful visual tool. Physically carrying the globe around the light source in a circle (i.e. make the Earth orbit the 'sun') but keeping its aspect the same will show exactly how the northern hemisphere alternates between tilting towards and away from the sun over the course of one year – it works best if you can actually make the globe completely orbit the light source (although someone will need to keep readjusting the direction of the light beam). At the same time, you could even delve into the sunlight intensity explanation by positioning an A4 piece of white card on the Earth at different points on the surface. It will be very clear to pupils that when one hemisphere is tilting away from the 'sun' the card looks quite dim because of low light intensity, which causes winter temperatures (Figure 18.9f).

Younger children can be asked to think about the different seasons by cueing them to think about the different things that happen in summer and in winter. For instance how local wildlife varies (especially birds and flowering plants), the clothes they wear, how long they play outside, how dark it gets, and differences in types of weather (snow, rain, wind, sunny, etc).

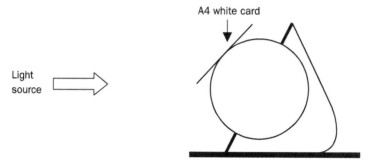

Figure 18.9f Holding an A4 white card at various points on a globe to show differences in light intensity

If the teacher suspects that some pupils believe that summer is caused by the Earth being closer to the sun, they should be informed that the Earth is actually at its closest point to the sun at the beginning of January, which is of course winter time for the UK.

Did you know?

Distance really can make a difference. A caveat must be mentioned at this point. When the Earth becomes closest to the sun in January this actually does have a warming effect on the Earth, but it is very small in comparison with the light intensity effect. It is a point of debate whether this fact should be shared with the children, as although it is scientifically acceptable it may act as a source of confusion and subsequently trigger a reversion back to the full-blown misconception that the Earth–sun distance causes seasonal change.

Sources: Baxter (1989); Parker and Heywood (1998); Sharp (1996).

18.10 Seasonal changes in daylight hours

Misconception

We have longer days in summer because the sun moves more slowly across the sky.

Scientific conception

This statement is incorrect because the apparent speed of the sun across the sky depends on how fast the Earth rotates (18.3). Since the Earth spins at a constant rate the sun travels across the sky at the same speed all year round.

Days are longer in summer and shorter in winter because the times that the sun rises and sets are constantly changing from day to day. The day which experiences the most daylight hours of the year falls at the time of the summer solstice, which is around 21 June in the northern hemisphere; the day that experiences the least is at the **winter solstice**, around 21 December. In the UK, during the period from 21 June until 21 December, days become shorter because from one day to the next the sun rises about 2 minutes later and sets about 2 minutes earlier, so around 4 minutes of daylight are lost with every passing day. Conversely, during the period from 21 December until 21 June, the sun rises earlier and sets later, so around 4 minutes of daylight are gained per day. Thus during the winter months days are shorter because the sun rises late and sets early, and in summer the long days are due to early sunrises and late sunsets (Figures 18.10a and 18.10b).

As well as differences in daylight hours, it can be noted from Figures 18.10a and 18.10b that in winter the sun's daily path describes an arc that is lower in the sky than

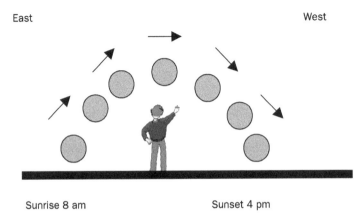

Figure 18.10a The sun's apparent motion during winter

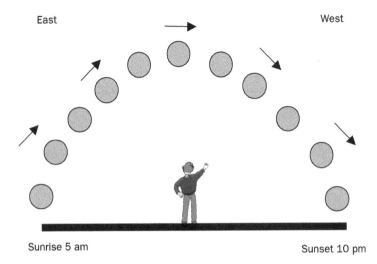

Figure 18.10b The sun's apparent motion during summer

during the summer. This is why during winter mornings when we are driving to school our visibility is sometimes hampered by extreme glare from the low sun.

Reconstruction

Using the same technique as described in 18.9 (an illuminated globe in a darkened room), the teacher can demonstrate the amount of time the UK spends in daylight by slowly spinning the globe and observing when the UK is illuminated, and when it is in darkness. This can be done for winter, with the northern hemisphere tilted away from the light source, and for summer, with it tilted towards the source. Using this method it should be clear to observers that the amount of daylight time experienced in summer outweighs that received in winter.

Anecdotal evidence elicited from pupils that supports seasonal variations in daylight hours could include doing an early morning paper round, walking home from school at different times of the year, and being allowed to play out later during the summer months.

If there is a competent photographer in the school ask them to take a long exposure shot of the sun during a fine day. Discourage pupils from doing this because of the danger of permanent eye damage as a result of looking directly at the sun.

Source: Sharp (1996).

18.11 How often do solar eclipses occur?

Misconception

There is a total solar eclipse every 28 days.

Scientific conception

For learners to be able to construct this misconception an understanding of the causality of solar eclipses is first required. The Earth, sun and moon lie roughly in the same hori-zontal plane in space; in fact the shape of the solar system as far out as Neptune resem-bles a round, flattish plate. Brighter pupils particularly might deduce from this fact that since the moon orbits the Earth every 28 days, it prevents sunlight from hitting the Earth when the three heavenly bodies become aligned as in Figure 18.11a. As the moon blocks sunlight from falling on the Earth this would be seen as a total solar eclipse during daylight hours, with areas of the Earth falling into darkness regularly every 28 days.

Records show, however, that solar eclipses are rare occurrences – there are between two and five per year, and total solar eclipses occur on average only once every 18 months. The reason for this apparent shortage of eclipses is that the orbits of sun/Earth and Earth/moon are not exactly aligned in the same plane, but differ slightly by 5°. Figure 18.11b shows this difference greatly exaggerated for effect. The Earth is the ball orbiting the sun, and for clarity the moon is not depicted although its orbit is the dotted oval that surrounds the Earth.

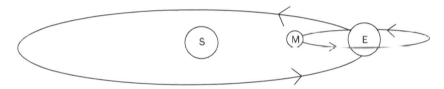

Figure 18.11a The sun, Earth and moon lie in exactly the same plane (misconception)

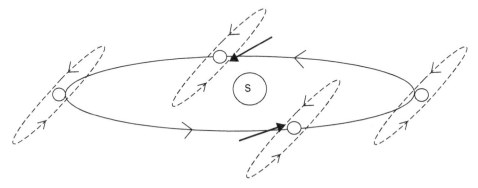

Figure 18.11b The Earth's orbit around the sun and the moon's orbit around the Earth are in slightly different planes. When the moon is in either of the positions indicated by the arrows it may stop some light from the sun falling onto Earth, casting a shadow on Earth and causing a solar eclipse

As the Earth orbits the sun, the plane of the moon's orbit stays in a constant relative orientation, i.e. keeps facing the same way (towards the left of the page in Figure 18.11b). Because of this, the only time the moon can block light from the Earth is theoretically twice a year if the moon happens to be at the precise locations, 6 months apart, as indicated by the arrows. There are further astronomical factors that influence when an eclipse can occur but are beyond the scope of this book, although Figure 18.11b makes it apparent, albeit in a limited way, why the moon cannot block light from the sun every 28 days.

Reconstruction

If this misconception crops up in class it is unlikely that any child-friendly explanation will be adequate without the use of three-dimensional physical props with which to model the two orbits under consideration. These can vary from simply using a dinner plate held at an angle circling a central 'sun', to more sophisticated constructions involving coat-hanger wire twisted into a circle with a ball (Earth) held in the middle.

If the class are not yet aware of the phenomenon of solar eclipses then the probability is that this misconception will not manifest itself.

Source: Zeilik *et al.* (1998).

18.12 How many planets are there in the solar system?

Misconception

Pluto is a planet.

Scientific conception

Since the 1930s astronomers had agreed that there were nine planets in the solar system, with Pluto being the outermost. In the 1990s, objects began to be discovered that lay beyond the orbit of Pluto but were not classified as planets because they were thought to be too small (they were much smaller than Pluto), and were called instead **trans-Neptunian objects** (TNOs). In 2003 the TNO *Sedna* was discovered, which is almost as large as Pluto, and was briefly regarded as being the tenth planet. The subsequent discovery of more TNOs having a similar size to Pluto presented the dilemma of whether or not to call all of these objects 'planets'. In 2006 the TNO *Eris* was discovered, which was actually larger than Pluto, prompting the International Astronomical Union to decide that only the innermost eight bodies were worthy of the name 'planet' because they were spherical and had cleared their surrounding space of debris – i.e. Mercury, Venus, Earth, Mars, Jupiter, Saturn, Uranus and Neptune. Anything else that was not a moon, including TNOs such as Pluto and Eris, were no longer classified as planets and instead were to be called dwarf planets.

Reconstruction

Traditionally pupils have rote-learned the names and order of the planets using mnemonics such as *My Very Eager Mother Just Served Us Nine Pizzas*. It is clear that fresh mnemonics need to be formulated to reflect Pluto's change in classification from full planet to dwarf planet status; perhaps *My Very Eager Mother Just Served Us Nachos*.

It does not help that some secondary sources such as textbooks, library books and videos still cite Pluto as being a planet, and for this reason pupils need to be advised to be on the lookout for these anomalies, and to be given a simple explanation of why Pluto is no longer considered to be a planet.

Source: Broughton *et al.* (2012).

18.13 How do the planets move?

Misconception

The planets and stars are stationary, forming part of the background of the night sky.

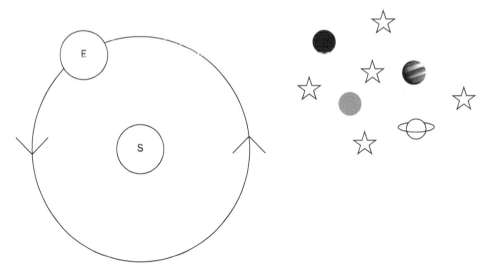

Figure 18.13 The Earth orbits the sun while planets and stars form a motionless backdrop in space (misconception)

Scientific conception

Children usually (and correctly) know that the Earth orbits the sun, while the stars do not. They sometimes incorporate all the other planets into this model, amalgamating them with the stars as stationary heavenly bodies that exist to form a backdrop to the night sky, and do not orbit the sun. In fact, all objects within the solar system are pulled by the sun's gravity and heavenly bodies including planets, asteroids and comets move in regular orbits, travelling around the sun at high speeds. However, the movement of these bodies across the night sky is very slow, though can be observed over a period of weeks and months as they journey through the constellations. The English word *planet* actually derives from the Greek *planēs*, meaning 'wanderer'.

The stars on the other hand exist outside of the solar system and so are not significantly influenced by the sun's gravity, therefore do not orbit the sun. Instead, they appear stationary to an observer on Earth and this is why over many days and weeks, planets can be seen to slowly move across a motionless backdrop of stars. Note that the movement of the planets described here is not the same as the *apparent* movement of the whole night sky due to the Earth's rotation. In the same way that the sun appears to move from east to west during the course of a day because the Earth spins (18.4), at night-time the Earth is still spinning so the night sky appears to moves in the same direction.

Related misconceptions include the belief that no planets can be observed without using a telescope or binoculars, where in fact several planets are very bright at certain times of the year and can be seen with the naked eye.

Reconstruction

Animations and videos sourced from the internet are useful and engaging visual tools for showing that the planets move around the sun, as are commercially available DVDs about the solar system. Together with activities and games used to learn the names of the planets (18.12), have children role play the solar system in a large space such as the playground or hall with individual children taking the roles of heavenly bodies and moving around a central sun. Children will need to be reminded that the model is not to scale, as the distances between planets would in reality be much larger.

During times of the year when planets such as Mars, Venus, Jupiter or Saturn can be seen with the naked eye, upper KS2 children can make weekly drawings at home in a logbook to show the movement of one or more of these planets through the constellations over a period of a couple of months. Websites such as www.skyandtelescope.com give clear information about where planets can currently be seen in the night sky. For instance at the time of writing, Jupiter appears bright and is visible just above the constellation *Taurus*.

Sources: Sharp (1996); Schoon and Boone (1998).

Notes

1. In the diagrams in this chapter, note that: the distances between bodies are not to scale; the sizes of bodies are not to scale, unless otherwise stated; and the orbits of the Earth and moon in reality are roughly circular but in the diagrams are sometimes viewed from a side-on perspective so appear as elongated ovals.
2. This diagram is a simplification and incorrectly implies that the Earth, sun and moon lie in exactly the same plane (see 18.11).

19
Energy

19.1 What is energy?

> **Misconception**
>
> *An Olympic athlete has lots of energy.*

Scientific conception

Like the words *animal, particle* and *light*, energy is one of those scientific terms that have a different meaning in everyday life. If someone 'has energy', they are thought to possess qualities such as liveliness, vitally and endurance. Taking part in a fitness programme will 'give people more energy', and when they become tired they 'run out of energy'. All of these everyday interpretations are quite different from the scientific meaning.

The concept of energy is not taught at primary level due to its complex and abstract nature. Because energy is not a material thing it requires a degree of imagination to conceptualize it, though, as will be discussed, the effects of energy can be readily observed. Although primary practitioners are not required to teach energy its presence is nevertheless implied in several parts of the primary Programme of Study, for example electricity, forces, chemical changes, photosynthesis, nutrition, growth and food chains. Energy is a fundamental cornerstone of all branches of science so it is preferable that teachers have some understanding of its underlying concepts. A traditional starting point is appreciating that there are commonly eight different 'types' of energy (Figure 19.1a).

The next thing to consider is that these different types of energy are not constant – given the right circumstances one type of energy can change into a completely different type of energy. A swimmer standing on a high diving board will have some gravitational potential energy because she is raised above the surface of the Earth. When she steps off the board she begins to travel downwards and so she loses gravitational potential energy, but gains kinetic energy because she is now moving. As she hits the

Type of energy	Example of context	Description
Kinetic	Moving car	All moving objects have kinetic energy; stationary objects do not.
Potential	Hot air balloon	*Gravitational potential energy (GPE).* Any object raised above the Earth's surface will have potential energy – it has the 'potential' to fall back down to Earth. Objects touching the Earth's surface have no potential energy, and when we lift an object up we 'give it' some potential energy.
	Taut bowstring	*Elastic potential energy (EPE).* Contained within systems such as a coiled spring or a stretched elastic band. Upon release, energy is set free and becomes (usually) kinetic energy.
		(GPE and EPE are also called 'stored energy'.)
Chemical	Food	Energy can be released during a chemical change. In a fire the chemical energy contained within wood/oxygen will change into heat energy and light energy.
Heat (thermal)	Hot bath	Heat energy is due to the vibrations and movements of particles such as atoms, molecules and electrons, or the movement of invisible waves (see 19.2).
Nuclear	Nuclear reactors	Energy contained within the nuclei of atoms. When utilized in atomic weapons it transforms into enormous amounts of kinetic, heat, light, sound and electrical energy.
Sound	Whistle	Energy produced by vibrating materials (see 17.3).
Light	Torch	Energy in the form of waves that is visible to the human eye (see 16.1).
Electrical	Mobile phone	Usually, the movement of free electrons through a conductor (see 15.3).

Figure 19.1a The different 'types' of energy

water with a splash the kinetic energy becomes sound and heat energy. Figure 19.1b illustrates a further example of energy changes. This way of thinking about energy is called the *energy transformation* model. The transformation model is the easiest for pupils to understand as it attempts to ground an abstract idea into something more concrete and digestible.

Energy is not just a quality of an object or system, it also can be measured and quantified. All forms of energy are measured in *joules* (J). For example, a 1 kg bag of granulated sugar contains 17 million J of chemical energy. In comparison (and surprisingly) a family car travelling at 70 mph (113 kph) only has 750 000 J of kinetic

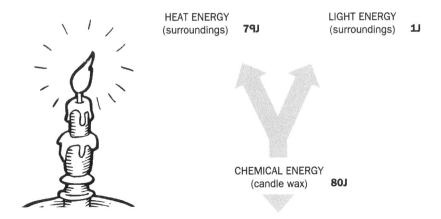

HEAT ENERGY
(surroundings) **79J**

LIGHT ENERGY
(surroundings) **1J**

CHEMICAL ENERGY
(candle wax) **80J**

Figure 19.1b Simple energy transformations in a burning candle

energy. As can be seen from Figure 19.1b, when one type of energy is transformed into other types there are no missing joules – all the different energies add up (79 + 1 = 80). This is the law of energy conservation, or *energy can neither be created nor destroyed*. Also this figure shows that a very small proportion of energy from the candle wax is transformed into useful light energy, the majority being wasted as heat energy; thus the candle is not energy-efficient.

The number of joules tells us the amount of energy that is present at a given time within a system. What is sometimes more useful is how quickly energy is being transformed – this is *power* (measured in watts, W). The power of a system is the number of joules being transformed every second. Therefore if the candle in figure 19.1b is burning 80 J of wax every second, then it is burning with a power of 80 W.

A different way of looking at energy is as something that never changes. Instead, it is moved or transferred from one place to another by a process. Considering Figure 19.1b, energy within the candle is transferred to the surroundings by the process of burning. This is the *energy transference model*, and the main difference between this model and the previously described energy transformation model is that the energy itself does not change. Instead, the energy can be thought of as a kind of unchanging object that is passed along a chain via processes such as heating, sound, moving and so on. It must be remembered, however, that energy is not a material thing.

The energy transformation model is easier for children to understand compared with the energy transference model. That said, there are more complex versions of the energy transformation model; strictly speaking, with the diving swimmer example mentioned earlier the whole *system* of swimmer/Earth gains gravitational potential energy and not just the diver. When pupils reach KS3 they learn a different definition of energy – a system that has energy has the capacity to do work. For instance, in a circuit if electrical energy is present within a motor, the motor can then do work. Conceptualizing this idea is difficult for the average KS3 (and even KS4) pupil.

A related misconception is the belief that *the world is running out of energy*. As sunlight reaches the Earth some of the energy is absorbed but some is also lost to space as heat so there is a constant balance. That said, imbalances are now thought to exist creating global warming so it could be argued that the Earth is in fact *gaining* energy (see 12.7). People who say the world is running out of energy are really referring to non-renewable sources such as fossil fuels, which once burned can no longer make useful forms of energy.

Reconstruction

As stated, energy is not part of the primary Programme of Study, although teachers may wish to touch on simple aspects of energy to stretch bright upper KS2 classes in the course of teaching related topics, such as how light energy from the sun is transformed into chemical energy within a plant during photosynthesis. It is recommended that a very basic transformation model is employed with children using analogies similar to those discussed in this chapter. Try to keep explanations as concrete as possible. Emphasize that energy is different from material things, i.e. solids, liquids and gases.

Simple activities can enable children to learn the different energy 'types' without venturing into transformations. Have a display of household objects such as food, a torch, a cell (battery), a wind-up car, a whistle, a spring-loaded jack-in-the-box and a pocket hand warmer, asking children to try and guess what kinds of energy are associated with each object.

Sources: Boyes and Stanisstreet (1990); Solomon (1982, 1983); Watts and Gilbert (1985).

19.2 The movement of heat

Misconception

Heat always rises.

Scientific conception

In English schools up to age 16 the concept of heat is simplified, being defined as *a type of energy that can be transferred from hotter to cooler places*. It is sometimes called thermal energy. Although some sources advise against this, and it is technically wrong, at this level it is simpler to grasp the concept of heat energy by imagining it to be something inside an object that is capable of moving, for instance along the solid handle of a hot cup of tea (**conduction**, see Figure 19.2b).

The idea that heat always has to rise is commonly held by pupils, and its sources may lie in familiar phenomena such as smoke travelling upwards, rising hot air balloons, and shimmering heat haze during a summer's day. However, in all of these cases it is actually *hot air* that is rising. Differences in density between blocks of air mean colder air will push underneath hotter air, which is analogous to the processes that drive **convection currents** (Figures 19.2a and 19.2b). It is similar to how a block

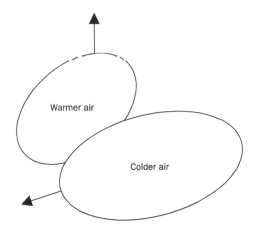

Figure 19.2a Parcels of air at different temperatures have different densities

Figure 19.2b The different ways that heat can move away from a cup of hot tea:
1 Radiation; 2 Convection; 3 Conduction

of wood released under water rises to the surface, being pushed upwards by water that rushes beneath it; water is denser than wood so will continue to undercut it until all of the water is underneath the block, and the wood is floating on the surface (14.3).

Because it moves from hotter to cooler areas, heat can move in any direction, not only upwards. Although the concept of heat energy is not taught at KS2, the fact that hot air rises is, e.g. during the water cycle, and pupils may think it is heat that is rising, not the air.

Another misconception concerning heat that is very common is the belief that if a glass of water that has been left on the side for a few hours to come to room temperature is then wrapped with an insulating material such as bubble wrap, then this causes the water to heat up. If the bubble wrap is also at room temperature then there are no temperature differences within the system, therefore no movement of heat occurs and so the water's temperature will not change. A different misconception is that if a block of ice is placed in the classroom and covered with insulating material then it melts more quickly. In fact the opposite happens because the material insulates the ice from the warmer air temperature of the room so the ice heats up more slowly than if it were unwrapped.

Figure 19.2c Heat snake. Cut out the snake along the thick black line then make a small hole in the head. Thread a length of cotton through the hole and tie above a heat source such as a hot radiator. The snake will whirl in the rising air currents

Reconstruction

At this level it is not necessary to introduce the concept of energy. However, an illustration resembling Figure 10.2b can be used to show that heat as an entity is able to travel in all directions, not merely upwards.

Demonstrations of hot air rising would help pupils visualize the idea that colder air undercuts warmer air, causing it to lift. Examples include 'heat snakes' (Figure 19.2c) and model hot air balloons. Releasing inflated party balloons under water provides a useful analogy of why hot air rises. These ideas can be introduced in tandem with experiments on floating and sinking.

However, these examples might only serve as sources for further confusion unless it is made clear that it is hot air and not technically heat that is rising. At this level it may merely be a case of correcting pupils who say 'heat always rises' by instead stating 'hot air rises'.

The basic ideas underlying heat insulation can be explained to KS1 children by reading the story book *The Emperor's Egg* by Martin Jenkins.

Using ice hands is an engaging way to perform experiments that test the speed of melting at room temperature when they are wrapped in different materials. To make an ice hand, fill a rubber washing-up glove or plastic/rubber disposable glove with tap water, tie off at the wrist with string or a strong elastic band, and place in the freezer.

Sources: Jenkins (2008); Tiberghien and Barboux (1980); Tiberghien *et al.* (1983).

Science glossary

AC See alternating current.

Accelerate Move faster.

Air resistance A type of friction that opposes the movement of an object through the air.

Allotrope Different forms of the same element; e.g. diamond and graphite are allotropes of carbon.

Alloy A mixture of two or more metals.

Alternating current (AC) Electric current that switches its direction of travel around a circuit very rapidly. Most domestic electricity supplies are AC.

Alveoli Air sacs found deep within the interior of the lungs; the site of gaseous exchange.

Amplitude (wave) The maximum distance moved by a vibration within a wave.

Angle of incidence Angle from the normal at which a light ray meets a surface.

Angle of reflection Angle from the normal at which a light ray reflects from a surface.

Antibodies Proteins made by the body that destroy or neutralize invading microbes and other foreign material.

Arterial Refers to blood carried away from the heart and towards other body tissues.

Arthropods Invertebrates with a hard external skeleton and jointed limbs; e.g. insects, spiders and crustaceans.

Atom The smallest 'bit' of an element that can exist.

Battery Several cells connected together.

Boiling A liquid changing into a gas; occurs at or above the material's boiling point (see also evaporation).

Breathing The actions of inhaling and exhaling; ventilates the lungs to allow gaseous exchange.

Capillaries Tiny blood vessels, a single cell thick.

Cartesian diver Device, often home-made, that allows the diving and ascending of an enclosed object subject to external pressure (see internet for further details).

Cell 1. Uses chemical energy to create voltage differences within a circuit, so allowing current to flow. 2. Building block of living things; many contain a nucleus, cell membrane and cytoplasm.

Cellular respiration Glucose and oxygen react together becoming carbon dioxide and water, liberating energy. Takes place within cells.

Centripetal force Inward force on an object describing a curved path acting towards the centre of rotation.

CGI Computer-generated images.

Chemical change A material changes into something completely different, losing its chemical identity; otherwise known as a chemical reaction.

Chlorophyll Green pigment found in plant cells that is important for photosynthesis.

Combustion Burning. A material reacts with oxygen, producing heat and light (flames are not necessarily generated).

Compressed air Air at a pressure greater than atmospheric pressure.

Condensation A gas changing into a liquid.

Conduction The passage of heat or electricity through a (usually solid) material.

Consumer Any non-plant organism within a food chain.

Contact force Force applied when objects are touching.

Convection current The circular movement of a fluid due to changes in density caused by heating and cooling.

CPR Cardiopulmonary resuscitation (heart massage); first aid for a patient with a stopped heart.

Current Electricity that moves around a circuit; measured in amperes or amps (symbol A).

DC See direct current.

Decelerate Slow down.

Density The mass of a material per unit volume.

Dew point The temperature at which water droplets start to condense to form dew.

Diffusion The movement of fluid particles from a higher to a lower concentration.

Digestion The breakdown of foodstuffs into simpler units before absorption.

Direct current (DC) Electricity moving in a single direction through a circuit.

Dispersion (wave) The separation of white light into different colours by using for instance, a prism.

Displacement The volume of liquid pushed aside by an object that is immersed in that liquid.

DNA Deoxyribonucleic acid.

Dormant Alive, though in a resting and inactive state, e.g. seed, bacterial spore, volcano.

Dwarf planet Heavenly body that is of sufficient size to exert enough gravity to become approximately spherical, but has not cleared its neighbouring space, and is not a moon. Smaller than a true planet; e.g. Pluto, Eris.

Eclipse Occurs when one heavenly body moves into the shadow of another.

Electricity (current) A flow of charge.

Electromagnetic radiation Travelling waves that carry energy. Different varieties exist including infra-red waves, radio waves, microwaves and light waves.

Electron Negatively charged subatomic particle.

Element A material that cannot be broken down into anything simpler without losing its chemical identity. The periodic table is a list of all known elements.

Energy The capacity to do work. Can exist in different forms, e.g. heat, light, kinetic, potential.

Enzyme A biological catalyst; allows a chemical reaction to proceed at a faster rate.

Epicentre The location on the Earth's surface immediately above the subterranean origin (focus) of an earthquake.

Epigenetics The study of inheritable changes in gene function that occur without a change in the DNA sequence.

Evaporation A liquid changing into a gas below its boiling point (see also boiling).

Evolution Theory that organisms developed from earlier, different species, usually via the process of natural selection.

Exoskeleton A rigid protective covering found on the outside of the bodies of some invertebrates.

Fault Fracture in rock that can become a point of weakness; earthquakes often originate from fault lines.

Floating Suspended in a fluid.

Flora The entire plant life of an ecosystem.

Fluid A liquid or a gas.

Food A substance that supplies energy to an organism during cellular respiration.

Force A push or a pull; measured in newtons (symbol N).

Fossil fuels Fuels that have been formed naturally from dead organisms, e.g. natural gas, coal, crude oil and its derivatives.

Freezing A liquid changing into a solid.

Frequency (wave) The number of vibrations occurring every second. Measured in hertz (symbol Hz).

Friction A force that opposes the forward motion of an object.

Gametes Reproductive cells; in animals, sperms and ova.

Gaseous exchange Occurs at surfaces where gases are swapped, e.g. lungs, leaf.

Gene The unit of inheritance. Carries information in the form of DNA sequence.

Genotype The genetic make-up of an organism; the entirety of their genes.

Geocentric Earth-centred.

Global warming The gradual rise in atmospheric temperature that has been taking place since the last quarter of the nineteenth century.

Globe map Usually spinnable map of the world superimposed on a sphere.

Glowing splint Thin taper of wood that is set alight then blown out, leaving a glowing ember; often used to test for the presence of oxygen.

Greenhouse gases Gases in the atmosphere that absorb heat and are thought to contribute to global warming, e.g. carbon dioxide, water vapour and methane.

Heat A type of energy that can be transferred from hotter to cooler places.

Heavenly body Natural object existing in space; e.g. star, planet, moon.

Heliocentric Sun-centred.

Homo sapiens The taxonomic name for the human species.

Inertia The resistance of an object to its present state of motion.

Interdependence (ecology) The dependence that organisms in an ecosystem have on each other for survival. For instance, a herbivore is dependent on plant species for food; when the herbivore dies it will decompose and provide nutrients for plants.

Invertebrate An animal without a backbone.

Ion A charged atom.

Irreversible change An alteration to something that cannot be undone.

Key (biological) A table or flowchart that aids the identification of unknown organisms.

KS1 Key Stage 1 (Years 1–2).

KS2 Key Stage 2 (Years 3–6).

KS3 Key Stage 3 (Years 7–9).

KS4 Key Stage 4 (Years 10–11).

Laterally Sideways.

LED Light-emitting diode; small electronic bulb, often coloured.

Longitudinal wave Waves where the vibrations are along the direction of travel, e.g. sound waves.

Macroscopic Visible to the naked eye; the opposite of microscopic.

Magnitude Size.

Mass The amount of matter of which an object is composed. Depends on the number and weight of the particles therein.

Matter Something consisting of particles.

Meaningful erroneous conceptual network Several related misconceptions linked within a learner's mind that make perfect sense because they all seem to fit well together.

Melting A solid becoming a liquid.

Microbe A microscopic organism; sometimes called a micro-organism.

Microscopic Something too small to be seen with the naked eye.

Mineral A naturally occurring 'pure' chemical that has been formed by geological processes.

Molecule Several atoms chemically joined together.

Moon A large, natural object that orbits a planet. The Earth has one moon.

Multicellular Made of more than one cell.

Multimeter A multi-function electrical device that can be used to measure current, voltage, resistance, etc.

Negative terminal The point where electrons exit a cell and enter the circuit; labelled with a minus sign.

Normal Imaginary line emerging at right angles from the point on a surface where, for instance, a light ray reflects.

Orbit The circular or elliptical (oval) path taken when one object in space circles another.

Ovum (plural *ova*) Egg cell; female gamete in animals.

Particle Used in primary science to describe atoms, molecules, ions and sometimes electrons.

Pathogen A microbe that causes a disease.

Pedagogy Method of teaching.

Phases of the moon The different shapes of the illuminated part of the moon as seen from Earth.

Phenotype The outward expression of the genes; e.g. blue eyes.

Photosynthesis Synthesis of food and oxygen from carbon dioxide and water.

Phylum (plural *phyla*) The taxonomic category immediately subordinate to kingdom.

Physical change A change that does not result in an alteration in the identity of a chemical; e.g. state change.

Pitch (sound) How high or low a sound is. Depends on the frequency of the sound wave.

Plane glass A flat, non-curved piece of glass.

Pneumatic Using air under pressure to do work.

Positive terminal The point where electrons enter a cell after leaving the circuit; labelled with a plus sign.

Potential difference The driving 'force' provided by a cell that causes current to move around a circuit.

Predator An animal that hunts another animal for food.

Prey An animal hunted by a predator.

Primary colours (science) Red, green and blue. All other colours can be derived when these basic three colours are mixed in different proportions.

Processes of life Activities that something must be capable of before it can be called 'living'.

Producer A green plant.

Projectile A thrown object that lacks its own propulsion after release.

Propagation (wave) A wave travelling through a material.

Pseudoscience A methodology that might claim to be scientific but is not; e.g. astrology.

Radiation Heat energy transmitted in wave form.

Reaction force Equal and opposite force acting in accordance with Newton's third law of motion.

Relative density The ratio of the density of a substance to the density of water.

Resistor Something within a circuit that resists current flow.

Retina Layer of light-sensitive cells at the back of the eye.

Reversible changes Situations where materials are altered but are able to change back later to their original form.

Rock Any natural material that is a product of geological processes and consists of an aggregate of more than one mineral.

Secondary colours Cyan, magenta and yellow. Are produced when two primary colours are mixed.

Sinking An object descending through a surrounding fluid because it has a greater density than the fluid.

Solar system The sun and all of its orbiting heavenly bodies, e.g. planets, moons, comets, asteroids, dwarf planets.

Spectrum The rainbow-like band observed when white light is dispersed into its constituent colours.

Sperm cell Male gamete in animals.

State change When a material changes from one state of matter to another, e.g. solid to liquid (melting).

State of matter At primary science level, solid, liquid or gas.

Steam Water in the gaseous phase at or above its boiling point (100°C with pure water at normal atmospheric pressure).

Stratosphere The layer of the Earth's atmosphere immediately above the troposphere. Extends upwards to an altitude of approximately 30 miles (50 km) above the Earth's surface.

Subatomic particles Particles that are smaller than atoms and exist within them, e.g. electrons, protons, quarks.

Summer solstice The day of the year when one hemisphere of the Earth is most tilted towards the sun; in the northern hemisphere, around 21 June.

Taxonomy The study of biological classification.

Tectonic plates The theory that the Earth's crust consists of giant plates of rock that are in slow but constant motion.

Terminal velocity The maximum velocity attained by an object freefalling through a fluid.

Thorax The middle part of an animal's body; in humans, the chest.

Top predator A predator that is not hunted by another predator; occupies the top space in a food chain/web.

Transmission (wave) Electromagnetic radiation travelling through a material.

Trans-Neptunian object (TNO) Heavenly body that orbits the sun beyond Neptune, e.g. Pluto.

Trophic level The position occupied by an organism in a food chain, e.g. producer, primary consumer.

Troposphere The lowest layer of the Earth's atmosphere. Extends from the Earth's surface upwards to an altitude of approximately 5 miles (8 km).

Unicellular Organism consisting of only a single cell.

Upthrust Upward force applied to any immersed or partly immersed body in a fluid.

Vacuum The absence of matter; a true empty space.

Venous Refers to blood carried towards the heart and away from other tissues.

Vertebrate An animal with a backbone.

Viscosity The 'thickness' of a liquid; e.g. treacle is very viscous.

Voltage Simply, the driving force that causes current to flow around a circuit. Measured in volts (symbol V).

Volume The physical space occupied by an object.

Water vapour Water in the gaseous phase below the boiling point (100°C for pure water at normal atmospheric pressure).

Wave A ripple of energy away from a source, e.g. sound, light, water, pulse.

Wavelength The distance between the same phase of a wave, e.g. compression to compression, peak to peak. Measured in metres (symbol m).

Weight The gravitational pull exerted by the Earth on an object.

White light Light from sources such as the sun, an electric light bulb or a torch. Appears as colourless but is a mixture of different-coloured light.

Winter solstice The day of the year when a hemisphere of the Earth is most tilted away from the sun; in the northern hemisphere, around 21 December.

Bibliography

Part One: Introduction

Allen, M. (2010) Learner error, affectual stimulation and conceptual change. *Journal of Research in Science Teaching*, 47, 151–173.

Avraamidou, L. and Zembal-Saul, C. (2005) Giving priority to evidence in science teaching: A first-year elementary teacher's specialized practices and knowledge. *Journal of Research in Science Teaching*, 42, 965–986.

Carle, E. (1969) *The Very Hungry Caterpillar*. London: Puffin.

Carter, L. (2008) Sociocultural influences on science education: Innovation for contemporary times. *Science Education*, 92, 165–181.

Ehrlén, K. (2009) Drawings as representations of children's conceptions. *International Journal of Science Education*, 31, 41–57.

Harlen, W. (2009) Enquiry and good science teaching. *Primary Science Review*, 106, 5–8.

Joung, Y. J. (2009) Children's typically-perceived-situations of floating and sinking. *International Journal of Science Education*, 31, 101–127.

Naylor, S., Keogh, B. and Mitchell, G. (2000) *Concept Cartoons in Science Education*. Sandbach: Millgate House.

Oliveira, A. W. and Sadler, T. D. (2008) Interactive patterns and conceptual convergence during student collaborations in science. *Journal of Research in Science Teaching*, 45, 634–658.

Otero, V. K. and Nathan, M. J. (2008) Preservice elementary teachers' views of their students' prior knowledge of science. *Journal of Research in Science Teaching*, 45, 497–523.

Phethean, K. (2009) When are you too old to play in science? *Primary Science Review*, 105, 12–15.

Piaget, J. (1929) *The Child's Conception of the World*. London: Routledge and Kegan Paul.

Posner, G. J., Strike, K. A., Hewson, P. W. and Gertzog, W. A. (1982) Accommodation of a scientific conception: Towards a theory of conceptual change. *Science Education*, 66, 211–227.

Vygotsky, L. S. (1962) *Thought and Language*. Cambridge, MA: MIT Press.

Zembal-Saul, C., Krajcik, J. and Blumenfeld, P. (2002) Elementary student teachers' science content representations. *Journal of Research in Science Teaching*, 39, 443–463.

Part Two: Biology

1 Concept of living

Arnold, B. and Simpson, M. (1979) The concept of living things. *Aberdeen College of Education Biology Newsletter*, 33, 17–21.

Bell, B. F. (1981a) *Animal, Plant, Living: Notes for Teachers*. LISP Working Paper 30, Science Education Research Unit, University of Waikato, Hamilton, New Zealand.

Bell, B. F. (1981b) When is an animal, not an animal? *Journal of Biological Education*, 15, 213–218.

Bell, B. and Barker, M. (1982) Towards a scientific concept of 'animal'. *Journal of Biological Education*, 16, 197–200.

Jewell, N. (2002) What's inside a seed? *Primary Science Review*, 75, 12–14.

Piaget, J. (1929) *The Child's Conception of the World*. London: Routledge and Kegan Paul.

Sere, M. G. (1983) *Premiers pas et premiers obstacles à l'acquisition de la notion de pression*. Working paper, LIRESPT, University of Paris VII, Paris.

Stavy, R. and Wax, N. (1989) Children's conceptions of plants as living things. *Human Development*, 32, 85–94.

Tamir, P., Gal-Chappin, R. and Nussnovitz, R. (1981) How do intermediate and junior high school students conceptualize living and non-living? *Journal of Research in Science Teaching*, 18, 241–248.

2 Classification

Allen, M. and Choudhary A. (2012) *Animal Classification by Early Years Children*. United Kingdom Science Education Research Conference. NSLC, University of York.

Bell, B. F. (1981) What is a plant? Some children's ideas. *New Zealand Science Teacher*, 31, 10–14.

Brass, K. and Jobling, W. (1994) Digging into Science – a unit developed for a Year 5 class. In P. J. Fensham, R. F. Gunstone and R. White (eds), *The Content of Science*, pp. 112–120. London: Falmer Press.

Braund, M. (1998) Trends in children's concepts of vertebrate and invertebrate. *Journal of Biological Education*, 32, 103–110.

Carle, E. (1969) *The Very Hungry Caterpillar*. London: Puffin.

Chen, S. H. and Ku, C. H. (1998) Aboriginal children's alternative conceptions of animals and animal classification. *Proceedings of the National Science Council (Part D)*, 8, 55–67.

Davies, N. (1997) *Big Blue Whale*. London: Walker Books.

Inagaki, K. and Hatano, G. (1987) Young children's spontaneous personification as analogy. *Child Development*, 58, 1013–1021.

Leach, J., Driver, R., Scott, P. and Wood-Robinson, C. (1992) *Progression in Conceptual Understanding of Ecological Concepts by Pupils Aged 5–16*. Centre for Studies in Science and Mathematics Education, University of Leeds, Leeds.

Patrick, P. and Tunnicliffe, S. D. (2011) What plants and animals do early childhood and primary students' name? Where do they see them? *Journal of Science and Educational Technology*, 20, 630–642.

Prokop, P., Prokop, M. and Tunnicliffe, S. D. (2008) Effects of keeping animals as pets on children's concepts of vertebrates and invertebrates. *International Journal of Science Education*, 30, 431–449.

Sequeria, M. and Freitas, M. (1986) 'Death' and 'Decomposition' of living organisms: Children's alternative frameworks. Paper presented at the 11th Conference of the Association for Teacher Education in Europe (ATEE), Toulouse, France, 1–5 September.

Shepardson, D. P. (2002) Bugs, butterflies, and spiders: Children's understandings about insects. *International Journal of Science Education*, 24, 627–643.

Stavy, R. and Wax, N. (1989) Children's conceptions of plants as living things. *Human Development*, 32, 85–94.

Tema, B. O. (1989) Rural and urban African pupils' alternative conceptions of 'animal'. *Journal of Biological Education*, 23, 199–207.

Trowbridge, J. E. and Mintzes, J. J. (1985) Students' alternative conceptions of animal classification. *School Science and Mathematics*, 85, 304–316.

Trowbridge, J. and Mintzes, J. (1988) Alternative conceptions in animal classification: A cross age study. *Journal of Research in Science Teaching*, 25, 547–571.

Waring, G. (2009) *Oscar and the Frog*. London: Walker Books.

Yen, C. F., Yao, T. W. and Mintzes, J. J. (2007) Taiwanese students' alternative conceptions of animal biodiversity. *International Journal of Science Education*, 29, 535–553.

3 Circulation

Bartoszeck, A. B., Machado, D. Z. and Amann-Gainotti, M. (2011) Graphic representation of organs and organ systems: Psychological view and developmental patterns. *Eurasia Journal of Mathematics, Science and Technology Education*, 7, 41–51.

Osborne, J. F., Wadsworth, P. and Black, P. J. (1992) *SPACE Research Report: Processes of Life*. Liverpool: Liverpool University Press.

Schoon, K. and Boone, W. (1998) Self-efficacy and alternative conceptions of science of preservice elementary teachers. *Science Education*, 82, 553–568.

Symons, A., Brass, K. and Odgers, S. (1994) Year 9 bodies. In P. J. Fensham, R. F. Gunstone and R. White (eds), *The Content of Science*, pp. 177–184. London: Falmer Press.

Westbrook, S. L. and Marek, E. A. (1992) A cross-age study of student understanding of the concept of homeostasis. *Journal of Research in Science Teaching*, 29, 51–61.

4 Breathing

Adeniyi, E. O. (1985) Misconceptions of selected ecological concepts held by some Nigerian students. *Journal of Biological Education*, 19, 311–316.

Arnaudin, M. W. and Mintzes, J. J. (1985) Students' alternative conceptions of the human circulatory system: A cross age study. *Science Education*, 69, 721–733.

Garcia-Barros, S., Martínez-Losada, C. and Garrido, M. (2011) What do children aged four to seven know about the digestive system and the respiratory system of the human being and of other animals? *International Journal of Science Education*, 33, 2095–2122.

Gellert, E. (1962) Children's conceptions of the content and functions of the human body. *Genetic Psychology Monographs*, 65, 293–405.

Osborne, J. F., Wadsworth, P. and Black, P. J. (1992) *SPACE Research Report: Processes of life*. Liverpool: Liverpool University Press.

Symons, A., Brass, K. and Odgers, S. (1994) Year 9 bodies. In P. J. Fensham, R. F. Gunstone and R. White (eds), *The Content of Science*, pp. 177–184. London: Falmer Press.

Tracana, R. B., Varanda, I., Viveiros, S., and Carvalho, G. S. D. (2012) Children's conceptions about respiration before and after formal teaching: Identification of learning obstacles. *International Organisation for Science and Technology Education*. Available at http://repositorium.sdum.uminho.pt/handle/1822/20882 [accessed 27 April 2013].

Westbrook, S. L. and Marek, E. A. (1992) A cross-age study of student understanding of the concept of homeostasis. *Journal of Research in Science Teaching*, 29, 51–61.

Yip, D. Y. (1998) Erroneous ideas about the composition of exhaled air. *School Science Review*, 80, 55–62.

5 Nutrition

Barker, M. (1985) *Teaching and Learning about Photosynthesis*. LISP, Working papers 220–9, Science Education Research Unit, University of Waikato: Hamilton, New Zealand.

Bell, B. F. and Brook, A. (1984) *Aspects of secondary students' understanding of plant nutrition*. Children's Learning in Science Project, Centre for Studies in Science and Mathematics Education, University of Leeds, Leeds.

Bjornsdottir, I., Almarsdottir, A. B. and Traulsen, J. M. (2009) The lay public's explicit and implicit definitions of drugs. *Research in Social and Administrative Pharmacy*, 5, 40–50.

Boyes, E. and Stanisstreet, M. (1990) Pupils' ideas concerning energy sources. *International Journal of Science Education*, 12, 513–529.

Brinkman, F. and Boschhuizen, R. (1989) Preinstructional ideas in biology: A survey in relation with different research methods on concepts of health and energy. In M. T. Voorbach and L. G. M. Prick (eds), *Teacher Education 5: Research and Developments on Teacher Education in the Netherlands*, pp. 75–90. London: Taylor and Francis.

Bruce, L. (2000) *Fran's Flower*. London: Bloomsbury Paperbacks.

Cakici, Y. (2005) Exploring Turkish upper primary level pupils' understanding of digestion. *International Journal of Science Education*, 27, 79–100.

Cruikshank, M. (2012) Fags, booze, drugs and children. Argyll: Argyll Publishing.

Dreyfus, A. and Jungwirth, E. (1988) The cell concept of 10th graders: Curricular expectations and reality. *International Journal of Science Education*, 10, 221–229.

Equit, M., Sambach, H., Niemczyk, J. and von Gontard, A. (2013) Children's concepts of the urinary tract. *Journal of Pediatric Urology*, 9, 648–652.

Fraiberg, S. (1959) *The Magic Years*. New York: Scribners.

Käpylä, M. K., Heikkinen, J. P. and Asunta, T. (2009) Influence of content knowledge on pedagogical content knowledge: The case of teaching photosynthesis and plant growth. *International Journal of Science Education*, 31, 1395–1415.

Lucas, A. (1987) Public knowledge of biology. *Journal of Biological Education*, 21, 41–45.

Mintzes, J. J. (1984) Naive theories in biology: Children's concepts of the human body. *School Science and Mathematics*, 84, 548–555.

Osborne, J. F., Wadsworth, P. and Black, P. J. (1992) *SPACE Research Report: Processes of Life*. Liverpool: Liverpool University Press.

Provo, J., Lamar, C. and Newby, T. (2002) Using a cross section to train veterinary students to visualize anatomical structures in three dimensions. *Journal of Research in Science Teaching*, 39, 10–34.

Smith, E. L. and Anderson, C. W. (1984) Plants as producers: a case study of elementary science teaching. *Journal of Research in Science Teaching*, 21, 685–698.

Smith, E. L. and Anderson, C. W. (1986) Alternative student conceptions of matter cycling in ecosystems. Paper presented to National Association of Research in Science Teaching.

Stavy, R., Eisen, Y. and Yaakobi, D. (1987) How Israeli students aged 13–15 understand photosynthesis. Unpublished manuscript, Tel Aviv University: Tel Aviv.

Turner, S. A. (1997) Children's understanding of food and health in primary classrooms. *International Journal of Science Education*, 19, 491–508.

Wandersee, J. H. (1983) Students' misconceptions about photosynthesis: A cross-age study. In H. Helm and J. D. Novak (eds), *Proceedings of the International Seminar: Misconceptions in Science and Mathematics*, 20–22 June, pp. 441–446. Ithaca, NY: Cornell University Press.

6 Feeding relationships

Barenholz, H. and Tamir, P. (1987) The design, implementation and evaluation of a microbiology course with special reference to misconceptions and concept maps. In J. D. Novak (ed.), *Proceedings of the 2nd International Seminar: Misconceptions and Educational Strategies in Science and Mathematics*, 26–29 July, pp. 32–45. Ithaca, NY: Cornell University Press.

Barman, C. R., Griffiths, A. K. and Okebukola, P. (1995) High school students' concepts regarding food chains and food webs: A multinational study. *International Journal of Science Education*, 17, 775–782.

Fradley, C. (2006) Welly-walks for science learning. *Primary Science Review*, 91, 14–17.

Gotwals, A. W. and Songer, N. B. (2010) Reasoning up and down a food chain: Using an assessment framework to investigate students' middle knowledge. *Science Education*, 94, 259–281.

Griffiths, A. K. and Grant, B. A. C. (1985) High school students' understanding of food webs: Identification of a learning hierarchy and related misconceptions. *Journal of Research in Science Teaching*, 22, 421–436.

Leach, J., Driver, R., Scott, P. and Wood-Robinson, C. (1992) *Progression in Conceptual Understanding of Ecological Concepts by Pupils Aged 5–16*. Centre for Studies in Science and Mathematics Education, University of Leeds.

Leach, J., Driver, R., Scott, P. and Wood-Robinson, C. (1996) Children's ideas about ecology 3: Ideas found in children aged 5–16 about the interdependency of organisms. *International Journal of Science Education*, 18, 129–141.

Maxted, M. A. (1984) Pupils' prior beliefs about bacteria and science processes: Their interplay in school science laboratory work. Unpublished MA thesis, University of British Columbia.

Munson B. H. (1994) Ecological misconceptions. *Journal of Environmental Education*, 25, 30–34.

Schollum, B. (1983) Arrows in science diagrams: Help or hindrance for pupils? *Research in Science Education*, 13, 45–49.

Shepardson, D. P., Wee, B., Priddy, M. and Harbor, J. (2007) Students' mental models of the environment. *Journal of Research in Science Teaching*, 44, 327–348.

7 Microbes and disease

Barenholz, H. and Tamir, P. (1987) The design, implementation and evaluation of a microbiology course with special reference to misconceptions and concept maps. In J. D. Novak (ed.), *Proceedings of the 2nd International Seminar: Misconceptions and Educational Strategies in Science and Mathematics*, 26–29 July, pp. 32–45. Ithaca, NY: Cornell University Press.

Byrne, J. (2011) Models of micro-organisms: Children's knowledge and understanding of micro-organisms from 7 to 14 years old. *International Journal of Science Education*, 33, 1927–1961.

Byrne, J. and Sharp, J. (2006) Children's ideas about micro-organisms. *School Science Review*, 88, 71–79.

Collins, R. (2005) *Germs*. London: Bloomsbury Paperbacks.

Dreyfus, A. and Jungwirth, E. (1988) The cell concept of 10th graders: Curricular expectations and reality. *International Journal of Science Education*, 10, 221–229.

Dreyfus, A. and Jungwirth, E. (1989) The pupil and the living cell: A taxonomy of dysfunctional ideas about an abstract idea. *Journal of Biological Education*, 23, 49–55.

Dymond, H. (2008) Picturing the world of microorganisms. *Primary Science Review*, 103, 25–28.

Keselman, A., Kaufman, D. R., Kramer, S. and Patel, V. L. (2007) Fostering conceptual change and critical reasoning about HIV and AIDS. *Journal of Research in Science Teaching*, 44, 844–863.

Leach, J., Driver, R., Scott, P. and Wood-Robinson, C. (1992) *Progression in Conceptual Understanding of Ecological Concepts by Pupils Aged 5–16*. Centre for Studies in Science and Mathematics Education, University of Leeds.

Maxted, M. A. (1984) Pupils' prior beliefs about bacteria and science processes: Their interplay in school science laboratory work. Unpublished MA thesis, University of British Columbia.

Nagy, M. H. (1953) The representation of germs by children. *Journal of Genetic Psychology*, 83, 227–240.

Natapoff, J. N. (1978) Children's views of health. *American Journal of Public Health*, 68, 995.

Prout, A. (1985) Science, health and everyday knowledge. *European Journal of Science Education*, 7, 399–406.

Santos, S. and Bizzo, N. (2005) From 'new genetics' to everyday knowledge: Ideas about how genetic diseases are transmitted in two large Brazilian families. *Science Education*, 89, 564–576.

Sequeria, M. and Freitas, M. (1987) Children's alternative conceptions about 'mold' and 'copper oxide'. In J. D. Novak (ed.), *Proceedings of the 2nd International Seminar: Misconceptions and Educational Strategies in Science and Mathematics*, 26–29 July, pp. 413–423. Ithaca, NY: Cornell University Press.

Smith, E. L. and Anderson, C. W. (1986) Alternative student conceptions of matter cycling in ecosystems. Paper presented to National Association of Research in Science Teaching.

8 Heredity and variation

Adeniyi, E. O. (1985) Misconceptions of selected ecological concepts held by some Nigerian students. *Journal of Biological Education*, 19, 311–16.

Biro, V. (2004) *Gumdrop and the Dinosaur*. Worksop: Award Publications.

Bishop, B. A. and Anderson, C. W. (1990) Student conceptions of natural selection and its role in evolution. *Journal of Research in Science Teaching*, 27, 415–427.

Deadman, J. A. and Kelly, P. J. (1978) What do secondary school boys understand about evolution and heredity before they are taught the topics? *Journal of Biological Education*, 12, 7–15.

Deniz, H., Donnelly, L. A. and Yilmaz, I. (2008) Exploring the factors related to acceptance of evolutionary theory among Turkish preservice biology teachers: Toward a more informative conceptual ecology for biological evolution. *Journal of Research in Science Teaching*, 45, 420–443.

Engel-Clough, E. and Wood-Robinson, C. (1985) Children's understanding of inheritance. *Journal of Biological Education*, 19, 304–310.

Hackling, M. W. and Treagust, D. F. (1982) What lower secondary students should understand about the mechanisms of inheritance, and what they do understand following instruction. *Research in Science Education*, 12, 78–88.

Hooper, M. (1996) *Dinosaur*. Cambridge: Cambridge University Press.

Jensen, M. and Finley, F. (1995) Teaching evolution using historical arguments in a conceptual change strategy. *Science Education*, 79, 147–166.

Kargbo, D. B., Hobbs, E. D. and Erickson, G. L. (1980) Student beliefs about inherited characteristics. *Journal of Biological Education*, 14, 137–146.

Meikle, W. E. and Scott, E. C. (2010) Why are there still monkeys? *Evolution: Education and Outreach*, 3, 573–575.

Nehm, R. H. and Schonfeld, I. S. (2008) Measuring knowledge of natural selection: A comparison of the CINS, an open-response instrument, and an oral interview. *Journal of Research in Science Teaching*, 45, 1131–1160.

Nicholson, C. (2009) The teaching of evolution in primary schools. *Primary Science Review*, 107, 13–15.

Taylor, N. and Jones, P. (2001) Animal adaptation through modelling. *Primary Science Review*, 66, 17–19.

Tsui, C. Y. and Treagust, D. F. (2007) Understanding genetics: Analysis of secondary students' conceptual status. *Journal of Research in Science Teaching*, 44, 205–235.

Part Three: Chemistry

9 Chemical changes in materials

Ahtee, M. and Varjola, I. (1998) Students' understanding of chemical reaction. *International Journal of Science Education*, 20, 305–316.

Bouma, H., Brandt, I. and Sutton, C. (1990) *Words as Tools in Science Lessons*. Chemiedidactiek, University of Amsterdam.

Çalik, M. and Ayas, A. (2005) A comparison of level of understanding of eighth-grade students and science student teachers related to selected chemistry concepts. *Journal of Research in Science Teaching*, 42, 638–667.

DES (1984) *Science in Schools. Age 15: Report No. 2*. Assessment of Performance Unit. London: HMSO.

Driver, R. (1985) Beyond appearances: The conservation of matter under physical and chemical transformations. In R. Driver, E. Guesne and A. Tiberghien (eds), *Children's Ideas in Science*, pp. 145–169. Milton Keynes: Open University Press.

Hand, B. M. and Treagust, D. F. (1988) Application of a conceptual conflict teaching strategy to enhance student learning of acids and bases. *Research in Science Education*, 18, 53–63.

Knox, J. (1985) A study of secondary students' ideas about the process of burning. MEd thesis, University of Leeds.

Meheut, M., Saltiel, E. and Tiberghien, A. (1985) Pupils' (11–12-year-olds) conceptions of combustion. *European Journal of Science Education*, 7, 83–93.

Papageorgiou, G., Grammaticopoulou, M. and Johnson. P. M. (2010) Should we teach primary pupils about chemical change? *International Journal of Science Education*, 32, 1647–1664.

Schoon, K. and Boone, W. (1998) Self-efficacy and alternative conceptions of science of preservice elementary teachers. *Science Education*, 82, 553–568.

Watson, J., Prieto, T. and Dillon, J. (1997) Consistency of students' explanations about combustion. *Science Education*, 81, 425–444.

10 Particles

Bouma, H., Brandt, I. and Sutton, C. (1990) *Words as Tools in Science Lessons*. Chemiedidactiek, University of Amsterdam.

Brook, A., Briggs, H. and Driver, R. (1984) *Aspects of Secondary Students' Understanding of the Particulate Nature of Matter*. Children's Learning in Science Project. Centre for Studies in Science and Mathematics Education, University of Leeds.

Gómez, E. J., Benarroch, A. and Marín, N. (2006) Evaluation of the degree of coherence found in students' conceptions concerning the particulate nature of matter. *Journal of Research in Science Teaching*, 43, 577–598.

Lee, K. W. L. and Tan, S. N. (2004) Atoms and molecules: Do they have a place in primary science? *Primary Science Review*, 82, 21–23.

Liu, X. and Lesniak, K. (2006) Progression in children's understanding of the matter concept from elementary to high school. *Journal of Research in Science Teaching*, 43, 320–347.

Nakhleh, M. B., Samarapungavan, A. and Saglam, Y. (2005) Middle school students' beliefs about matter. *Journal of Research in Science Teaching*, 42, 581–612.

Novick, S. and Nussbaum, J. (1978) Junior high school pupils' understanding of the particulate nature of matter: An interview study. *Science Education*, 62, 273–281.

Nussbaum, J. (1985) The particulate nature of matter in the gaseous state. In R. Driver, E. Guesne and A. Tiberghien (eds), *Children's Ideas in Science*, pp. 124–144. Milton Keynes: Open University Press.

Papageorgiou, G., Stamovlasis, D. and Johnson, P. M. (2010) Primary teachers' particle ideas and explanations of physical phenomena: Effect of an in-service training course. *International Journal of Science Education*, 32, 629–652.

Piaget, J. and Inhelder, B. (1974) *The Child's Construction of Quantities*. London: Routledge and Kegan Paul.

Renstrom, L., Andersson, B. and Marton, F. (1990) Students' conceptions of matter. *Journal of Education Psychology*, 82, 555–569.

Sere, M. G. (1985) The gaseous state. In R. Driver, E. Guesne and A. Tiberghien (eds), *Children's Ideas in Science*, pp. 105–123. Milton Keynes: Open University Press.

Skamp, K. (2005) Teaching about 'stuff'. *Primary Science Review*, 89, 20–22.

Stains, M. and Talanquer, V. (2007) Classification of chemical substances using particulate representations of matter: An analysis of student thinking. *International Journal of Science Education*, 29, 643–661.

11 States of matter

Ahtee, M. and Varjola, I. (1998) Students' understanding of chemical reaction. *International Journal of Science Education*, 20, 305–316.

Bar, V. (1986) *The Development of The Conception of Evaporation*. The Amos de Shalit Science Teaching Centre, The Hebrew University of Jerusalem.

Bar, V. and Galili, I. (1994) Stages of children's views about evaporation. *International Journal of Science Education*, 16, 157–174.

Brook, A. and Driver, R. (in collaboration with Hind, D.) (1989) *Progression in Science: The Development of Pupils' Understanding of Physical Characteristics of Air Across the Age Range 5–16 Years.* Centre for Studies in Science and Mathematics Education, University of Leeds.

Dove, J. (1998) Alternative conceptions about the weather. *School Science Review*, 79, 65–69.

Frankel-Hauser, J. (1998) *Science Play.* Nashville, TN: Ideal Publications.

Galili, I. and Bar, V. (1997) Children's operational knowledge about weight. *International Journal of Science Education*, 19, 317–340.

Goodwin, A. (2003) Evaporation and boiling: Trainee science teachers' understanding. *School Science Review*, 84, 131–141.

Jones, B. L. and Lynch, P. P. (1989) Children's understanding of the notions of solid and liquid in relation to some common substances. *International Journal of Science Education*, 11, 417–427.

Leite, L., Mendoza, J. and Borsese, A. (2007) Teachers' and prospective teachers' explanations of liquid-state phenomena: A comparative study involving three European countries. *Journal of Research in Science Teaching*, 44, 349–374.

Osborne, R. J. and Cosgrove, M. M. (1983) Children's conceptions of the changes of state of water. *Journal of Research in Science Teaching*, 20, 825–838.

Oversby, J. (2004) Science knowledge: Representing liquids. *Primary Science Review*, 83, 27.

Ross, K. and Law, E. (2003) Children's naive ideas about melting and freezing. *School Science Review*, 85, 99–102.

Russell, T. and Watt, D. (1990) *SPACE Research Report: Evaporation and Condensation.* Liverpool: Liverpool University Press.

Russell, T., Longden, K. and McQuigan, L. (1991) *SPACE Research Report: Materials.* Liverpool: Liverpool University Press

Stavy, R. (1994) States of matter: Pedagogical sequence and teaching strategies based on cognitive research. In P. J. Fensham, R. F. Gunstone and R. White (eds), *The Content of Science*, pp. 221–236. London: Falmer Press.

Stavy, R. and Stachel, D. (1984) *Children's Ideas about Solid and Liquid.* Israeli Science Teaching Centre, School of Education, Tel Aviv University.

12 Earth science

Boyes, E. and Stanisstreet, M. (1993) The 'greenhouse effect': Children's perceptions of causes, consequences and cures. *International Journal of Science Education*, 15, 531–552.

Boyes, E., Stanisstreet, M. and Papantoniou, V. S. (1999) The ideas of Greek high school students about the 'ozone layer'. *Science Education*, 83, 724–737.

Brass, K. and Duke, M. (1994) Primary Science in an integrated curriculum. In P. J. Fensham, R. F. Gunstone and R. White (eds), *The Content of Science*, pp. 100–111. London: Falmer Press.

Ford, D. J. (2005) The challenges of observing geologically: Third graders' descriptions of rock and mineral properties. *Science Education*, 89, 276–295.

Francis, C., Boyes, E., Qualter, A. and Stanisstreet, M. (1993) Ideas of elementary students about reducing the 'greenhouse effect'. *Science Education*, 77, 375–392.

Frankel-Hauser, J. (1998) *Science Play.* Nashville, TN: Ideal Publications.

Happs, J. C. (1985a) *Mountains.* LISP Working Paper 202, Science Education Research Unit University of Waikato: Hamilton, New Zealand.

Happs, J. C. (1985b) Regression in learning outcomes: Some examples from Earth sciences. *European Journal of Science Education*, 7, 431–443.

Kali, Y., Orion, N. and Eylon, B. S. (2003) Effect of knowledge integration activities on students' perception of the earth's crust as a cyclic system. *Journal of Research in Science Teaching*, 40, 545–565.

King, C., Fleming, A., Kennett, P. and Thompson, D. (2005) How effectively do science textbooks teach earth science? *School Science Review*, 87, 95–104.

Koulaides, V. and Christidou, V. (1999) Models of students' thinking concerning the greenhouse effect and teaching implications. *Science Education* 83, 559–576.

Marques, L. and Thompson, D. (1997) Portuguese students' understanding at ages 10–11 and 14–15 of the origin and nature of the Earth and the development of life. *Research in Science and Technological Education*, 15, 29–51.

Nussbaum, J. (1985) The Earth as a cosmic body. In R. Driver, E. Guesne and A. Tiberghien (eds), *Children's Ideas in Science*. Milton Keynes: Open University Press.

Ross, K. and Shuell, T. J. (1993) Children's beliefs about earthquakes. *Science Education*, 77, 191–205.

Russell, T., Bell, D., Longden, K. and McGuigan, L. (1993) *SPACE Research Report: Rocks, Soil and Weather*. Liverpool: Liverpool University Press

Rutin, J. and Sofer, S. (2007) Israeli students' awareness of earthquakes and their expected behaviour in the event of an earthquake. *School Science Review*, 88, 57–62.

Rye, J. A., Rubba, P. A. and Wiesenmayer, R. L. (1997) An investigation of middle school students' alternative conceptions of global warming. *International Journal of Science Education*, 19, 527–551.

Schoon, K. and Boone, W. (1998) Self-efficacy and alternative conceptions of science of preservice elementary teachers. *Science Education*, 82, 553–568.

Shepardson, D. P., Choi, S. and Niogi, D. (2011) Seventh grade students' mental models of the greenhouse effect. *Environmental Education Research*, 17, 1–17.

Skamp, K. R., Boyes, E. and Stanisstreet, M. (2009) Global warming responses at the primary secondary interface: 1 Students' beliefs and willingness to act. *Australian Journal of Environmental Education*, 25, 15–30.

Whitburn, N. (2007) Earth science in the classroom. *Primary Science Review*, 96, 30–34.

Part Four: Physics

13 Forces

Alonzo, A. C. and Steedle, J. T. (2009) Developing and assessing a force and motion learning progression. *Science Education*, 93, 389–421.

Bar, V., Zinn, B., Goldmuntz, R. and Sneider, C. (1994) Children's conceptions about weight and free fall. *Science Education*, 78, 149–169.

Bar, V., Zinn, B. and Rubin, E. (1997) Children's ideas about action at a distance. *International Journal of Science Education*, 19, 1137–1157.

Champagne, A., Klopfer, L., Solomon, C. and Cohen, A. (1980) *Interactions of Students' Knowledge with their Comprehension and Design of Science Experiments*. Technical Report, University of Pittsburgh.

Driver, R. (1983) *The Pupil as Scientist?* Milton Keynes: Open University Press.

Driver, R., Squires, A., Rushworth, P. and Wood-Robinson, V. (1994) *Making Sense of Secondary Science: Research into Children's Ideas*. London: Routledge.

Frankel-Hauser, J. (1998) *Science Play*. Nashville, TN: Ideal Publications.

Gunstone, R. F. and White, R. T. (1981) Understanding of gravity. *Science Education*, 65, 291–299.

Howe, C., Taylor Tavares, J. and Devine, A. (2012) Everyday conceptions of object fall: Explicit and tacit understanding during middle childhood. *Journal of Experimental Child Psychology*, 111, 351–366.

Jones, A. T. (1983) Investigation of students' understanding of speed, velocity and acceleration. *Research in Science Education*, 13, 95–104.

Minstrell, J. (1982) Explaining the 'at rest' condition of an object. *Physics Teacher*, 20, 10–14.

Montanero, M., Suero, M. I., Pérez, A. L. and Pardo, P. J. (2002) Implicit theories of static interactions between two bodies. *Physics Education*, 37, 318–323.

Murphy, J. (1982) *On the Way Home*. London: Macmillan Children's Books.

Osborne, R. (1984) Children's dynamics. *The Physics Teacher*, 22, 504–508.

Pfundt, H. and Duit, R. (1994) *Bibliography: Students' Alternative Frameworks and Science Education*. Kiel: IPN.

Piaget, J. (1970) *The Child's Conception of Movement and Speed*. London: Routledge and Kegan Paul.

Reynoso, E., Fierro, E., Torres, G., Vicentini-Missoni, M. and Pérez de Celis, J. (1993) The alternative frameworks presented by Mexican students and teachers concerning the free fall of bodies. *International Journal of Science Education*, 15, 127–138.

Ruggiero, S., Cartelli, A., Dupre, F. and Vicentini-Missoni, M. (1985) Weight, gravity and air pressure: Mental representations by Italian middle school pupils. *European Journal of Science Education*, 7, 181–194.

Russell, T., McQuigan, L. and Hughues, A. (1998) *SPACE Research Report: Forces*. Liverpool: Liverpool University Press.

Stead, K. and Osborne, R. (1980) *Gravity*. LISP Working Paper 20, Science Education Research Unit, University of Waikato, Hamilton, New Zealand.

Terry, C. and Jones, G. (1986) Alternative frameworks: Newton's third law and conceptual change. *European Journal of Science Education*, 8, 291–298.

Vicentini-Missoni, M. (1981) Earth and gravity: Comparison between adults' and children's knowledge. In W. Jung, H. Pfundt and C. J. von Rhoneck (eds), *Proceedings of the International Workshop on Problems Concerning Students' Representation of Physics and Chemistry Knowledge*, 14–16 September, pp. 223–253. Ludwigsburg: Pädagogische Hochschule.

Viennot, L. (1979) Spontaneous learning in elementary dynamics. *European Journal of Science Education*, 1, 205–221.

Viennot, L. and Rozier, S. (1994) Pedagogical outcomes of research in science education: Examples in mechanics and thermodynamics. In P. J. Fensham, R. F. Gunstone and R. White (eds), *The Content of Science*, pp. 237–254. London: The Falmer Press.

Waring, G. (2007) *Oscar and the Cricket*. London: Walker Books.

Watts, D. M. (1982) Gravity: Don't take it for granted. *Physics Education*, 17, 116–121.

14 Floating and sinking

Bar, V., Zinn, B., Goldmuntz, R. and Sneider, C. (1994) Children's conceptions about weight and free fall. *Science Education*, 78, 149–169.

Biddulph, F. and Osborne, R. (1984) Pupils' ideas about floating and sinking. Paper presented to the Australian Science Education Research Association Conference, May, Melbourne.

Carr, M., Barker, M., Bell, B., Biddulph, F., Jones, A., Kirkwood, V., Pearson, J. and Symington, D. (1994) The constructivist paradigm and some implications for science content and pedagogy. In P. J. Fensham, R. F. Gunstone and R. White (eds), *The Content of Science*, pp. 147–160. London: Falmer Press.

Galili, I. and Bar, V. (1997) Children's operational knowledge about weight. *International Journal of Science Education*, 19, 317–340.

Hewson, M. (1986) The acquisition of scientific knowledge: Analysis and representation of student conceptions concerning density. *Science Education*, 70, 159–170.

Joung, Y. J. (2009) Children's typically-perceived-situations of floating and sinking. *International Journal of Science Education*, 31, 101–127.

Mullet, E. and Montcouquiol, A. (1988) Archimedes' effect, information integration and individual differences. *International Journal of Science Education*, 10, 285–301.

Parker, J. and Heywood, D. (2000) Exploring the relationship between subject knowledge and pedagogic content knowledge in primary teachers' learning about forces. *International Journal of Science Education*, 22, 89–111.

Rowell, J. A. and Dawson, C. J. (1977) Teaching about floating and sinking: An attempt to link cognitive psychology with classroom practice. *Science Education*, 61, 245–253.

She, H.-C. (2002) Concepts of a higher hierarchical level require more dual situated learning events for conceptual change: A study of air pressure and buoyancy. *International Journal of Science Education*, 24, 981–996.

15 Electricity and magnetism

Armitage, R. (2007) *The Lighthouse Keeper's Lunch*. London: Scholastic Books.

Bar, V., Zinn, B. and Rubin, E. (1997) Children's ideas about action at a distance. *International Journal of Science Education*, 19, 1137–1157.

Chiu, M. H. and Jing-Wen Lin, J. W. (2005) Promoting fourth graders' conceptual change of their understanding of electric current via multiple analogies. *Journal of Research in Science Teaching*, 42, 429–464.

De Posada, J. (1997) Conceptions of high school students concerning the internal structure of metals and their electric conduction: Structure and evolution. *Science Education*, 81, 445–467.

Driver, R. (1983) *The Pupil as Scientist?* Milton Keynes: Open University Press.

Finley, F. N. (1986) Evaluating instruction: The complementary use of clinical interviews. *Journal of Research in Science Teaching*, 23, 635–650.

Fredette, N. and Lockhead, J. (1980) Student conceptions of simple circuits. *Physics Teacher*, 18, 194–198.

Garnett, P. J., Garnett, P. J. and Treagust, D. F. (1990) Implications of research on students' understanding of electrochemistry for improving science curricula and classroom practice. *International Journal of Science Education*, 12, 147–156.

Glauert, E. B. (2009) How young children understand electric circuits: Prediction, explanation and exploration. *International Journal of Science Education*, 31, 1025–1047.

Meyer, K. (1991) *Children as experimenters: Elementary students' actions in an experimental context with magnets*. Unpublished doctoral dissertation, University of British Columbia, Vancouver.

Osborne, J. F., Black, P. J., Smith, M. and Meadows, J. (1991) *SPACE Research Report: Electricity*. Liverpool: Liverpool University Press.

Osborne, R. (1985) Building on children's intuitive ideas. In R. Osborne and P. Freyberg (eds), *Learning in Science*, pp. 41–50. Auckland: Heinemann.

Osborne, R. J. (1982) Bridging the gap between teaching and learning. Paper presented at the New Zealand Science Teachers' Association Conference, Hamilton, New Zealand.

Osborne, R. J. (1983) Towards modifying children's ideas about electric current. *Research in Teaching and Technological Education*, 1, 73–82.

Paatz, R., Ryder, J., Schwedes, H. and Scott, P. (2004) A case study analysing the process of analogy-based learning in a teaching unit about simple electric circuits. *International Journal of Science Education*, 26, 1065–1081.

Rhoneck, C. von (1981) Students' conceptions of the electric circuit before physics instruction. In W. Jung, H. Pfundt and C. J. von Rhoneck (eds), *Proceedings of the International Workshop on Problems Concerning Students' Representation of Physics and Chemistry Knowledge*, 14–16 September, pp. 194–213. Ludwigsburg: Pädagogische Hochschule.

Shipstone, D. M. (1984) A study of children's understanding of electricity in simple DC circuits. *European Journal of Science Education*, 6, 185–198.

Shipstone, D. M. (1985) *Circuits*. In R. Driver, E. Guesne and A. Tiberghien (eds), *Children's Ideas in Science*. Milton Keynes: Open University Press.

Tiberghien, A. and Delacote, G. (1976) Manipulations et représentations de circuits électriques simples par des enfants de 7 à 12 ans. *Revue Française de Pédagogie*, 34, 32–44.

Waring, G. (2009) *Oscar and the Bird*. London: Walker Books.

16 Light

Anderson, C. W. and Smith, E. L. (1983) Children's conceptions of light and colour: developing the concept of unseen rays. Paper presented to the annual meeting of the *American Educational Research Association*, Montreal, Canada.

Driver, R., Squires, A., Rushworth, P. and Wood-Robinson, V. (1994) *Making Sense of Secondary Science: Research into Children's Ideas*. London: Routledge.

Feher, E. and Meyer, K. R. (1992) Children's conceptions of colour. *Journal of Research in Science Teaching*, 29, 505–520.

Feher, E. and Rice, K. (1985) Showing shadow shapes: Activities to elicit and dispel some preconceptions. Paper submitted to *Science and Children*.

Fetherstonhaugh, T. and Treagust, D. F. (1990) Students' understanding of light and its properties following a teaching strategy to engender conceptual change. Paper presented to the annual meeting of the American Educational Research Association, Boston, 16–20 April.

Galili, I. and Hazan, A. (2000) Learners' knowledge in optics: Interpretation, structure and analysis. *International Journal of Science Education*, 22, 57–88.

Guesne, E. (1978) Lumière et vision des objets: Un exemple de représentation des phénomènes physiques préexistant à l'enseignement. In G. Delacote (ed.), *Physics Teaching in Schools*, pp. 265–273. London: Taylor and Francis.

Guesne, E. (1984) Children's ideas about light. In E. J. Wenman (ed.), *New Trends in Physics Teaching*, Vol. IV, pp. 179–192. Paris: UNESCO.

Guesne, E. (1985) Light. In R. Driver, E. Guesne and A. Tiberghien (eds), *Children's Ideas in Science*, pp. 10–32. Milton Keynes: Open University Press.

Guest, G. (2003) *Alternative Frameworks and Misconceptions in Primary Science*. University of the West of England. Available at http://sci-tutors.gnxt.net/downloads/professional_issues/teaching/misconceptions/alternative_frameworks.pdf [accessed 29 March 2012].

Martinez-Borreguero, G., Pérez-Rodríguez, A. L., Suero-López, M. I. and Pardo-Fernández, P. J. (2013) Detection of misconceptions about colour and an experimentally tested proposal to combat them. *International Journal of Science Education*, 35, 1299–1324.

Osborne, J. F., Black, P. J., Smith, M. and Meadows, J. (1990) *SPACE Research Report: Light.* Liverpool: Liverpool University Press

Ramadas, J. and Driver, R. (1989) *Aspects of Secondary Students' Ideas about Light.* Children's Learning in Science Project, Centre for Studies in Science and Mathematics Education, University of Leeds.

Şahin, Ç., Ipek, H. and Ayas, A. (2008) Students' understanding of light concepts in primary school: A cross-age study. *Asia-Pacific Forum on Science Learning and Teaching*, 9, 1–19.

Settlage, J. (1995) Children's conceptions of light in the context of a technology-based curriculum. *Science Education*, 79, 535–553.

Tiberghien, A., Delacote, G., Ghiglione, R. and Metalon, B. (1980) Conceptions de la lumière chez l'enfant de 10–12 ans. *Revue Française de Pédagogie*, 50, 24–41.

Waring, G. (2006) *Oscar and the Moth.* London: Walker Books.

Watts, D. M. (1985) Student conceptions of light: A case study. *Physics Education*, 20, 183–187.

Watts, D. M. and Gilbert, J. K. (1985) *Appraising the Understanding of Science Concepts: Light.* Department of Educational Studies, University of Surrey: Guildford.

17 Sound

Asoko, H. M., Leach, J. and Scott, P. H. (1991) A study of students' understanding of sound 5–16 as an example of action research. Paper prepared for the symposium on Developing Students' Understanding in Science at the Annual Conference of the British Educational Research Association at Roehampton Institute, 2 September 1990, London.

Eshach, H., and Schwartz, J. L. (2006) Sound stuff? Naïve materialism in middle-school students' conceptions of sound. *International Journal of Science Education*, 28, 733–764.

Linder, C. J. (1993) University physics students' conceptualisations of factors affecting the speed of sound propagation. *International Journal of Science Education*, 15, 655–662.

Linder, C. J. and Erickson, G. (1989) A study of tertiary physics students' conceptualisations of sound. *International Journal of Science Education*, 11, 491–501.

Waring, G. (2007) *Oscar and the Bat.* London: Walker Books.

Watt, D. and Russell, T. (1990) *SPACE Research Report: Sound.* Liverpool: Liverpool University Press.

Whittaker, A. G. (2012) Pupils think sound has substance – well sort of. *School Science Review*, 94, 109–111.

Wittmann, M., Steinberg, R. and Redish, E. (2003) Understanding and affecting student reasoning about sound waves. *International Journal of Science Education*, 25, 991–1013.

18 Earth and space

Arnold, P., Sarge, A. and Worral, L. (1995) Children's knowledge of the earth's shape and its gravitational field. *International Journal of Science Education*, 17, 635–641.

Baxter, J. (1989) Children's understanding of familiar astronomical events. *International Journal of Science Education*, 11, 502–513.

Broughton, S. H., Sinatra, G. M., and Nussbaum, E. M. (2012) 'Pluto has been a planet my whole life!' Emotions, attitudes, and conceptual change in elementary students' learning about Pluto's reclassification. Available at http://digitalcommons.usu.edu/cgi/viewcontent.cgi?article=1287andcontext=teal_facpub [accessed 25 May 2013].

Bryce, T. G. K. and Blown, E. J. (2012) Children's concepts of the shape and size of the earth, sun and moon. *International Journal of Science Education*, 3, 388–446.

Davies, R. W. (2002) There's a lot to learning about the Earth in space. *Primary Science Review*, 72, 9–12.

Ehrlén, K. (2009) Drawings as representations of children's conceptions. *International Journal of Science Education*, 31, 41–57.

Jones, B. L., Lynch, P. P. and Reesink, C. (1987) Children's conception of the Earth, Sun and Moon. *International Journal of Science Education*, 9, 43–53.

Lias, S. and Thomas, C. (2003) Using digital photographs to improve learning in science. *Primary Science Review*, 76, 17–19.

Nussbaum, J. (1985) The Earth as a cosmic body. In R. Driver, E. Guesne and A. Tiberghien (eds), *Children's Ideas in Science*, pp. 170–192. Milton Keynes: Open University Press.

Nussbaum, J. and Novak, J. D. (1976) An assessment of children's concepts of the Earth utilising structured interviews. *Science Education*, 60, 535–550.

Osborne, J. F., Wadsworth, P., Black, P. J. and Meadows, J. (1993) *SPACE Research Report: The Earth in Space*. Liverpool: Liverpool University Press.

Parker, J. and Heywood, D. (1998) The earth and beyond: Developing primary teachers' understanding of basic astronomical events. *International Journal of Science Education*, 20, 503–520.

Plummer, J. D. (2009) Early elementary students' development of astronomy concepts in the planetarium. *Journal of Research in Science Teaching*, 46, 192–209.

Sadler, P. M. (1987) Misconceptions in astronomy. In J. D. Novak (ed.), *Proceedings of the 2nd International Seminar: Misconceptions and Educational Strategies in Science and Mathematics*, 26–29 July, pp. 422–425. Ithaca, NY: Cornell University Press.

Schoon, K. and Boone, W. (1998) Self-efficacy and alternative conceptions of science of preservice elementary teachers. *Science Education*, 82, 553–568.

Sharp, J. G. (1996) Children's astronomical beliefs: A preliminary study of Year 6 children in south-west England. *International Journal of Science Education*, 18, 685–712.

Shen, J. and Confrey, J. (2007) From conceptual change to transformative modeling: A case study of an elementary teacher in learning astronomy. *Science Education*, 91, 948–966.

Taylor, I., Barker, M. and Jones, A. (2003) Promoting mental model building in astronomy education. *International Journal of Science Education*, 25, 1205–1225.

Trumper, R. (2006) Teaching future teachers basic astronomy concepts – seasonal changes – at a time of reform in science education. *Journal of Research in Science Teaching*, 43, 879–906.

Trundle, K. C., Atwood, R. K. and Christopher, J. E. (2007) A longitudinal study of conceptual change: Preservice elementary teachers' conceptions of moon phases. *Journal of Research in Science Teaching*, 44, 303–326.

Vosniadou, S. and Brewer, W. F. (1990) A cross-cultural investigation of children's conceptions about the Earth, the Sun and the Moon: Greek and American data. In H. Mandl, E. De Corte, N. Bennett and H. F. Friedrid (eds), *Learning and Instruction: European Research in an International Context*, pp. 605–629. Oxford: Pergamon Press.

Zeilik, M., Schau, C. and Mattern N. (1998) Misconceptions and their change in university-level astronomy courses. *The Physics Teacher*, 36, 104–107.

19 Energy

Boyes, E. and Stanisstreet, M. (1990) Pupils' ideas concerning energy sources. *International Journal of Science Education*, 12, 513–529.

Jenkins, M. (2008) *The Emperor's Egg*. London: Walker Books.

Paik, S. H., Cho, B. K. and Go, Y. M. (2007) Korean 4- to 11-year-old student conceptions of heat and temperature. *Journal of Research in Science Teaching*, 44, 284–302.

Solomon, J. (1982) How children learn about energy, or, does the first law come first? *School Science Review*, 63, 415–422.

Solomon, J. (1983) Messy, contradictory and obstinately persistent: A study of children's out of school ideas about energy. *School Science Review*, 65, 225–233.

Tiberghien, A. and Barboux, M. (1980) Difficulté de l'acquisition de la notion de temperature par les élèves de 6ème. In *Compte-rendus des Cinquièmes Journées Internationales sur l'Education Scientifique*. Chamonix: France.

Tiberghien, A., Sere, M. G., Barboux, M. and Chomat, A. (1983) *Étude des representations préalables de quelques notions de physique et leur évolution*. Rapport de recherche, LIRESPT, University of Paris VII, Paris.

Watts, D. M. and Gilbert, J. K. (1985) *Appraising the Understanding of Science Concepts: Energy*. Department of Educational Studies, University of Surrey.

Index

Illustrated references are in *italics*; glossary references are in **bold**.

PRIMARY SCIENCE
Teaching the Tricky Bits

Neil Rutledge

9780335222285 (Paperback)
2010

eBook also available

The book provides a combination of engaging, practical lesson ideas and
subject knowledge to help you teach the trickiest parts of primary science
such as materials and their properties, magnetism, circuits, forces and life
processes. The book includes a range of accessible ideas, hints and tips
with a focus on providing a skills-based, problem-solving approach to
learning.

Each topic area includes advice on:

- How to link the topic with other areas of learning
- Identifying and challenging common misconceptions
- How to effectively pre-assess the learners' ideas to best meet their
  needs
- Practical activities for challenging and developing children's ideas
- Explanatory models to help pupils consolidate their understanding

OPEN UNIVERSITY PRESS
McGraw - Hill Education

www.openup.co.uk